WHEN GOD WHISPERED MY NAME

Smyth & Helwys Publishing, Inc.
6316 Peake Road
Macon, Georgia 31210-3960
1-800-747-3016
©2022 by Kathy Manis Findley and Kay Wilson Shurden, editors
All rights reserved.

Image on the cover and page x is *Labyrinth* by Leslie Crane
Reprinted courtesy of the artist.
Leslie Crane Photography
lesliecranephotography.com

Library of Congress Cataloging-in-Publication Data

Names: Findley, Kathy Manis, editor. | Shurden, Kay Wilson, editor.
Title: When God whispered my name : stories of journey told by Baptist women called to ministry / Kathy Manis Findley, editor, Kay Wilson Shurden, editor.
Description: Macon, GA : Smyth & Helwys Publishing, 2022. | Includes bibliographical references.
Identifiers: LCCN 2022015021 | ISBN 9781641733731 (paperback)
Subjects: LCSH: Baptists--Clergy--Biography. | Women clergy--Biography.
Classification: LCC BX6493 .W47 2022 | DDC 286.092/52
[B]--dc23/eng/20220512
LC record available at https://lccn.loc.gov/2022015021

Disclaimer of Liability: With respect to statements of opinion or fact available in this work of nonfiction, Smyth & Helwys Publishing Inc. nor any of its employees, makes any warranty, express or implied, or assumes any legal liability or responsibility for the accuracy or completeness of any information disclosed, or represents that its use would not infringe privately-owned rights.

Praise for *When God Whispered My Name*

"*When God Whispered My Name* shares the stories of women with diverse backgrounds, recalls the diverse ways they were called, tells the diverse ways they minister, and reveals the diverse ways they have been challenged. Yet they have a sense of sisterhood with others on the journey of ministry."

—*Carolyn Blevins*

"Women ministers, including my friend of almost 60 years, Carolyn [Staley], have enriched my life and the lives of countless others. I hope their stories will encourage others who feel the call to follow it with humility, peace, and love."

—*Former President Bill Clinton*

"This book is a collection of faithful and, at times, fierce testimonials of Baptist women who heard and responded to the call of God. For some, the still, small, voice moved them to confront cultural and religious obstacles. For others, the call was a fire, stirring up in their very bones. For all, it was a voice too certain to be ignored, too necessary to be handled as anything less than sacred. We too get to listen in to these divine conversations and as such are inspired to consider our own holy summons."

—*C. Gregory DeLoach, MDiv, DMin*
Dean, Mercer University McAfee School of Theology

"I gladly endorse this timely book of firsthand accounts from reverent women who heard, pondered, struggled, and answered the whispers of God's Spirit that led them into ministry. The honest reflections about their trials, tragedies, and triumphs makes this book a 'must read'!"

—*Wendell Griffen*
Pastor at New Millennium Church

"There is power in a story well told, a sacredness that speaks to shared experiences, and draws us closer to God and to one another. *When God Whispered My Name* is full of such stories. Equal parts inspiring, sobering, and challenging, the stories of these women bear witness to the Good News that flourishes when one dares say yes to God's call. This timely volume is sure to offer hope, encouragement, and community to women and men who are wrestling with that same mysterious call from God and those seeking to empower them."

—*Mandy McMichael*
Associate Director and J. David Slover Assistant Professor of Ministry Guidance, Baylor University

"The voices and stories which live in these pages are powerful reminders of Peter's Pentecost proclamation that God pours out God's spirit on God's daughters and on God's sons, with no regard for whether they are daughters or sons; thanks be to God."

—*Chuck Poole*
Senior Pastor, Northminster Baptist Church

This beautifully diverse, soul-disclosing collection of call stories captures the breadth of experiences embodied by women in ministry among Baptists. From Arkansas to Cuba, from Georgia to Uganda, what a gift to be invited into the heart journeys of nineteen women who persevered in order to respond to God's call. For anyone who may be curious about the inspiring, heart-breaking, brave, and faithful inner workings of the journey for Baptist women in ministry, this book is for you.

—*Meredith Stone*
Executive Director
Baptist Women in Ministry, Abilene, Texas

WHEN GOD WHISPERED MY NAME

Stories of Journey
Told by Baptist Women
Called to Ministry

KATHY MANIS FINDLEY &
KAY WILSON SHURDEN, EDITORS

Also by Kathy Manis Findley

Voices of Our Sisters

The Survivor's Voice: Healing the Invisible Wounds of Violence and Abuse

Emilie's Journey: A Love Story from the Bayou

Also by Kay Wilson Shurden

Women on Pilgrimage

Call Waiting: God's Invitation to Youth (with Larry L. McSwain)

For the foremothers who made these journeys possible,
For their courage and persistence to prophesy, against all odds,

For the dreams they dreamed—
the ones that fell into the dust, unknown, unrealized,
and the ones that took flight on the wings of the morning,
those dreams-in-flight that rose high above, lifted by Spirit.

And we looked up to see the dreams,
when before we had looked down;

Yes, we looked up into the sky and saw them,
and held them close.

—KMF

Acknowledgments

I am grateful to my husband, Walter Shurden, whose support and understanding of the important role of women in Baptist life, including the pastorate, has been vital to me; and to my spiritual direction group, the *Wild Women*, who always provide support and encouragement for my creative ventures.

—*Kay Wilson Shurden*

I must acknowledge the many ways my husband Fred helped me bring this book to life. He has been my muse and my champion, always. For this book, he was technical advisor, editor, proofreader, computer guru, photo editor, scheduler, taskmaster, and stalwart encourager. Without him, this book would have never seen the light of day. I also acknowledge my Sunday school class, *Voices*, for being my sisters on the journey who help me find my voice. They empower me to search, to discover, to tend to my soul, to embody my best self, and to always be open to creative inspiration.

For the many women who contributed to this book, we are eternally grateful. For their time, their giftedness, their candor, their humor, their words, and their lives, we say "Thank you!" Special thanks to the writer of our foreword, Dr. Bill J. Leonard, and the writer of our afterword, Rev. Suzii Paynter March.

This book would not have been possible without the colleagues and friends who have helped us as readers, editors, advisers, and encouragers: Dr. Mandy McMichael and Dr. Elizabeth Flowers, Baylor University; Dr. Dee Bratcher, Mercer University; Mr. Marvin Black; Rev. Paula Clayton Dempsey, Alliance of Baptists; Mark Wingfield, Baptist News Global; and Rev. Dr. Meredith Stone, Baptist Women in Ministry.

I am grateful for the support of my brother, Andrew, who always believes in me. Life as I know it today might not have been possible without the living kidney donors who gave me the gift of life, Greg Adams and Corita Forster. And finally, I thank the ones whose contributions to my life and to this book cannot be measured—my son, Jonathan, and my grandchildren, loves of my heart.

—*Kathy Manis Findley*

. . . I will pour out my Spirit upon all flesh,
and your sons and your daughters shall prophesy.
—Acts 2:17, NRSV

A depiction of the labyrinth of Chartres Cathedral in France. The eleven-circuit Chartres Labyrinth, almost certainly built in the early thirteenth century, became a symbol for pilgrims who walk the labyrinth as part of their pilgrimage to the holy land.

Let us continue walking the sacred path,
gently moving ourselves toward the center,
that space where we might find the center of our souls,
and the center of God's holy presence.

"While my male contemporaries seemed to have a straight shot, my way has been circuitous just like walking a labyrinth requires many twists and turns before arriving at center."
—*Rev. Dr. Rhonda Abbott Blevins*

"As for the shape my calling may take in the future, I am entrusting the labyrinth to God."
—*Rev. Julie Pennington-Russell*

Contents

Foreword
On Spirit-Infused Callings
Dr. Bill J. Leonard
1

Preface
On Building Bigger Rooms
Dr. Kay Wilson Shurden
7

Introduction
On Treasure Boxes of Memories
Rev. Kathy Manis Findley
11

The First Story
With a Story to Tell
Rev. Nancy Hastings Sehested
19

The Second Story
Bloom Where You Are Planted
Rev. Dr. C. Lynn Brinkley
29

The Third Story
Following God's Next Right Step
Rev. Julie Whidden Long
39

The Fourth Story
Never Too Late
Rev. Carolyn Yeldell Staley
51

The Fifth Story
Continuing the Legacy of Goodness and Love
Rev. Dr. Anika T. Whitfield
67

The Sixth Story
If God Can Speak through a Donkey
Rev. Dr. Rhonda Abbott Blevins
85

The Seventh Story
Holy Whispers
Rev. Kathy Manis Findley
99

The Eighth Story
A Divine Ajíaco: My Calling to Ministry
Rev. Dr. Cristina García-Alfonso
123

The Ninth Story
Coming and Going and in the Meantime
Rev. Carolyn Hale Cubbedge
133

The Tenth Story
Reflecting on Winds of Change
Rev. Dr. Christine Y. Wiley
147

The Eleventh Story
Dancing on Earth as It Is in Heaven: My Rhythm of Divine Calling
Rev. Jenna Sullivan
155

The Twelfth Story
Empowered by My Promised Inheritance
Rev. Sheila D. Sholes-Ross
163

The Thirteenth Story
My Child's Heart Remembers
Rev. Mica Togami
175

The Fourteenth Story
Awakening to My Call
Rev. Dr. Jann Aldredge-Clanton
185

The Fifteenth Story
Magic and Mystery
Rev. LeAnn Gunter Johns
201

The Sixteenth Story
Grateful for Who I Am and What I Do
Pastora Ruth Eunice Rodríguez de Orantes
213

The Seventeenth Story
On Being a Soul Friend
Melody Carroll Harrell
231

The Eighteenth Story
If the Shoes Fit
Rev. Kelsey Stillwell
245

The Nineteenth Story
This Labyrinthine Calling
Rev. Julie Pennington-Russell
257

The Continuing Story
Then, Now, and Dreams to Come
Rev. Kathy Manis Findley
269

Afterword
On the Meaning of Baptist-ness
Rev. Suzii Paynter March
273

Foreword

On Spirit-Infused Callings

Dr. Bill J. Leonard

This book echoes with the voices of women who live out their callings as ministers in multiple contexts of Christian community. Their stories intersect and diverge across regions, denominations, educational institutions, and family settings. While not all of them continue to serve within Baptist congregations, each of them has some element of a "Baptist past" that both nurtured and distanced itself from their calling to ministry. Their stories bear witness to the gifts of spiritual formation they received in Baptist traditions and the testimony that each of them bring inside and outside those traditions.

Concerning the participation of women in ordained Christian ministry, Baptists have often tried to have it both ways. They nurtured girls and boys with a calling to commit their lives to Jesus Christ for salvation, discipleship, and mission with imperatives such as "Discern and follow God's will for your life; do whatever God tells you to do." They taught young people to sing and incarnate "hymns of commitment" like "Wherever He Leads I'll Go" and "I Surrender All" as mandates for following the Spirit's guidance. Yet when some of those women took them at their word, experienced "the call" to Christian ministry, and had the audacity to seek ordination, Baptists cut theological bait on them, implicitly revising hymns and commitments to "Wherever He Leads MEN Go" or "I Surrender SOME." (By the way, for generations, most other American denominations acted similarly in one way or another, and some still do.)

Responding to the 2010 ordination of Libby Grammar Garrett, Reverend Dr. Pam Durso, then director of Baptist Women in Ministry and now president of Central Baptist Seminary, wrote, "The earliest known ordination of a Baptist woman was that of M. A. Brennan, who in 1876 was ordained as a minister by the Bellevernon Freewill Baptist Church in Pennsylvania."[1] Durso also documented the 1882 ordination of May Jones by the Baptist Association of Puget Sound in Washington as the time a woman was ordained in what is now the American Baptist Churches, USA; and the 1964 ordination of Addie Davis at the Watts Street Baptist Church, Raleigh, North Carolina, as the first for Southern Baptists.

Multiple twenty-first-century Baptist groups either ordain women or affirm the ordination of women. These include the North American Baptist Conference; the Baptist General Association; the American Baptist Churches, USA; the Alliance of Baptists; the Cooperative Baptist Fellowship; the National Baptist Convention, USA; and the Progressive National Baptist Convention. The General Association of Regular Baptists, Independent Baptists, and Southern Baptists do not approve of female ordination.

African American scholar TeResa Green offers a response to opposition toward women's ordination that encompasses the Black church and beyond, noting,

> Black male ministers' arguments against women pastors are questionable because they compare twenty-first century African American women, many with graduate degrees and extensive theological training, to uneducated first century women. The social and political interests of many Black ministers appears to control their conclusions when challenging the right of women to pursue the role of pastor.[2]

---

1. Pam Durso, "Baptist Women Ministers: A Bit of History for an Ordination Service," December 14, 2010, Baptist Women in Ministry, bwim.info/baptist-women-ministers-a-bit-of-history-for-an-ordination-service-by-pam-durso/.

2. TeResa Green, "A Gendered Spirit: Race, Class, and Sex in the African American Church," *Race, Gender & Class* 10/1 (2003): 121. www.jstor.org/stable/41675063.

Southern Baptists are a case in point. The Southern Baptist Convention (SBC) revised its confession of faith, the Baptist Faith and Message 2000, to state, "Each congregation operates under the Lordship of Christ through democratic processes. In such a congregation each member is responsible and accountable to Christ as Lord. Its scriptural officers are pastors and deacons. While both men and women are gifted for service in the church, the office of pastor is limited to men as qualified by Scripture."

Apparently, Southern Baptists decided that a congregation's "democratic processes" ended where women sought ordination. An earlier, more elaborate statement appeared in 1984, when "messengers" to the SBC's annual meeting approved a "Resolution on Ordination and the Role of Women in Ministry" stating, in part,

> WHEREAS, The Scriptures attest to God's delegated order of authority (God the head of Christ, Christ the head of man, man the head of woman, man and woman dependent one upon the other to the glory of God) distinguishing the roles of men and women in public prayer and prophecy (1 Cor. 11:2-5); and WHEREAS, The Scriptures teach that women are not in public worship to assume a role of authority over men lest confusion reign in the local church (1 Cor. 14:33-36); and WHEREAS, While Paul commends women and men alike in other roles of ministry and service (Titus 2:1-10), he excludes women from pastoral leadership (1 Tim. 2:12) to preserve a submission God requires because the man was first in creation and the woman was first in the Edenic fall (1 Tim. 2:13ff).

The passage from 1 Timothy states, "But I suffer not a woman to teach, not to usurp authority over the man, but to be in silence. For Adam was first formed, then Eve. And Adam was not deceived, but the woman being deceived was in the transgression" (1 Tim 2:12-14, KJV). As those 1984 messengers understood it, the curse of Eve remains, preventing her daughters from "usurping" male authority in home or pulpit, a curse that even Christ's redemptive work cannot atone.

Sometimes we Baptists can believe ourselves right about the Bible while being wrong about the gospel. (Southern Baptists should have learned that from their "biblical" support of chattel slavery alone.)

Yet, knowingly or unknowingly, Paul provided a radically alternative theological vision when he wrote, "as in Adam all die, in Christ are all made alive" (1 Cor 15:22, KJV). And in those words all curses die. Indeed, if women are too cursed to be called, they may be too cursed to be saved.

The Reverend Women in this volume exemplify Paul's liberating assertion. In Christ, they are "all made alive," and they strengthen Christ's church by their prophetic witness and the courage of their Spirit-infused calling. We read their stories gladly, grateful for the grace that overtakes us through their journeys.

Bill J. Leonard is founding dean and professor of divinity emeritus (1999–2018) at Wake Forest University School of Divinity. His education includes a BA from Texas Wesleyan University; an MDiv from Southwestern Baptist Theological Seminary; and a PhD from Boston University. He is affiliated with the American Baptist Churches (USA), the Cooperative Baptist Fellowship, and the Alliance of Baptists.

His research focuses on church history with particular attention to American religion, Baptist studies, and Appalachian religion. He is the author or editor of some twenty-five books, including *God's Last and Only Hope: The Fragmentation of the Southern Baptist Convention* (1990); *Christianity in Appalachia* (1999); *Baptist Ways: A History* (2003); *The Challenge of Being Baptist* (2010); *Can I Get a Witness? Essays, Sermons and Reflections* (2013); and *A Sense of the Heart: Christian Religious Experience in the U.S.* (2014). His newest book, *The Homebrewed Christianity Guide to Church History: Flaming Heretics and Heavy Drinkers*, was published in July 2017.

He has received numerous honors and awards including the Judson-Rice Award, *Baptists Today*, April 17, 2015; *Historian of Baptists and American Religion: A Legacy of Conscience and Dissent, Essays in Honor of Bill J. Leonard*, edited by C. Douglas Weaver, National Association of Baptist Professors, May 2015; Religious Liberty Award, Baptist Joint Committee for Religious Liberty, June

2014; Distinguished Alumni Award, Texas Wesleyan University, Fort Worth, Texas, October 2013; and the Lifetime Service Award, Community Service Awards, the *Winston-Salem Chronicle*, March 19, 2011.

Dr. Leonard serves on the board of the *Journal of Disability and Religion*, the *Baptist Quarterly* (England), the Day1 Preaching Network, the Institute for Rural Journalism and Community Issues, and the Governing Board of the Cooperative Baptist Fellowship. His sabbatical research focuses on a new book, tentatively titled *Security or Idolatry? A History of Religion and Firearms in the U.S.* Leonard writes a twice-monthly column for *Baptist News Global*, is an ordained Baptist minister, and is a member of First Baptist Church, Highland Avenue (American Baptist Churches, USA) in Winston-Salem, North Carolina.

Preface

On Building Bigger Rooms

Dr. Kay Wilson Shurden, editor

This is not a "whiny" book. The women ministers who wrote these stories are not whiners, crying over what the church would not allow them to do.

These are stories by women who faced barriers to their call to ministry, and they either hurdled those barriers or sashayed around them. Some of these women stayed within the church and claimed their rightful place in the pulpit. Some, on the other hand, made their way into a world hungry for their spiritual gifts. Like Jesus when he saw that the religious institution of his day wasn't big enough to include everyone, these women went outside where they were included and where they could include others.

These stories are from women who built bigger rooms, big enough to hold all the people because they matter. The church rooms they grew up in weren't large enough, so they knocked down walls and invited people in who had previously been excluded. Even when they served as ministers in churches that welcomed women as pastors, they helped transform their churches into larger rooms—not always larger crowds, but more diverse groups. Their churches looked more like the world.

You will find that each story is different. Each woman is unique and her response to her calling is unique. Gifts differ. Personalities differ. One commonality is that they all began as Baptists. They found love and acceptance at a local Baptist church. It was their starting place and to a great extent their stopping place.

Baptist churches have no defined hierarchy: no bishops, presbytery, or external ruling body. Because Baptist churches operate freely in our octopus-like culture, they are too often radically reshaped by that culture's nonsense.

Traditionally, women have not been preachers or even deacons in some Baptist churches. They taught Sunday school, especially children, cooked fellowship meals, visited the sick, beautified the sanctuary, and sought to enlarge the church's vision by promoting missions. But they sat on the sidelines for the big stuff. The pulpit was off limits, as was the board of deacons or the church council where all the decisions were made.

The women who wrote the stories in this book helped change the culture of Baptist churches. And their indisputable callings gave them courage to obey a higher, inner voice that their churches often failed to hear.

This is definitely *not* a book of whining. This is a book of celebration, an invitation to encourage women to speak out wherever they can. Even in church. Even in the pulpit.

Kay Wilson Shurden was born in 1937 in Greenville, Mississippi. She graduated from Mississippi College with a BS in elementary education, from Louisiana College with an MA in English, and from the University of Tennessee with an EdD in curriculum and instruction. She did post-doctoral study at Louisville General Hospital in marriage and family therapy.

Kay had an evolving career, beginning as an elementary school teacher in public schools. After obtaining her master's degree in English, she taught and supervised student teachers at Carson-Newman College for seven years. She became interested in counseling while studying at the University of Tennessee and entered post-doctoral study in marriage and family therapy. Upon completion of this program, she joined the faculty at Mercer University School of Medicine, where she taught medical students about family dynamics and began, with a colleague, a program in marriage and family therapy. She also saw clients for therapy in the clinic at the medical school.

Dr. Shurden continues to have a special interest in women's issues and in spirituality. She has studied the enneagram, a spiritual and psychological tool of understanding personality. She has spoken in churches and at retreats. She edited *Women on Pilgrimage* and cowrote *Call Waiting*. Both books deal with issues of women's development and sense of call.

Since her retirement, she leads a spiritual direction group of women who seek to move past cultural conditioning of roles for women and determine their own life path. Kay is married to Walter Shurden, who is retired from serving as chair of the religion department and director of the Center for Baptist Studies at Mercer University. They have been married sixty-four years and have three grown children, six grandchildren, and one great-grandchild. The Shurdens live in Macon, Georgia.

Introduction

On Treasure Boxes of Memories

Rev. Kathy Manis Findley, editor

Welcome to these pages—sad and soulful, deeply serious and sometimes whimsical. As you read, be prepared for the serendipities. Right out of a sad moment, you'll find humor, fun, and even a little laughter. I invite you to fall into the stories, to enter into the lives of these women, and to "listen" to the expressions of their souls. I hope these stories of journey create a sacred pause for you, a few moments of contemplation and a quiet space for thinking about the ways Spirit whispers *your* name.

Bill Leonard appropriately named the ministries of our writers, "Spirit-Infused Callings." His description of their ministries is reality, for they are Spirit-infused. They had to be to follow their path to ministry. Baptist women called to ministry are seldom, if ever, launched after seminary graduation into vocational ministry. They may wait, explore, seek out their contacts and then perhaps wait some more. Unlike their male counterparts in ministry, their journey will not follow a straight path. Instead the waiting will one day lead them to follow a more sacred path, a path that is circuitous, fluid, and free. Likely the women will follow a labyrinthine path—a path that is circular and never straight—a path where one never gets lost or follows the wrong road because the destination is the center.

Taken together, these stories create what I call a *collective telling*, individual stories merging to chronicle a consequential story of Baptist history/herstory spanning more than sixty years. The writers pay tribute to Baptist life as they experienced it, giving testimony to the spiritual nurture they received as children. It is about girls learning the Bible as soon as they were old enough to memorize "God is love." It is about their earliest worship experiences, the Vacation Bible Schools they loved, the prayers they learned, the hymns they sang, and the pews on which they fidgeted every Sunday.

Just as important as the *collective telling*, the writers offer a deeply *personal telling*, a view into their lives. For months, they searched through treasure boxes of memories to write their stories. They plumbed the depths of their lives to reveal their joys and sorrows. The telling was a harrowing experience for some of them, and yet it was also a solace to pause along their journey's path and find new meaning.

Most importantly, the individual stories are about their "heart stuff"—the call they sensed, the struggle to discern it, the rejections and betrayals along the way, the spiritual community that surrounded and blessed them, and, finally, the creativity, courage, persistence, patience, commitment, and compassion that propelled them into ministry, sometimes against all odds.

While gathered in a virtual meeting, one of the writers asked, "How can I tell my story with truth and kindness?" Together we endeavored to do just that: to tell our stories with truth and kindness. It is the heart stuff—all of it—that makes this collection unique.

And Your Daughters Shall "Prophesy" ('präfə͵sī)

I will pour out my Spirit on all flesh, and your sons and your daughters shall prophesy. (Acts 2:17, NRSV)

There's just something about the word "prophesy" that reminds church women that men prophesy, but prophesying women might encounter some pushback. From my roots of Greek Orthodoxy all the way to my unlikely conversion that made me thoroughly Baptist, I knew beyond any doubt that women could not prophesy and could not *ever* be priests or pastors! My earliest message: *Know your place, young lady!*

While hunkering down in my *allowed place*, I learned that female Baptist ministers trying to live life in *our* places had foremothers who refused to stay in *their* places. From a young age, Baptist girls learned that they had at least one formidable foremother—Lottie Moon. Much has been written about this remarkable woman, Charlotte Digges "Lottie" Moon, a Southern Baptist missionary who spent nearly forty years living and working in China as a teacher and evangelist.

Lottie Moon believed her calling was to be "going out among the millions" as an evangelist. Instead, she found herself teaching forty schoolchildren. She came to view herself as part of an oppressed class. In an article titled "The Woman's Question Again," published in 1883, she wrote,

> Can we wonder at the mortal weariness and disgust, the sense of wasted powers and the conviction that her life is a failure, that comes over a woman when, instead of the ever-broadening activities that she had planned, she finds herself tied down to the petty work of teaching a few girls?[1]

I imagine that Lottie Moon did not believe that teaching girls was "petty work," but over time, her teaching paled in comparison to her dream of evangelizing all of China. Eventually she set out to pursue some of those "ever-broadening activities," choosing to follow God's call rather than men's expectations of her as a woman. In 1885, she gave up teaching in the school and moved into China's interior to evangelize. "It is said that her converts numbered in the hundreds."[2] Author Regina Sullivan says that Lottie Moon was a pioneer for gender equality. Moon wrote from China in 1893, "What women have a right to demand is perfect equality."[3] Certainly Lottie Moon was a woman ahead of her time, one who both acted according to her

---

1. Regina D. Sullivan, "Myth, Memory, and the Making of Lottie Moon," in Jonathan Daniel Wells and Sheila R. Phipps, eds., *Entering the Fray: Gender, Politics, and Culture in the New South* (Columbia: University of Missouri Press, 2009), 5, 11–41; quote on 11.

2. "Lottie Moon," *Wikipedia*, April 25, 2021, en.wikipedia.org/wiki/Lottie_Moon.

3. Sullivan, "Myth, Memory, and the Making of Lottie Moon," in *Entering the Fray*, 17.

calling and used her influence to advocate on behalf of women who were facing similar oppression. Yet, on her trips back to the States, she was conventional, even refusing to speak to audiences where men were present, a hint that her life was a complicated contradiction.

Quite often, Baptist women called to ministry identify with Moon's oppression as well as her complicated contradiction, knowing that our call could well cause similar frustration. She serves as both exemplar and encourager for many who have followed in her footsteps to "prophesy" both at home and abroad.

A stirring hymn that many of us learned as young Baptist girls is "We've a Story to Tell to the Nations."[4] Like the story of Lottie Moon, this hymn's inspiring text touched our hearts and helped us believe we could be missionaries in exotic, faraway lands. We learned that those lands were called "the mission field," and some of us set our minds to go. We were taught to learn the Bible, to give our offerings, to be kind, to pray, to care about all people, to teach, to speak, and to sing. We were also told that someday, when we were older, God would call us to do something. The problem is that some of us grew into young women destined to experience rejection when we announced that we *were* called to do something. That something was a call to ministry—a "God whispered my name" moment that may well have been a call to prophesy, at least for some of us.

Dr. Susan M. Shaw, professor of women, gender, and sexuality studies at Oregon State University in Corvallis, Oregon, writes prolifically about the journeys of Baptist women who aspired to ministry:

> We practiced public speaking skills, and we listened intently when leaders told us, "You can be anything God calls you to be . . . ." When you tell little girls they can be anything God calls them to be, they grow up to be women with powerful voices calling the church to be and do. When God calls, there's nothing the SBC [Southern Baptist Convention] or any other force can do to stop them.[5]

---

4. H. Ernest Nichol, "We've a Story to Tell to the Nations," *Hymnary.org* (Baptist Hymnal 1991, 2007), hymnary.org/text/weve_a_story_to_tell_to_the_nations.

5. Susan M. Shaw, "GAs Gone Bad: Baptist Women You Should Be Reading," *Baptist News Global*, June 10, 2021, baptistnews.com/article/gas-gone-bad-baptist-women-you-should-be-reading/.

Indeed! The women featured in this book are among the many who found their voices, and the words they write present a captivating portrayal of their lives. Unstoppable, they take you along on their journeys to ordained ministry and inspire you with their persistence and courage, commitment and creativity. Some of them were told they absolutely could not "prophesy" because only sons could do that, never daughters. And yet, like Lottie Moon, they did it anyway.

Diverse Stories

Nevertheless, they persisted! Some of the women who share their stories of journey in this book traveled a hard way of rejection while others enjoyed a clearer, friendlier path. They are a diverse group—Black, White, Latinx, Japanese; LGBTQIA; young, old, and in between. They align themselves with the Cooperative Baptist Fellowship, the Alliance of Baptists, the American Baptist Churches USA, Church Without Walls Global Reach Ministries, Progressive National Baptist Convention, National Baptist Convention USA, and the Covenant Baptist United Church of Christ. Some are ecumenical Baptists. They represent more than five decades of ministry and illustrate the ways their ministries impacted the Baptist landscape and influenced Baptist history/herstory. Their stories are written while sitting with pen and paper or clicking on a computer keyboard in towns and villages and cities all over this country and beyond—from the southern United States to the north, from the west coast to the east coast, and even beyond the borders of the United States to El Salvador.

The book's foreword is written by a consummate historian of all things Baptist, Dr. Bill J. Leonard. He draws us into the Baptist history that surrounded these women through call and journey. As he gathers their thoughts and emotions, he places them in the context in which they occurred, juxtaposing them with the firmly and sometimes stubbornly held convictions of Baptists and Baptist churches.

The book's afterword, written by Rev. Suzii Paynter March, reveals the many ways the writers continue to make a positive impact in their ministry settings, their communities, and the world.

Soul Stories

The women narrators bring this book to life. Their stories fill every emotional space with wisdom and poignancy. Their stories are sad and happy, sometimes pensive, at times unrestrained. These are women—Baptist women—who have found their voices. Their stories are compelling. Their stories are inspiring. Their soul stories fill this book with life.

They are stories that might just create life-giving moments for you. Their stories recount how they heard someone or something whispering their name and how they identified the whisper as coming from a Spirit beyond them and yet inside them, all at once. Their stories narrate an acceptance of call to religious vocation that demanded living out their commitment through various types of ministry. Some preach and prophesy; some teach and lecture; some offer pastoral care; some write; some offer spiritual direction; some create sweet music. All immerse themselves in sacred presence with people in need.

You will walk beside these women on journeys that follow rocky paths. You will also walk beside those who followed pleasing paths through welcoming valleys. You will watch them as their persistence and creativity move them into acts of love and compassion, at times in the face of discouragement, threat, and uncertainty.

Stories of Journey

As you read, you may laugh or weep. You may find yourself cheering or booing. You may fully understand the women's stories, or you may become thoroughly confused. Stories of call can be confusing at times; articulating them to others can be even more convoluted. I challenge you to honor the experiences and stories shared here, even when you cannot fully understand. May you feel their sorrow and celebrate their joy. Our highest hope is that, as you read, you will sense . . .

- the deep aspirations of women who are able to ascend to higher ground, even from their lowest places;

- the ways they creatively and persistently create a clear path to minister to the people who need to hear their prophetic word;
- the grace of how they follow Spirit whispers throughout their journey;
- and how, in the end, they know deep in their souls that they are God's daughters called to minister to God's people in their neighborhoods, in their cities, and to every nation.

These women do have "a story to tell to the nations," and they are telling it in so many ways, in so many places, to many and diverse people who need to hear messages of gospel and grace.

Even upon my slaves, both men and women, in those days I will pour out my Spirit; and they shall prophesy. (Acts 2:18, NRSV)

I invite you to pause on your journey as you encounter these women on theirs. Eavesdrop on their pilgrimages. Delight in their sharing of stories. Hear with your heart the depth of their words, and, in your moments of reading, try to experience and understand what a calling from God, a whisper of Spirit, means.

Kathy Manis Findley is an ordained Baptist minister with Greek Orthodox roots. She graduated from the University of Alabama and Southern Baptist Theological Seminary and later did graduate study in victimology at Washburn University in Topeka, Kansas. She spent her thirty-eight-year ministry serving as a pastor, hospital chaplain, trauma counselor, and missionary to Uganda. She is certified in victimology, trauma intervention, and child forensic interviewing.

Kathy is active in the Alliance of Baptists, where she formerly served on the board of directors. She served two terms as president of Baptist Women in Ministry. She is an avid watercolor artist, iconographer, and blogger. Kathy is the author of two serious books, *Voices of Our Sisters* and *The Survivor's Voice: Healing the Invisible Wounds of Violence and Abuse*, and, just for fun, one Kindle novel,

Emilie's Journey: A Love Story from the Bayou. She has been married to Fred Findley for fifty-two years and is the mother of one son, Jonathan, and the doting grandmother of Jawan, Jordan, Kaden, Jalen, and Skylar.

The First Story

With a Story to Tell

Rev. Nancy Hastings Sehested

I grew up hearing women preachers in my Baptist church in Texas. I was captivated by the way they weaved the biblical story with stories from their communities. I was mesmerized by their ability to tell the story of Jesus' love shining forth in the people around them. Their preaching often closed with our fervent singing of a hymn we knew by heart: "We've a story to tell to the nations, a story of truth and mercy, a story of peace and light."[1] I longed to have experiences with a story to tell. Those preaching women were called missionaries, with their messages named "talks" or "testimonies" instead of sermons. They spoke in the fellowship hall in the basement rather than upstairs in the sanctuary. My trouble began when I walked one flight up and spoke from the pulpit sanctuary. Location. Location. Location.

My first location in the church was as a preschooler sitting in small circles as a "Sunbeam,"[2] a class where a missionary spirit was nurtured and we fervently sang "Jesus wants me for a Sunbeam, to shine for him each day." The biblical story was vividly portrayed on a flannel board with colorful moving pieces. When old enough to read,

---

1. H. Ernest Nichol, "We've a Story to Tell to the Nations," *Hymnary.org* (Baptist Hymnal 1991, 2007), hymnary.org/text/weve_a_story_to_tell_to_the_nations.

2. Southern Baptist Convention, "Sunbeams," December 25, 2021. This program of the SBC Woman's Missionary Union (WMU) was designed to teach preschoolers about missions.

I played biblical games called "sword drills" during Sunday night Training Union. It was the church's version of a non-contact competitive sport—but with military imagery (*draw swords! charge!*)—and a fun way to learn the books of the Bible. I dutifully completed the weekly checklist of my spiritual practices with the eight-point record system: arrived on time, completed daily Bible readings, attended worship and Sunday school, etc.

As a child I leaned on my mother's shoulder during long and boring sermons in Sunday services. Her small Bible was opened on her lap. It was the one given to her by my dad as a Christmas present before their wedding. She cherished it for all sixty-two years of her married life. It was a New Testament translation by Helen Barrett Montgomery, the remarkable social reformer and educator. Montgomery became the first woman president of the Northern Baptist Convention in 1921. She decided to translate the New Testament from the original Greek into more current language so that her "street urchins" (as she called them) could more easily understand the words. The translation was printed in 1924 by the American Baptist Publication Society.

In the front cover page of my mother's copy are words handwritten by her: "Man's approval is pleasant but not essential." The words were transmitted through her supportive arm into my resting head. Those words have served me well throughout forty years of ministry.

My dad was a minister and teacher who observed the rabbinical practice of daily studying the sacred texts. He taught with his hand outstretched to the congregation, holding his open Greek New Testament and simultaneously translating the verses into English. In his late eighties, he had his computer configured to type English, Hebrew, and Greek so he could continue his biblical work. Even with the diminishment of age, when his eyes blurred and his mind slipped, his hands still held his Bible, opened on his lap.

When my parents died, I kept the treasures of their beloved testaments. I also kept the German Bible that my dad was given while stationed in Germany during WWII. The book of Esther was ripped out. My dad explained that the Nazis didn't want anyone to read the story of the Jewish people being saved from death by an uprising of their own people. I wanted to be like Queen Esther.

Perhaps it was the spirit of Esther that urged me to go to the principal's office in the sixth grade. I told him it wasn't fair that only boys were the crossing guards at school. Girls could do it too. The principal smiled across his huge desk and said, "No, Nancy. Only boys can be crossing guards." I decided that the principal simply needed to see it to believe it. We girls got organized. We told the boys that if they'd give us the yellow-striped belts to wear one morning, we'd give them some Hostess Twinkies. Sure enough, it worked. We walked the children safely across the street. The principal changed his mind and girls became crossing guards too. It's unfortunate that it did not happen as easily with women ministers in the Southern Baptist Convention.

From that experience, I learned that it does not take much to stir up trouble. I learned that if you want to get things changed, it's best not to try to do it alone. It helps to have others join you in the struggle. Sometimes it is easier to say no to one voice in a private setting than to many voices in a public setting. I also learned that acting courageous has little to do with feeling courageous. As with faith, we step out with all the truth that is within us in spite of knocking knees.

It was the fall of my seventh grade year. I stared at the magazine photo of the young girl. We were born the same year, 1951. She had a coat with a Peter Pan collar, just like me. She had short, curly bangs, just like me. She sang in her Baptist church choir, just like me. But her skin color was not like me. A bomb had killed her and three other girls while they prepared for Sunday morning worship. Her name was Denise McNair.

I tore out her picture and stuck it between the pages of my Bible. Each night as I said my prayers, I held the picture of Denise and asked God to stop the bombs that killed young girls. Then I prayed that God would show me a way to help.

As the days passed, I added more pictures to my nightly ritual. Magazines from 1963 were stacked on our coffee tables with photos of the guns, the whips, the fire hoses, the dogs, the bombs, and the angry faces. I spread them out on my bed. I couldn't make sense of it.

I wrote to the president of the United States, twelve pages in my best handwriting with my favorite blue cartridge ink pen. I wanted him to know that we were all created equal and God's message of love was that we didn't need to fight. I concluded the letter with "Mr. President, if you need any help with getting this message out, I'm available. You can reach me in Dallas, Texas." I addressed the envelope to President Kennedy at the White House and placed it in the mailbox.

With each nightly prayer, my dreams increased. I imagined the president contacting me, pleased with my offer. I pictured myself speaking in school auditoriums, in church halls and sanctuaries, and even in stadiums, but weeks passed and no invitation arrived.

On November 22, President Kennedy visited my hometown. The television monitor in my seventh grade classroom showed the president and first lady as they walked off Air Force One and into the motorcade. A short time later we heard the wobbly voice of the principal: "Boys and girls, the president of the United States has been shot. You will all go home now."

I joined my parents, my brothers, and my sister in our den, huddled in front of the television as we listened to the horrifying news of the assassination. We sat in silence until my mother picked up an envelope and said, "Nancy, you got a letter today. It's from the White House."

I ran to my room to open the letter alone and read these words: "The president wants me to thank you for your letter. He and this Administration are dedicated to taking every necessary and proper step to end discrimination in all parts of our national life. . . . He appreciates your public spirit and concern for our national principles. . . . Your constructive leadership in this will be important, now and in the years to come." It was signed by Lee C. White, assistant special counsel to the president. For an impressionable twelve-year-old, the letter on that fateful day was enough to make a vow to God to be a peacemaker. And I imagined Denise McNair was my patron saint, if Baptists could have saints.

Where does a person go to become a peacemaker? Seminary seemed like a good idea. Union Theological Seminary in New York

City was the choice. For the first time, I heard women who were called preachers and pastors preach in the chapel services. None were Baptists, but that didn't matter to me. At the time I could not imagine myself being a part of any denomination. I also was not dreaming of being a pastor. I imagined working in a community center or social service agency.

I had seminary professors who encouraged the exploration of many avenues to live my call. Liberation, feminist, and womanist theology was high on the agenda of the seminary. I roamed into classrooms filled with mind-expanding ideas from James Cone, Dorothee Sölle, Katie Cannon, James Forbes, Walter Wink, Gustavo Gutiérrez, James Sanders, Raymond Brown, and Beverly Harrison. During my first semester, I watched in disbelief as some women students walked out of a lecture when the professor exclusively used male pronouns for God. I wondered if they could do that and pass the course. I was learning. The next time around I joined them.

On Reformation Sunday in that fall of 1974, I wore an armband to serve as an usher for an ecumenical service at Riverside Church. My professor Carter Heyward was one of the three priests who were celebrants for the Communion service. She was one of the "Philadelphia Eleven" who was considered "irregularly ordained" in the Episcopal Church on the Feast of Saints Mary and Martha a few months before in July.[3] Someone marred the service by spitting into a Communion cup. Nevertheless, most of the people who gathered that day were joyful, swept up in the holy hope of the turning of a new day for the church.

I watched Rev. Heyward embody courage and clarity as she met the resistance of the leadership in her diocese. I learned that misogyny is expressed in many forms, but it is always centered on power and control of women. The opposition to women priests in the Episcopal Church focused on their disobedience to the hierarchy. They were barred from the consecration of the elements in the Eucharist because that is where the power resided. In my Baptist world, the power place was considered the pulpit. Thus it became the place to resist women ministers.

---

3. "The Philadelphia Eleven," episcopalchurch.org/glossary/philadelphia-eleven-the/.

Seminary proved to be a good training ground for my journey into the Baptist world of resistance to women in leadership in the church. Plus, it was the place where I started to imagine pastoring as an avenue for embodying the grand story of God's liberation movement.

Equipped with a call, a degree, and high hopes, I looked for work. The timing was not good. Few churches of any denomination were calling women as pastors. After three years, I became the associate pastor of Oakhurst Baptist Church in Decatur, Georgia. They gladly ordained me, but it was not without some inner turmoil. As a Baptist I wondered why anyone should be ordained. Weren't we all called by God to live fully our faith as a part of the priesthood of believers? Wasn't our baptism our ordination, marking us to serve in Christ's mission in the world? What did it mean to be ordained in an institution that claimed an egalitarian way of being servants of God but was shaped in a pyramidic leadership style?

After much discernment within my church and the wider community, I was ordained with my life partner, Ken, on Reformation Sunday in 1981. It was confirmation that a personal calling needs not only an inner conviction but also a public recognition and affirmation by a community. I also began to understand ordination not as being set apart for power over the people but as being set apart for power *with* the people. Ordination offered the unique honor of weaving in and around the community to bear witness to the sightings of the Holy Spirit.

In 1987, I was called as pastor of the Prescott Memorial Baptist Church in Memphis, Tennessee. I made an unexpected dramatic entrance into that pastorate. At the time, the president of the Southern Baptist Convention was Adrian Rogers, pastor of Bellevue Baptist Church in Memphis. It was also the season that the denomination was condemning women in pastoral leadership. I liked to say that I moved into Mr. Rogers's neighborhood, but he did not like me just the way I am. It seemed that the denominational leaders wanted to be clear about the kinds of churches that would not be tolerated.

The annual meeting of the Shelby County Baptist Association met, bringing a motion to disfellowship the church for calling a woman as pastor. While the motion was being debated, I rose to speak for my three-minute rebuttal. Suddenly a motion was made to cut off the debate. It passed. I was stunned. Every Baptist bone in me rose up. I blurted into the microphone, "Mr. Moderator, since I am at the center of this controversy, I ask that I be allowed to speak." The yells from the around the sanctuary rang out. "Too late." "Too late." Then Rev. Rogers rose and said, "In the name of Christian courtesy, I think we should allow this little lady to speak." I walked to the pulpit and gave my testimony. I concluded with a reading of Jesus' words from Luke 4: "The Spirit of God is upon me, to preach good new to the poor." I closed the Bible and said, "Today this Scripture has been fulfilled in your hearing." Then I watched as the majority of people in the room voted to "disfellowship" the church.

After the meeting, the man who brought the motion to sever ties with our church came to me and said, "I hope you didn't take this personally." Well, yes, I did. "I am a person," I responded. But in one sense he was right. His attack was far greater than me personally. It was an attack on all women. The disfellowshipping act was yet another way to control and oppress women. It was yet another indication of the abuse of power. The action was wrapped in the language of biblical authority. It was a thin veneer. It was an act of justifying the subjugation and submission of women.

My church maintained courage and never wavered in the clarity of their call to me as their pastor. We became a national flash point of debate about women ministers. The church was maligned as disobedient to God's word because they said women were "first to sin in the Edenic fall." I was called "Jezebel," "whore of Babylon," "destroyer of family," "heretic," "an abomination." Some people sent me letters citing verses of the Bible on women's submission to men, just in case I'd overlooked them. However, I also received an avalanche of support from individuals and congregations all around the country.

In the public conversations, I learned to duck when anyone started their remarks with "The Bible says . . . ." At first I enjoyed the volley of biblical verses as much as anyone. The memorized verses of my youth came in handy. But it did not take long for me to lose my enthusiasm for such debate. I started asking, "What are you afraid of?" It was never answered except with a sharp word about obeying God's word. The Bible is still being dragged into the public arena to give undue authority to prejudices and injustices.

I knew that I was not going to change minds by my knowledge, my experience, or my whimsical responses. I stopped seeking to justify my calling. Instead I leaned on the one verse that is all the justification and affirmation I ever needed: "The winds of the Spirit blow where they will" (John 3:8). It blew on Shiphrah and Puah, who defied Pharaoh and his violent ways (Exod 1:15-21). It blew on Esther, who daringly saved her people (Esth 4:14). It blew on Mary, who birthed the Incarnate One without benefit of biblical precedence. It blew on the women at the tomb who were the first preachers of the resurrection. The wild winds of Spirit blow where they will. I felt them blow on me.

Sometimes people have asked me how I walked through that time of being the target of hatred. I was fortunate. Unlike some women, I had the support of family, friends, and church. I also had the story of Jesus. He was nearly thrown off a cliff by his hometown folk for his sermon on including people whom they thought should be excluded. The Jesus story still empowers me to step up and speak up.

About a year after the church was disfellowshipped, I was in Sweden for the first International Baptist Peace Fellowship, hosted by Swedish Baptists. I was surprised that there were so many women pastors in their country. I remarked that the Swedes were leading the way in social progress. One of the pastors responded by saying, "This is not progress. It is a sign of the weakness of the church that so many women are pastors. If it was still strong, more men would still be leaders."

The words struck me as a clarifying explanation. In some places we were breaking through the stained-glass ceiling, but that ceiling was already cracked and beginning to fall down upon us all. As in other professions, when status and salary are diminished in once male-dominated occupations, women are hired to do the same work or more but with less pay and less prestige.

Over time I felt the crumbling of the institution. While we've been changing the landscape, it has been changing us. I learned that the institution that claimed me could not save me. I put extra pressure on myself as a pioneer to prove that women could do the work. I grew weary. It became clear that I could not sustain the pace that I set for myself.

I stepped away from church for a while. But I didn't step away from my calling. I became a prison chaplain, still intent on discovering the ways the Spirit was popping up with hope and healing in hopeless places. My congregation comprised 800 men and 350 staff. In that village of the damned, I became their pastor for thirteen years. It forced me to ask the hardest questions of my faith. What did I truly believe about redemption, forgiveness, and grace? Was transformation possible with people who had maimed and murdered? I stayed on high alert, not only for the possibility of violence breaking out but also for the possibility of the Spirit breaking in. The Spirit blows where it will, even in a high-security prison.

During that time, I also became a founding co-pastor of a new community of faith. With Joyce Hollyday and my husband Ken, we formed a church. We started the church during Advent 2001, a few months after the horrors of 9/11. We named it Circle of Mercy for two notable reasons: because the world is desperately in need of mercy and because a circle invites us all to practice this holy calling.

There is a proverb: "They tried to bury us. They didn't know we were seeds." I have been blessed to see so many seeds sprout. I have lived long enough to reap the harvest of forty years. I am grateful that I have been being able to practice preaching, teaching, blessing babies, honoring the dead, holding the hands of the dying, weeping with those who weep, and rejoicing with those who rejoice. I've lived to see gifted women in ministry bring new life to the church, the academy, hospitals, and prisons. I've seen the wisdom of women as pastoral counselors and professors. I've witnessed the skills of women leading nonprofits and doing advocacy work. Women have expanded the conversation in theology, prophetically calling us all to see both the injustices as well as the redemption in our religious traditions. I cannot but bow in thanksgiving.

After forty years, I have now retired from my positions. But I have not retired from my calling. The winds of the Spirit still blow with a story to tell.

Nancy Hastings Sehested served as a state prison chaplain in a maximum-security prison for men in North Carolina. She was also co-pastor of the Circle of Mercy Congregation, an ecumenical church in Asheville, North Carolina, which is affiliated with both the United Church of Christ and the Alliance of Baptists. Nancy earned a master of divinity from Union Theological Seminary in New York City and received the seminary's Distinguished Alumni Award in 1992. An ordained Baptist minister, she has pastored churches in Atlanta, Memphis, and Asheville during the past twenty-five years. She is a frequent guest preacher and lecturer at churches, colleges, and conferences around the country and abroad. Nancy has written extensively for religious journals and periodicals, is featured in an anthology of sermons by women titled *And Blessed Is She*, and recently published *Marked for Life: A Prison Chaplain's Story*. Married to Ken Sehested, she is proud to be a grandmother.

The Second Story

Bloom Where You Are Planted

Rev. Dr. C. Lynn Brinkley

I have always been inspired by the phrase "Bloom where you are planted."[1] The Bishop of Geneva, Saint Francis de Sales (1567–1622), is credited with the quote. This quote has been the guidepost for my ministry. A constant reminder that no matter where God plants me, it is there that I must serve, bloom, thrive, and present the best version of myself. I have discovered value in being faithful in messy and muddy places as God cultivates my next opportunity to grow.

I didn't grow up in the church. I wanted to, but family dynamics made it impossible. I was the youngest of four, raised by a single parent who worked three jobs from hours 7-3, 3-11, and 11-7. That is not an exaggeration. There was hardly any time for my mom to rest, let alone take four children to church on Sunday morning. Thankfully, I had a praying grandmother and an aunt who took me in and nurtured me each summer. These women were instrumental in introducing me to the faith. On hot summer days in rural North Carolina, I watched Grandma Mary model Christian hospitality. "Who come?" is how she greeted visitors who knocked on her door.

---

1. Bishop of Geneva, Saint Francis de Sales (1567–1622), idiomation.wordpress.com/tag/saint-francis-de-sales/.

Once the "who" was identified, guests were welcomed inside for Southern cuisine, a cold glass of lemonade, and *Days of Our Lives* on a black-and-white television for entertainment. My grandmother's gift of hospitality was a source of inspiration for my first publication, *Manners and Money: A Manual on Preaching Etiquette*.[2]

My grandmother and Aunt Clara knew my mom worked a lot, so they made sure I was introduced to the Black church, Vacation Bible School, and celebratory worship. Although I wasn't a frequent churchgoer, I prayed often as a child. I vividly remember this prayer: "God, I don't know if Jesus is good or bad, but I pray for him too." I am glad I eventually learned how truly good Jesus is.

Not belonging to a "home church" was a thorn in my side. Church always fascinated me, and I didn't understand why our family didn't go. It didn't register to me at the time that my mom probably needed to *Selah* (to rest or stop) on the Sabbath Day. Nevertheless, it hurt not being connected to a community of faith. I remember my peers in middle school talking about a great time they had at a recent youth retreat. I felt excluded from that conversation and desperately wished I had gone too. I even walked away from my peers so they wouldn't notice the tears that welled up in my eyes. This feeling of detachment from the local church continued into my young adult years.

From the Patrol Car to the Pulpit

In summer 1988, I entered college. Parties and Duke basketball dominated my attention. Church was not in the equation. I readily admit that I was distracted as a young adult and often engaged in sinful behavior. It wasn't until my senior year that a light bulb came on and I began to take my studies more seriously. I finished my final semester with a 4.0, only by God's amazing grace.

Prior to graduating, I served as a student intern with campus police despite the fact that I wasn't interested in law enforcement. I wanted to be a meteorologist or a sports anchor on television. I went home one weekend and ran into one of my high school teachers. I told Mr. Stevens I wanted to be a news reporter and he responded,

---

2. Lynn C. Brinkley, *Manners and Money: A Manual on Preaching Etiquette* (Norman, OK: Nurturing Faith, 2015).

"That's not a good profession; you shouldn't do that." But that was what I wanted to do. Some days, I still wish I had.

Regrettably, I went back to North Carolina State, a university that leads in agriculture education, a place where I should have bloomed, but I changed my major to Sociology because my professor said I should. After earning my bachelor's degree, I was hired by the campus police department and sent to basic law enforcement training to become a certified police officer. This was the first professional job offer I had, so I took it! I have three major takeaways from my experience in law enforcement. (1) I never want to work in that field again. (2) There are more good cops than bad. (3) The bad cops are really bad.

Black Lives Matter

In 2021, as I reflect on my past experience as a police officer in the aftermath of the deaths of Ahmaud Arbery, Breonna Taylor, George Floyd, and so many others, I firmly believe Black Lives Matter! As a former police officer who has had my life in danger on more than one occasion, I believe blue lives matter. And yes, I believe *your* life matters! Why is it so difficult for others to hear with empathy the cries of Black, Indigenous, people of color (BIPOC) when we say "The struggle is real"? Being followed in department stores, being pulled over by the police without just cause, and fearing for your life in certain settings is real! And no uniform or badge shielded me from that reality.

After my brief career in law enforcement, I went into the nonprofit sector trying to find my vocation, my voice, and my passion. I served as a foster care supervisor and a lead case manager for a juvenile program, but nothing seemed to fit who God was calling me to become. I began to wrestle with my purpose and considered joining the Air Force, but God called me beside a dumpster.

Divinity School and Seminary

My call to ministry happened right outside of Taylor Hall on the campus of Campbell University. It was August 24, 2004, shortly after 5:00 p.m. I had just finished my last divinity school class for the day. As I was exiting the back of Taylor Hall, I walked beside a trash dumpster (it's still there). When I passed the dumpster, I had an epiphany. I don't know why the Spirit chose to speak to me beside a dumpster. I have always been a trash talker, so that could have some bearing. What I do recall is that the sun was shining bright that day. I didn't hear a loud voice. The trumpet didn't sound. The earth didn't quake, but a still, small voice clearly revealed, "You are going to work at Campbell one day." This vision was so strong that I went home and wrote about it in my journal. I then placed the journal back on the shelf and never thought about it again until February 2007 (put a pin here). I am a big fan of journaling! I think it is important to journal and record "God moments" or significant things that happen in your life. I journaled the vision at the dumpster in which the Spirit spoke to me on August 24, 2004, and I thought no more about it until three years later.

In February 2007, I was leaving class, this time on the third floor of Taylor Hall, and my preaching professor, Dr. Roy DeBrand, approached me and said, "You know Faith's position is open. I think you should consider applying for it!" When Dr. DeBrand encouraged me to apply for the position as director of student services at the Divinity School, my mind immediately went back to August 24, 2004, and the vision I received by the dumpster that I was going to work at Campbell University in the future. What did this mean? I had to start praying. I had to decide if God was calling me. I didn't want to leave my job at the time because it was safe. I was a supervisor, the pay was good, and I worked close to home. I was comfortable. Should I apply and work in an environment where I would be the only woman of color on staff? How would my colleagues receive me? How would the students receive me? Was I good enough? The answer was yes. The call by the dumpster was not a mistake. I was able to bloom!

I am deeply indebted to Campbell University Divinity School for preparing me for ministry. I am reminded of 1 Corinthians 3:6 in which Paul says, "I have planted, Apollos watered; but God gave the increase." This verse always reminds me of my time at Campbell and how "a few good men" invested in my ministry. Rev. Jesse L.

Timmons, pastor of my grandmother's home church in Chadbourn, North Carolina, helped to plant me by introducing me to Campbell Divinity School and escorting me to student orientation. Dr. Roy DeBrand affirmed my gifts as a preacher and watered my preaching ministry by being a supportive father in ministry and getting me "gigs." And Dr. Mike Cogdill, dean of the divinity school, took the bold step to hire me. I was still a semester away from graduating with my master of divinity degree. There were others equally qualified, but Dr. Cogdill believed in my August 24, 2004, journal entry and said, "Forgive me if I say this the wrong way. We have always needed diversity on our staff, but I want you to know today that we are hiring you because of you, and for no other reason." Through these male mentors, God gave the increase! It was time to bloom.

By answering the call to pursue theological education, I have preached in chapels and churches of diverse denominations across the country and the world. I have taught at the Baptist World Congress in Durban, South Africa. I was appointed as vice president of the ministers' division of the General Baptist State Convention of North Carolina, and I currently have the pleasure of serving with the Baptist Joint Committee as the first African American chair of their executive committee. But there is always room to blossom.

In 2010, I decided to pursue a doctorate of ministry degree (DMin). My original intent was to attend Drew University. However, I wanted to remain faithful to my job at Campbell, and Drew's cohort schedule would not allow me to do both. I was led to Gordon Conwell Theological Seminary (GCTS) in South Hamilton, Massachusetts, by my assigned mentor at Campbell Divinity School, Rev. Dr. Terry L. Henry, senior pastor of Macedonia Missionary Baptist Church in Wilmington, North Carolina. Terry had completed his DMin at GCTS and recommended the program to me, so off I went. I entered a cohort that included legendary preaching professor Dr. Haddon Robinson, seventeen men, and me. Some of the men in the cohort didn't believe in women in ministry. Some of them felt I shouldn't be there. But when graduation day came, only six of us walked across the stage, and I was one of them. Bloom where you are planted!

Ordination Pains

My doctoral studies were rewarding but caused a strain on my already troubled marriage. My quest to become an ordained minister was the last straw. The process was prolonged and painful. My spouse was also my pastor, who held the keys to my becoming "Reverend." I was told, "We don't have a quorum to have a meeting to approve your ordination," or meetings kept getting postponed. There was always some excuse for over a year (I counted) that blocked my ordination from going forward. Here I was, serving in my local church, serving in a leadership role at a divinity school, working on a doctor of ministry degree, and I couldn't get my church, my pastor, my spouse, to authorize my ordination. I even had peers in my doctoral program who urged me to come to their church. Two of my African brothers, Joseph Oniyama and Mamusha Fenta, said, "Come to our church. We will ordain you on the spot!" This was a dark and hurtful moment in ministry. A time when I felt my petals falling to the ground to be buried in mud.

I wanted to live and not die, so I made the painful decision to leave my marriage and my church. It was at that time that Rev. Jesse L. Timmons, the former pastor of my grandmother's home church, invited me to ordination classes at a local association where he was now serving as moderator. My ordination process took an entire year to complete. Each month, I drove almost an hour to participate in early Saturday morning ordination classes. It was a long, arduous process, but I stayed faithful to it. I bloomed where I was planted for that entire year, and I received my certificate of ordination. I am thankful for the many years Rev. Timmons invested in my ministry. He even purchased a new laptop for me when the one I had used for preaching engagements stopped working. I am certain that I have been able to thrive because of the male mentors in my life, and I regret that I didn't have any women mentors during my early years of ministry. There weren't any women in major leadership positions in the church or our local associations. I never had a female mentor to turn to until I met Pam.

Mentors and Me

Pam Durso called and invited me to serve on the Baptist Women in Ministry's leadership team in 2014. I didn't know Pam personally, but I had heard a lot about her. Her name still lingered in the halls of Campbell University Divinity School, where she had previously served as a professor of Church History. Pam was the first woman in ministry who invested in me. Pam nurtured, advocated, and connected me in so many ways. Not only did Pam invite me to serve on BWIM's leadership team; she introduced me to the Baptist Joint Committee and always managed to place me in the room where it happens. I am deeply grateful for the time Pam called, once again, and offered me my current position as associate director of Baptist Women in Ministry. It is through Pam Durso that I discovered how vital it is for women in ministry to have other women in their lives as mentors.

Lessons Learned

When this book is published, I will be fifty-two years old, serving in the ministry now for twenty-one years. I have learned some valuable lessons along the way, but I am still learning how to navigate this odd and wondrous calling. I will share a few:

(1) I am learning that having a mentor is important, and being a mentor is paramount.

(2) I am learning that I have a role to play in the pursuit of justice. The death of George Floyd was a national awakening moment, but Mr. Floyd's death particularly hit home when I realized he was born in my hometown of Fayetteville, North Carolina. The death of George Floyd awakened my soprano voice for advocacy. Black Lives Matter!

(3) I am learning that my personal well-being is vital to being my authentic self. I am happy entertaining myself, although I used to struggle with eating alone or seeing others eating alone. Now, one of my greatest gifts of wellness I can give myself is eating alone at a nice restaurant with outdoor seating, listening to Yo-Yo Ma.

(4) I am also learning that less is more. I always did more because I felt the pressure as a Black woman to go beyond what was required.

I felt I needed to do more in order to be seen, taken seriously, and respected. I didn't have the luxury of doing less because more was expected of me. I am finally at a place where I am learning that I am enough!

(5) I am learning that my daughter Taylor is now a young adult. If I have done my job as a mother, I have prepared her well, so there is no need for me to control her life's narrative. She does a pretty good job of it on her own.

(6) I have learned that breakups are a part of life. I sure wish that wasn't true, but we have to be prepared. Someone we love will hurt, disappoint, or leave us.

(7) The greatest lesson I have learned is to be faithful where I am planted—to offer to the Lord, my family, my job, my studies, and my local church my best. To stay planted until another door of opportunity opens. As my Aunt Ann, a retired lieutenant colonel who passed away in 2020 due to Covid-19, would always say, "When the door opens, you better have your bags packed and ready to go!"

Lynn Brinkley has been associate director of Baptist Women in Ministry since January 2020. Lynn previously served as director of church, alumni, and student relations at Campbell University Divinity School in Buies Creek, North Carolina, where she had been on staff since May 2007. Since 2012, she was an adjunct instructor, teaching in both Campbell University Divinity School and the Christian Studies Department. Lynn earned a doctor of ministry degree from Gordon Conwell Theological Seminary in May 2014, a master of divinity degree from Campbell University Divinity School in May 2008, a master of science degree from the University of Tennessee-Chattanooga in May 1997, and a bachelor of science and sociology degree from North Carolina State University in May 1992.

Lynn is the vice-president of the ministers' division for the General Baptist State Convention of North Carolina, serves on the board of Baptist Joint Committee (BJC), and is currently co-chair of BJC's executive committee. She serves as associate minister at First Baptist of Fayetteville, North Carolina, and was ordained on May 4, 2014. Lynn was a board member of the Baptist Women in Ministry of North Carolina, and from 2015 to 2018 she served on Baptist Women in Ministry's Leadership Team. A frequent guest preacher at churches of diverse denominations, Lynn is also the author of *Manners and Money: A Manual on Preaching Etiquette*. Lynn's daughter, Taylor, is a 2020 graduate of North Carolina A&T State University in Greensboro, where she majored in mechanical engineering; she has been commissioned as a second lieutenant in the Air Force.

The Third Story

Following God's Next Right Step

Rev. Julie Whidden Long

I can't pinpoint the moment when I fell in love with the church. Barbara Brown Taylor writes in her book, *Leaving Church*, that she can't remember the exact moment when she fell in love with God.[1] I resonate with her, but for me it was the community of faith that captured my heart. In my early years, God was a little harder to put my finger on, more of a generous authority figure than a close companion. The people of the church—they were the ones I could put my arms around. The church welcomed me in, affirmed me, gave me space to figure out who I was becoming, and became extended family for me. The church—the people—embodied God for me, and it was through loving church that I learned to love God and the life of faith.

I can identify the moment I first fell in love with a particular church—during my youth group years. My family had been a part of First Baptist Church of Fitzgerald, Georgia, since I was born, but during my middle and high school years, church youth group became a transformative place for me. Blane and Barbara Jacobs were the heart of our youth group. Blane held the title of minister of music

---

1. Barbara Brown Taylor, *Leaving Church* (San Francisco: HarperSanFrancisco, 2006), 22.

and youth, and his wife Barbara was employed by the church as his part-time associate, but their ministry was a partnership through and through. They were fun, creative, caring, and deeply invested in the lives of the young people with whom they worked. Under their leadership, our youth group thrived. I found "my people" there, friends who shared values and had fun together and leaders who encouraged us to live our faith and were open to our big questions. I could not get enough of church.

During a time in my adolescent development in which I asserted my independence and pushed away from my parents, I found family at church. It's hard to say whether I was drawn there out of a deep spiritual identity and call that was at the core of who I was, or if the church's profound influence on me nudged me toward ministry. It probably goes both ways.

As I approached high school graduation and considered future educational plans, three of my ministers—youth minister Blane, our associate pastor Gerald Thomas, and our pastor Gene Wilder—came to me individually and asked if I had ever considered a call to ministry. As much as I loved church, I had not. Maybe it was because I didn't have any women ministry role models and I couldn't imagine that for myself (Barbara Jacobs had functioned in pastoral ways but had not been recognized by the church as a minister in any formal sense). I was a good student, particularly in math, and I planned to choose a field that required academic rigor. I had no idea that ministry could be that path. I worried if I would live up to my family's expectations. I didn't know how I felt about the social implications of being "set apart"—that seemed like a lonely place to be. Deep down, I feared what saying yes to God's call might mean. So I tucked those encouragements from my ministers away and continued with my own plan.

As I prepared to go to college, I chose Mercer University and enrolled in the School of Engineering. At Mercer, a historically Baptist school, all students were required to take a religion class. By the spring semester of my freshman year, I discovered that I didn't have much passion for engineering. But when I took my Introduction to New Testament class with Walter (Buddy) Shurden, I felt lit up by the teaching, the subject matter, and the way of thinking that differed from the hard sciences. I absolutely loved it and knew I needed to leave the engineering school and move into the College of Liberal Arts.

The summer following my freshman year, I served as the summer children's minister at First Baptist Fitzgerald. I could not imagine a better summer job—getting paid to work with children at my beloved home church under the supervision of Blane Jacobs. I loved every minute.

As I returned to Mercer in the fall, I took another class with Dr. Shurden, enjoying it as much as the previous one. One day, he returned a paper I had written with a note scribbled on it asking me to come see him in his office. Though he had always been warm to me and I had scored well on the paper, I was terrified. When I visited him, he offered a few writing tips and then invited me to sit down and talk. He asked about my experience working at the church that summer and if I thought I was being called to ministry. I'm pretty sure I burst into tears as I confessed that I had been wrestling with a sense of call and didn't know what to do with it. He told me, "When I am talking to people who think they may be called to ministry, I ask them three questions: What can't you shake? If you could choose a book to read about any subject, what would you choose? What do others (besides your parents) say that you should do?" As I pondered my answers to those questions, clarity came and I embraced a call to ministry and all that would entail.

As I talked to my parents in the days ahead, I framed my decision as a change of major, not as a call to ministry. My family focused on education and achievement and held high expectations for me. My parents were regular church attenders but not deeply involved, and neither parent talked about their faith openly. In keeping with that tone, our conversation was more professionally focused than spiritually centered. I noticed resistance at first, although they tried hard not to show it. It wasn't about my gender; I came from a long line of independent, empowered women who were leaders in their male-dominated fields. Their concerns were valid: was this a serious career option, or was this merely wishful thinking that I could get a job hanging out at church as if I was still in youth group? This path was not one they expected for me, and I imagine they felt some of the tension I held about whether I was squandering my intellect.

Eventually my parents came around after seeing me in action and hearing others speak of my giftedness for ministry. Years later I heard a story from my paternal grandfather, himself a devoted church leader with a deep sense of piety. He told me that my father had expressed to him his concern and uncertainty about my call to ministry early on. My octogenarian fundamentalist Baptist grandfather told his son, "If God is calling her into ministry, you do not need to stand in the way." My grandfather was always supportive of me as a minister, giving me my first set of biblical commentaries. Although I don't embrace the books' scholarship or theology and have never used them, they remain a treasure to me.

In college, I held a pretty specific idea of what my ministry would look like—serving as a children's minister in a local congregation. To gain experience, I volunteered in a local congregation when I was away at school, First Baptist Church of Christ in Macon, Georgia, leading a preschool missions class and a fifth and sixth grade Sunday school class. During the summers, I continued to serve as First Baptist Fitzgerald's summer children's minister. Longtime children's ministry leaders in both of these places formed me and mentored me. As I considered next steps, professors and mentors encouraged me to continue my education in seminary.

I enrolled at Mercer's McAfee School of Theology in Atlanta and worked part-time as a children's minister at a small church near the Atlanta airport. I still loved children's ministry, but seminary exposed me to a myriad of ways of doing ministry. I loved the academy, so I focused my master of divinity with an academic research concentration, thinking it would broaden my options to pursue PhD work. Yet I continued to feel drawn to the local church. Seminary helped me to take the knowledge I was learning and apply it to the work of ministry. While those years broadened my scope and expanded my ideas, they also affirmed my sense of devotion to congregational ministry.

Meanwhile, I fell in love with a fellow student, Jody Long, and as we realized that we wanted to marry, my decisions about my future became *our* decisions. We both worked in congregational ministry, and we knew that we didn't want to serve in different places as we began our life together. As he approached graduation (one year before me), I nudged him toward an open youth ministry position at my beloved college church in Macon. He was called there, and several months later, I took a part-time children's ministry position there as well, anticipating that we would soon marry and serve in ministry together. The church took a risk in hiring me, as Jody and I were not yet engaged. But I think all parties sensed that the Spirit was in it and that it would work.

It did work, resulting in a long tenure for us both. My position turned full-time upon my graduation, and Jody and I married that summer. We were so excited and grateful for the chance to serve in ministry areas to which we felt called and equipped, in a wonderfully supportive and healthy church that was committed to being a teaching congregation for young ministers.

We worked there together, at First Baptist Church of Christ in Macon, for fourteen years. During those years, our responsibilities grew, titles changed, and callings developed. As other staff members transitioned, I took on more administrative and pastoral responsibilities. I developed a broader calling to pastoral leadership, not only to ministry with children. While working with children and their families and giving specific focus to their faith formation remained central and life-giving to me, I found that I also loved other areas of congregational leadership. I developed as a preacher and found deep fulfillment in pastoral care spaces. I saw my gifts in strategic thinking and planning and emerged as the staff member who "kept the trains running on time." I found profound meaning in developing deep relationships over time and being a part of the most significant moments of people's lives—births, baptisms, weddings, funerals. Helping people make meaning out of these rites of passage and important seasons became among the most personally significant work I did.

Once, a first grader in my ministry drew a picture for me. In the picture, I was standing on the front steps of the church holding something in my hand that looked like a stick. I asked her about it. "It's a magic wand," she said, "because you help make the magic happen at church." I posted that drawing on my office bulletin board, and it became a guiding image for me about my calling—to help make the magic happen for people. I began to understand my specific purpose and giftedness in creating space for people to encounter the sacred in life and to make meaning of it. Sometimes that came in the form of planning retreats or children's events, often in intentionally crafting rituals and language for dedications or baptisms or bedside moments or funerals or weddings or sermons. While I wasn't naïve or idealistic enough to think I would retire doing the same thing in the same place I started, for many years my ministry at First Baptist was a vocational "sweet spot" for me. I was thriving. I loved what I was doing in a good and healthy place where I was surrounded by people who loved me and challenged me to grow and excel. Working with my husband was a gift. He was my biggest cheerleader, my most honest critic, and a creative partner when I needed to brainstorm or flesh out an idea. I was in love with my work, and I put my whole heart into it.

At the same time, my deep love for my work could be too much of a good thing. I tend to be the type of person who gives my full effort to whatever I am doing. If I am going to commit to something, I want to do it well. Our church historically had a reputation and culture of excellence as well. I held high expectations for myself and those I worked alongside. I grew frustrated when I felt like others dropped the ball. I over-functioned for other staff members, covering what they dropped, overcompensating for gaps and weaknesses, working to maintain a reputation of professionalism and competency. I felt like, as the detail-oriented staff member and the only female minister, I carried the bulk of the emotional labor and mental load. I tended to be the one who kept all the moving parts in mind, knowing the details of how each event or initiative we planned affected the others and what people needed to be involved. While my colleagues were competently doing their own jobs, somehow I felt like I was the one holding it all together.

I was aware that I needed to set some self-care boundaries, and I did—taking Fridays off, using all of my vacation time each year, screening phone calls and emails during my time off, surrounding myself with ministry peers with whom I could be real and on whom I could lean for support. I thought I was doing many of the right things, maybe not all the time, but faithfully.

In the last two to three years of my ministry at First Baptist, I struggled with burnout and compassion fatigue, and I wondered how long I could keep up the pace. As my own children entered school and we became tied down to a Monday-Friday schedule during the school year, the Sunday church obligations made it difficult to get any meaningful or substantial time away as a family. With both Jody and I serving in youth and children's ministry, our summer schedule was slammed full as well. We staggered weeks of youth camp, youth choir tour, children's camp, VBS, mission trips, denominational conferences, and more so that one parent was home with our own children while the other was away with church kids. We passed like ships in the night for weeks at a time. While I loved my work, the rhythms felt more and more unsustainable. I began to lose pieces of my creativity and needed a drastic change.

I thought an upcoming sabbatical would help, and the time away was a helpful reset. But when I found myself exhausted again three weeks after returning, I knew that something had to give. My husband was in an interview process for a new ministry position in a denominational setting. When he was offered a job that allowed us more financial freedom, I asked to give up my broader pastoral and administrative responsibilities to return to part-time children's ministry. I focused on a particular ministry that was life-giving for me while removing some of the responsibilities that had begun to feel overbearing. The specificity of my work helped me to get the distance needed to let go of some of my over-functioning in other areas.

Six months later, a ministry opportunity came my way. Pam Durso, then executive director of Baptist Women in Ministry (BWIM), offered me a brand-new position. As associate director of BWIM, I would support her work in all of the initiatives of the organization while focusing on developing a mentoring program for new ministers and call discernment retreats for college and seminary students. I would work from home, not have to move my family, receive a salary increase, and work with an organization and leader that I had long been involved with and admired.

The opportunity felt like a lifeboat, coming to rescue me from drowning. I hardly had to consider whether I would accept it, although I must confess that my heart was never truly in it. I chalked that up to grief around leaving church ministry and nervousness about trying something new and decided to press forward anyway, because it still somehow felt like the next right step.

Upon later reflection, I found language around my ambivalent feelings about this new ministry opportunity. Leaving church and going to BWIM was much more of a call "away from" than a call "to." I did not particularly want to leave church ministry. I deeply loved my ministry and the people in that particular church, and I wanted so badly to make it work. But I realized I could no longer work in that system and be healthy. I experienced much grief in leaving that position, but as much as I resonated with Barbara Brown Taylor's feeling of falling in love with God and the church, I also connected with another reflection on call in her book: "the call to serve God is first and last the call to be fully human."[2] I needed to take a step toward being a whole, healthy human.

I began my new ministry with BWIM learning the ropes through conversations, reading history and organizational documents, and imagining what this new position and the programs I held responsibility for would look like. I felt grateful for a slower pace, catching my breath and having time to rest, recover, and reflect on the past fourteen years of full-time congregational ministry. Six weeks into my BWIM work, my family learned that my mother had advanced colon cancer. Her illness and death unfolded quickly in the course of less than a month. On the day after my mom received her diagnosis, I broke my foot, requiring surgery and grounding me from walking or driving for nine weeks. I felt like the carpet had been pulled out from under me as I found myself literally broken and in acute grief compounded by my vocational grief. The freedom and flexibility of my work life was such a gift; I could not imagine going through

---

2. Taylor, *Leaving Church*, xi.

all of that in the midst of a busy Advent season as a congregational minister.

While I appreciated and enjoyed the slower pace and the chance to create something new, I struggled to feel energized and connected to my new work. Working from home felt isolating. I realized how much I valued face-to-face encounters and a depth of relationships with those with whom I ministered, and cultivating those relationships with the scattered "congregation" of a national organization would take time. The travel required to build those connections took me away from my husband and children more often than I wished, and I felt like I was missing out on things at home. While I loved and believed in the organization and the work we were doing, I realized a few months in that this way of doing ministry would not be a long-term fit for me. Knowing my grief was a part of my unsettledness, I tried to give it time to see if my love for the work could grow.

I also wrestled with my sense of calling; while I didn't doubt that I was still called to ministry, I struggled with whether I had misread God's calling to this particular setting. I wondered if I would ever find another ministry position that I loved as much as my time at First Baptist. I had so many questions: Was my nostalgia clouding my memories of the difficulties and challenges there? Was my calling focused to congregational ministry after all? What was it, specifically, that I was called to do? Was that calling changing? What did it mean for me to be faithful to God's call in this new season?

As I reflected, I affirmed some of the gifts and passions that I had experienced in previous seasons of ministry. I remembered that guiding image of meaning-making and realized my value of investing deeply in relationships that provide the chance to share in the most sacred moments of people's lives. I missed engaging with children and knew that I needed to create spaces in my life to continue to work with them. I reaffirmed that I do my best work in collaboration with others, and I missed the energy of working closely with a team. I love creating and improving initiatives and processes. Problem-solving and strategic thinking invigorate me.

I stuck it out through the first year, but soon thereafter I determined that my staying in the position half-heartedly was not serving me or the organization. The timing was right, as a couple of my projects were wrapping up and new long-term initiatives would soon launch. I worried that I was leaving too soon: Should I wait longer or try harder to make it work? What would this short tenure look like on my resumé? Would my departure raise red flags about the organization? Ultimately, I decided, having experienced the unexpected loss of both parents in their sixties, that life is too short to be stuck, unhappy and unfulfilled. My recent inheritances gave us the financial security for me to step away to try something new once again.

At BWIM, one of my responsibilities included developing a mentoring program for young or new ministers. As I explored how to train mentors to lead their groups, I learned more about how the field of coaching could inform our approach. I underwent coach training to pass my learning on to the mentors in the program.

The more I studied coaching and coached others, the more I realized how much I liked it. Coaching uses deep listening and thoughtful questioning to help people determine how to achieve goals and be who they want to be. A coach does not approach the conversation as an expert but empowers the person being coached to realize their own answers and potential. I discovered how much this style of coaching connects with my values as a leader and was surprised at how naturally coaching came to me. I had been coaching all along in congregational ministry as I counseled, equipped volunteers, supervised staff, and had conversations with individuals about their faith or life journey. The training helped me to hone those skills and reminded me of some of the parts of ministry that I most enjoyed.

I decided to launch a coaching practice that would become my primary avenue of ministry. My niches have become coaching women in ministry as well as people engaging in vocational discernment or transition. Creating my own business has given me the flexibility and creativity for other ministry-related endeavors, including designing coaching groups around topics, consulting with congregations, writing curriculum and collaborating on book projects, and supply preaching. I love the freedom and time I have to say "yes" to these types of projects that were previously hard to add to a full plate.

I also pursued a part-time position at my children's elementary school as a Family Engagement Facilitator, connecting parents and families with ways to partner in supporting their child's learning and growth at school. The school job matches my desire to work with children and families and involves me in a collaborative team environment while offering employment benefits and a stable, though small, income.

A year and a half in to this new model of ministry (most of it in the midst of a global pandemic), I must confess that I continue to wrestle with calling. I still feel called, though I question the best ways to live that out and sometimes still feel as if I still am in a liminal season. What I do feel confident about is this: in every season, I have seen enough of God's light and have felt enough of the Spirit's tug to know, when it is time, the next right step. So far, every time I have taken a leap, I have landed; each time I have felt like I was stuck, a way forward opened.

I have learned that my call to ministry is not solely dependent on where I draw a paycheck. In discovering that work is less important than I once thought it was, I have found other spaces in life that are as meaningful. I am spending this season exploring and creating those other spaces that offer significance for my life. While I deeply value the place of the church in my story, I no longer believe, in Barbara Brown Taylor's words, that God's address is the church.[3] While I always knew God lived outside of the church, I experienced God most deeply in the people and rituals within her walls. That is changing for me as I discover the Holy in places where I previously devoted less attention—in nature, in my body, in books, in my dearest people.

Anyone who has been in love long enough can tell you that over time, the excitement and passion and energy of those early days of the relationship start to wane. Growing in their place is a love that is steady and committed, familiar and comfortable, although punctuated at times with disappointment, betrayal, frustration, or

---

3. Barbara Brown Taylor, "Finding God Outside the Church Walls," *Christian Century*, July 9, 2020, christiancentury.org/article/how-my-mind-has-changed/finding-god-outside-church-walls.

indifference. It takes work—intentional time and attention and care and respect—to continue to nurture and deepen the love that remains.

I still wear my vows to Christ's church like I wear my wedding band, as a sign of the covenant of love that I have entered into. As I learn and grow and change, this call has grounded me in who I have been and challenged me to pay attention to who I am continually being created to be. It connects me with the Spirit that always calls us forth and gives us enough light to see the next right step.

Julie Whidden Long is an ordained Baptist minister and certified empowerment coach. She has served congregations in Georgia for nearly twenty years in the roles of associate pastor and minister to children and families and as associate director of Baptist Women in Ministry. She currently lives out her ministry calling through coaching clergy and other leaders, consulting with congregations, writing, and pulpit supply. Julie is the author of *Portraits of Courage: Stories of Baptist Heroes* and has contributed chapters or sermons to several other publications. Julie is a graduate of Mercer University (BA) and Mercer's McAfee School of Theology (MDiv) and serves on Mercer University's Board of Trustees. She and her husband, Jody Long, live in Macon, Georgia, with their two children.

The Fourth Story

Never Too Late

Rev. Carolyn Yeldell Staley

My ministry journey has been long, winding, and sometimes treacherous. I am grateful that, more recently, women who hear God's call to ministry travel calmer journeys with many roads to follow. Some of them even follow a straight path, directly through seminary and ordination to places of ministry of all kinds. That type of journey was not available to me. I never saw a woman preaching in the pulpit, although women sang and gave testimonies. Everyone's story is unique. I hope my story might inspire those who hear a late-life call to ministry, even to preaching ministry.

The desire to hear God's call has been a part of life for me for as long as I can remember. Retracing the years, I can see God's call through every career step—motherhood, teaching, public service, missions, performance, and church ministry. In each instance I have felt God's call as an opportunity to serve. Eventually, the pathway to seminary, ordination, and preaching opened for me—right in God's good time.

I felt God's call from a young age. My father was a Baptist preacher in Arkansas and Mississippi. My mother was a Bible study teacher and mission leader. I had three siblings, and most of our family activities were centered at church. My siblings and I played church instead of playing house or school as other children did. We arranged our small chairs in the backyard and created a sanctuary. We took turns leading the service. One of us preached, and another led the singing. We also took up the offering, and our offertory hymn was "Put Another Nickel In."[1]

It's funny that I can remember, as a preschooler, thinking about theological issues. I remember being concerned that Baptists, Methodists, and Presbyterians believed differently. At age five I asked my mother, what if they were right and we had it wrong? I wondered if everyone was going to heaven.

Mother told me that at age four, I came into the kitchen, sat on a step stool, and, swinging my legs, announced, "I'm going to heaven today!" She remembers being stunned when she replied, "Oh, Carolyn Ann, don't say that!" Years later, she told me she worried that maybe I had some premonition about my own death. Polio was rampant and a vaccine had not yet been discovered. We lined the toilet seat at the gas station with paper to be sure we were safe on our travels. I'm sure my innocent pronouncement about heaven was a real concern for my mother.

When I was six years old, I accepted Christ as my Savior. I knew the basics—that Jesus loves me, died for me, and wanted me to trust and follow him and to give him my heart. I understood that when I died, I would go to heaven. I knew this was a big step in my life. I told Mother about my decision as she was making posters for a Women's Missionary Union meeting: "I have decided I want to trust Jesus."

She stopped and told me that was so wonderful, and she said, "Let's go into the living room and kneel down and pray." We knelt by the sofa and prayed a prayer of joy. I was so happy, and I understood, even as a child, the simple, clear message I had heard about becoming a Christian. Little did I imagine a journey that would lead me to places and people all over the world.

One of my most precious keepsakes is a letter my mother wrote to her mother, Georgia Bell Boswell. She had saved it for me. In it she told about my walking forward at the close of the service, taking Daddy's hand and telling him I wanted to trust Jesus. She said she

---

1. Stephen Weiss and Bernie Baum, "Music! Music! Music!" *Wikipedia*, October 19, 2021, en.wikipedia.org/wiki/Music!_Music!_Music!.

didn't prompt me in any way and that on the first verse I stepped out of the pew and walked to the front. She said I sat on the front pew to await the end of the hymn. Then Daddy said, "Today we have this little one coming to accept Christ as her savior, Carolyn Ann Yeldell." Then he grinned and started to get teary and couldn't continue. The minister of music concluded the service while Daddy sat beside me on the pew. When Daddy went to greet the worshipers at the church's front door, I remember standing beside him. I cried and cried, and although I know I was a dramatic and emotional child, I also remember that I was deeply happy. Mother wrote that many people in the church were also crying with joy, moved by Daddy's emotional response.

My earliest opportunities for expressing God's call to ministry were through music. I started piano study at age six and loved it. I first wanted to be a concert pianist and then, after college, an opera singer. The immediate opportunities to use my music gifts were in church. I played piano for worship services in junior and senior high school. At age sixteen, I began directing children's choirs.

In college, I majored in piano and voice, first at Ouachita Baptist University and later at Indiana University. I was soloist for a Christian Science Church while in college, and I directed church choirs for campus churches. I taught Bible study classes. Being in the pulpit felt comfortable and normal. Serving as a summer missionary to Venezuela was the first mission travel experience out of many in my future. I felt like God's call was pulling me in so many directions, and I had no idea where my journey would lead me.

As a young adult living in northern Indiana, I continued to serve as a church musician in Lutheran, Methodist, and Jewish congregations, leading choirs and playing piano and organ. I was cantorial soloist in two temples and taught music in Lutheran and Catholic universities. Serving as music director in Jewish temples for thirty years was an enlightening time of spiritual growth. As a young girl, I had been taught to share the story of Christ with everyone. I struggled with how God wanted to use me with the Jewish community. One Sabbath night before services, I prayed for God's leadership in how I could be a witness. The unmistakable answer came: "Just love."

I did share my faith with rabbis and others who were eager to talk about Christianity. One rabbi told me that I had a responsibility to share my faith with him. He went on to earn a graduate degree in Christian studies. He later told me that he came to believe that Jesus is the Christ and to share that with his temple board, even as he continued to serve as a rabbi. I found this amazing.

When I taught voice at Valparaiso University and served as cantorial soloist at Sinai Temple in Michigan City, Indiana, the congregation sponsored my European trip with the university choir as soloist. They asked me to visit Dachau, lead a memorial service, and come back to tell about it. The Lutheran students came face to face with the challenge of their church's silence during the Nazi rule of Germany in WWII as they shared in the memorial service at the crematorium at Dachau. It was for me a time of faith discovery and growth as I again recognized that God was always calling and opening doors.

Jerry Staley and I were married while in graduate school. Jerry has been completely supportive and encouraging of my career choices, including ministry. I often held a regular full-time job plus a church music position and temple soloist work on weekends. My journey led me down many paths—mothering; public service; university and private teaching in Indiana, Kentucky, and Arkansas; performing; and church ministry.

We had three children in the decade that followed, Sarah, Mary, and William. One of life's greatest blessings has been watching our children grow in life, careers, and faith and then have children of their own who have also accepted Christ as their Savior. My children graced me with the blessing of baptizing two grandchildren during the period of Covid-19 church closures. I thought my heart would burst at our baptism service in the swimming pool!

I also thought my heart would burst when we lost our ten-month-old grandson Freeman to pulmonary hypertension. He spent most of his life in the hospital, and I spent part of every day with him there to love him and to minister as I could. It was the saddest day of our lives when he died in 2016. His life continues to inspire through a handicapped playground and a medical device our son William and daughter-in-law Misti designed.

As I completed the master of music degree from Indiana University School of Music, the natural next step was a career in vocal performance. I began entering vocal competitions and won some important ones. In the midst of performing, I was also trying to discern my call. I sang with the University of Chicago Rockefeller Chapel Choir and traveled to Chicago for rehearsals and services for three years. As I cared for our young children, I taught voice lessons at home and began university voice teaching.

We moved to Arkansas, where I enjoyed public service as the director of two state agencies, the Arkansas Arts Council and the Governor's Commission on Adult Literacy. I also served as director of touring programs for the Arkansas Arts Center. An early interest planted during high school to go into public service also tugged at my heart. While I filed away a hope to run for office someday, I approached these agency positions as ministry opportunities to bring access to arts programs and to encourage adults to return to school to learn basic reading and writing skills. I continued church and temple ministry on weekends.

A performing career continued to open for me. But even as God allowed me to get closer, I began to experience obstacles. After our son Will was born in 1981 in Little Rock, I sang in Strauss's *Der Rosenkavalier* with the Tulsa Opera. My family planned to come for the performance, but my husband was hospitalized with blood poisoning. Our children, ages ten, seven, and one year, had to be taken in by family and friends. Without an understudy, I was unable to come home and care for my family. This gave me a valuable, close look at the life I was exploring. I found myself at the end of performances walking offstage and wondering what difference I was making. A diva doesn't think this way. I knew God's hand was in all of this.

Later in 1985, world-renowned singer Marilyn Horne took me under her wing and arranged for me to sing at Carnegie Hall with the San Francisco Opera. During this time, I was ill at ease about the call to sing professionally, and several incidents lent clarity that it wasn't my destiny. Thankful to have had the opportunity to explore it closely, I chose not to pursue it further. Many people couldn't understand why I'd turn my back on a performing career, but I felt sure that it wasn't my call.

The year 1994 brought a new opportunity for me to listen for God's call in an unexpected way. My childhood friend, President Clinton, wanted me to be part of his administration. He and Hillary asked me to organize the inaugural prayer service and to sing. That was such a remarkable experience, but I wasn't sure if moving to DC was right. The president asked me to consider taking a position at the National Institute for Literacy; this was not a presidential appointment but rather by board selection. So I voiced a new kind of prayer: "God, I am going to do my best to get this job. If it's where you want me to be, open every door. If not, put up every barrier."

I was hired, and we loved this new adventure where I served for nine years. We were able to have many thrilling experiences during the Clinton presidency. Most importantly, it also opened the door for seminary. I had wanted to attend seminary for years but never had access to one nearby so I could tend to family as well. The John Leland Center for Theological Studies opened in 1998 as an alternative to historic Baptist seminaries, which had begun to foster a more conservative view than many Baptists could support. I enrolled in the graduate theological studies program in 2000 and graduated in 2003.

In 2000, I began serving as associate minister at Briggs Baptist Church in Bethesda, Maryland. I was licensed and ordained to ministry there, and Jerry was ordained as a deacon. Teaching voice lessons at the Washington Conservatory of Music housed at Briggs Church was a richly rewarding experience. I continued to serve at Briggs until we moved back to Little Rock in 2005 when I accepted the post of associate pastor at Pulaski Heights Baptist Church.

On May 19, 2002, I was ordained to ministry. It was special to me that two churches asked to ordain me, McLean Baptist Church and Briggs Memorial Baptist Church. While ordination was at Briggs Church, I had been music minister and chair of deacons at McLean Baptist, so both churches were pivotal in my ministry.

The ordination service was deeply moving. My family traveled to DC to attend. Many friends and family participated in the service. Friend and Rabbi Joseph Edelheit sent a Hebrew Bible, the Tanakh, and a letter that was read in the service.

My childhood friend President Clinton also sent a letter that was read in the service: "Your commitment to serving the spiritual needs of others and celebrating God through music is invaluable in fostering an atmosphere of compassion and fellowship. By embracing this profound challenge, you are helping to shape a part of our world for generations to come." At the bottom of the letter, he added a handwritten note to say, "I am so proud of you. We have been friends for nearly forty years, and I believe this is what you were meant to do." Those words continue to mean a great deal to me.

Graduation from seminary was a happy day. These years of theological studies had been among the most grueling of my life, but I learned so much. My professors were among the best anywhere and made certain I received a thorough historical and theological education. I recall the semester that I took Old Testament history and twenty-first-century theological thought. I was astounded that I was studying everything from the creation of the world to feminist theology and liberation theology in one six-month period. It was dizzying but thrilling.

My friendship since age sixteen with President Clinton also offered some incredible moments of hearing God's call. He was my next-door neighbor and classmate, and we have remained close friends through the years. For many years I have sent Scripture passages to him with notes of encouragement. When he was president, he went to Russia during the same weeks I traveled there to sing with the Sverdlovsk Symphony as soprano soloist with conductor Sarah Caldwell for the Verdi Requiem Mass. His mother died during this time, and I was able to share with the orchestra members about our friendship and to share about our Christian faith. I called Bill from Russia, and together we planned the music for her service.

The Sverdlovsk Symphony chamber orchestra and I were invited to perform for President Clinton in Moscow. That evening President

Yeltsin invited President Clinton to his dacha[2] for dinner. I visited with Clinton later that night, and he told me they talked about the current status of religion since the fall of Communism in 1991. Clinton shared with me his conversation with Yelstin, who sought his advice about building a working democracy. What fascinated me most was their long talk about religion.

Yeltsin asked Bill, "You're a Christian, aren't you?" The president told him, "Yes, my faith is the most important thing in my life." Yeltsin responded, "I have to do something about all these Christians coming to Russia. They're ruining our country and our culture. Everyone is becoming a born-again Christian, and they are being re-baptized and putting crosses around their necks."

He worried about the influx of Baptists and other Christian groups and said the people of Russia were flocking to Western religious faith in droves. Bill told him he shouldn't try to control people's beliefs. "Democracy doesn't work that way," he said. "Either you're free or you're not. You can't have it both ways. You need to allow Christians to come into your country, and you have to allow the Russian people the freedom to choose their faith."

I shared with Clinton how symphony member Vladimir came to the symphony hall the previous Sunday with his wife and daughter on the way from church. His daughter had just been confirmed and baptized and she wanted to show me a cross necklace that was given to her on this special occasion. Vladimir shared that having the opportunity now to have a personal faith made it more meaningful.

In May 2007 after Yeltsin's death, I was interviewed by *Time Magazine* and also wrote a reflection for the Baptist Joint Committee. I shared this thought: "What a remarkable exchange this was. In sharing his faith with Yeltsin that Christian workers should be allowed to come as missionaries, Clinton helped keep the doors to Russia open for the spread of Christianity." Yeltsin had come close to closing Russia to Christian missionaries, but the policy was not implemented. I hoped the conversation Bill had with Yeltsin had

---

2. "A dacha (Russian: дача) is a seasonal or year-round second home, often located in the exurbs of Russian-speaking and other post-Soviet countries" ("Dacha," *Wikipedia*, en.wikipedia.org/wiki/Dacha).

made a difference for him personally and had also affected his respect for personal religious freedom. Again, I heard God's voice in affirming that this friendship has been a part of God's plan in my life.

Serving in missions in Angola, Zambia, and later in India had a profound impact on my sense of God's work in the world and the ways churches might be actively involved. I was invited to travel to Angola and Zambia to help start women's adult literacy programs in local churches. Cooperative Baptist Fellowship worker Lonnie Turner, who led HIV/AIDS work in sub-Saharan Africa, asked me to go because of my work in literacy in Arkansas and as deputy director of the National Institute for Literacy in Washington, DC. I went in 2003, 2004, and 2006.

The challenge in Angola was that Portuguese was the national language, and some of the people spoke tribal languages. With translators, my classes began learning the alphabet. The students were thrilled to hold pencil and paper and begin to learn basics, even how to write their names. For them, it was a profound joy to learn basic words they used in church, like "God" and "Jesus."

My first trip to Angola revealed the desperate needs of people living in internal displacement camps. War refugees from the Democratic Republic of the Congo had been given land to settle and rebuild their lives, but little else. They were given small huts, but they needed access to water and irrigation tools, seeds, and supplies to try to grow their own food. They begged for needles, thread, and fabric. Few had shoes. Seminary pastors asked for shirts and ties to wear. Paper and pencils and basic teacher supplies were needed for the classes. The people had lost hope. Their despair brought another call from God, and I came home determined to collect items to take back with me the following year.

The church in Cabinda, Angola, was located on the oceanfront and had open windows that looked out across the sea. It was spectacularly beautiful, as were the voices of the people as they sang. As I sang "The Love of God" in worship one night, the men started singing a low choral accompaniment. The richness of their tone sounded like a pipe organ. Looking out over the ocean, I sang, "Could we with ink the oceans fill, and were the skies of parchment made . . . to write the love of God would drain the oceans dry."[3] It's a memory I'll hold forever.

In 2003, God called me to India with a team from the Baptist World Alliance. Our purpose was to visit the Christian communities in the Northeastern Manipur, Nagaland, and Mizoram to encourage them. The area was under government pressure to end their attempts at independence. Christianity was illegal. Army troops lined the highways, and we felt a heavy military presence as we traveled. Because many kidnappings had occurred, I felt unnerved to be seated in the small hotel lobby when a government leader came in surrounded by his heavily armed military aides.

Traveling to the northeast was treacherous. We drove military-type vehicles to help navigate the terrible unpaved roads. The single-lane roads wound around mountainsides and steep cliffs. As we approached a blind curve, our driver would slow down and honk in case we were meeting an oncoming vehicle. As we rode, our heads bumped against the roof. When we rounded a mountain and I looked down over a steep drop-off, I wondered if we'd make it home alive. I was honestly prepared and ready to die. God was with us.

After we moved back to Little Rock in 2005, when called to serve as minister of education, missions, and outreach at Pulaski Heights Baptist Church, I traveled to Zambia in 2006 for continued work in literacy and a focus on building wells. Access to water in Zambia was a dire need. Women and children walked for miles carrying large containers to fetch water and bring it home for cooking, bathing, and garden irrigation. Churches helped raise funds to build at least one well in a rural area. Children in Vacation Bible Schools contributed. We were able to present a check to a local church for a new well, and within the three weeks there, I could see great progress in the installation. Photos sent later made me enormously happy to see the well operational at last. The mission work was satisfying. I could imagine living there, I thought. I had been told that a visit to Africa would change my life forever. It did!

---

3. Frederick M. Lehman, "The Love of God," *Baptist Hymnal 2008*, #111, *Hymnary.org*, hymnary.org/hymn/BH2008/111.

In both Angola and Zambia, women were enrolled in literacy classes because they were their families' teachers. It was taboo to speak to their husbands about matters of marital faithfulness, but many were growing more comfortable in moving this traditional boundary line. It was commonplace for tribal men to frequent the brothels of sex workers. AIDS had claimed the lives of millions, and young children were left to raise their siblings.

The problems of malnutrition and poor education were also rampant. A lack of clean water exacerbated the health crisis. The hope was that if people learned the basics of reading, they would be able to understand leaflets about HIV/AIDS. I worked with church pastors to begin programs that could continue after my team left, and I left literacy materials for duplication. Churches helped make sets of alphabet flashcards to leave. I asked African seminary friends to write sermons about HIV/AIDS that I could distribute, in hopes that pastors would become more comfortable speaking about it in the pulpit. President Clinton also agreed to explore mobile medical vans with AIDS medicines for service to remote areas.

These trips were life-changing for me. I felt a love and kinship with the people I met. We sang and danced together and celebrated in worship. We shared meals, and they taught me many of their traditions of cooking and arts and crafts. I tried to learn to carry large baskets on my head as they did routinely each day, and I heard their laughter as I walked. We built bonds of friendship and understanding.

In 2005, my interest in public service was sparked. I felt called to run for state representative. The same teachers in high school who instilled the importance of public service in Bill Clinton's life had been my mentors too. I held on to the idea that a role in public service would be a way to help the poor and oppressed. Coming home to Arkansas to serve in church ministry also included a long-held hope that maybe I could run for office someday.

One night as I attended a race-relations service, I was tapped on the shoulder by a member of the state legislature who said to me, "Did you know that the representative in your district is running unopposed?" I felt a call to step up to this opportunity. I received the blessing of my pastor and church leadership, explaining to them that I felt this was part of my calling and ministry to serve as a voice for the oppressed and under-represented. I had criticism from two or three members, but most members were supportive. I ran a strong race but lost in a close election. Still, I had fulfilled this dream. I also realized that public life had changed dramatically since my youth, and I wondered if it was still the right place to make a difference. Many doors opened to draw me into public service on issues including education, the death penalty, immigration, and hunger. Serving in state and federal agencies had also given me public service experience. I had followed God's leading and had been obedient. As with exploring a performance career, God had allowed me to have the experience.

In 2014, I resigned from my associate pastor role at Pulaski Heights Baptist to make room in the budget for a youth minister. When Methodist friends learned I was resigning, they told me if I wasn't ready to stop ministry, there were Methodist churches needing a pastor. I went through the Methodist credentialing, more seminary study required for Methodist history and polity, and was called to serve a United Methodist congregation nearby. God had continued speaking through my Methodist friends.

Interestingly, I always felt supported by congregations I served as minister of music, education, outreach, and missions. No one ever mentioned anything about my being a woman in the pulpit. Likely, this was because I served in the more traditional areas of ministry for women that did not include preaching.

The first and only hints of opposition about my gender came after I was called to be ordained to gospel ministry. What was most disheartening was that the criticism was mostly from women. In my early adult life, I shared with a senior woman deacon in our church that I felt called someday to serve as a deacon. She told me that now was not the right time because I should make my home and family my priority. A man in a leading Baptist church told me that for a woman to be a deacon would be okay, as long as we rewrote the Bible. I felt stung and speechless. A couple with me overheard him and later exclaimed in disbelief, "Did you hear what he just said to

Carolyn?" I was comforted that I wasn't the only one taken aback. But I realized what a common attitude this was in some churches. It seemed unlikely to change. Later I was ordained as deacon at McLean Baptist Church, Virginia.

In 2002, as my ordination approached, my mother told me that skeptical women in her Southern Baptist church in Mississippi asked her how she felt about my ordination. Mother told them, "That's between Carolyn and God." I appreciated her love and support. My father had passed away, but I always felt his love and support would be there too. Another friend said, "What God has called, we don't touch."

When I joined the staff of Pulaski Heights Baptist Church in Little Rock in 2005, a woman who identified as Southern Baptist told me she appreciated my "teaching" when I preached. She supported me as minister of education, outreach, and missions and was complimentary of my sermons, but only as a teacher and not as an ordained preacher. Any negativity I ever experienced about ministry was quickly overcome by the strong sense of God's calling on my life. I vowed to stay true to God's calling and to continue my God-ordained journey.

The simple advice I would give to any women feeling called to ministry would be to stay true to God's call. That will always prove to be a rock of ages for you in overcoming self-doubt and criticism. Also vow to keep an open heart and mind as you seek to grow spiritually and intellectually. Let love be the guiding principle in your ministry, and remember that ministry can take many forms at different times throughout your journey.

Know that God's call to ministry doesn't come only to young people. I always served where called, but the opportunity to attend seminary didn't come until I was fifty-four years old. I was ordained to gospel ministry at age fifty-six. That was when these doors opened for me.

Today my life ministry is primarily focused on service to churches as supply pastor, helping our farmer's market ministry, and helping my husband Jerry after his stroke in 2018. I enjoy writing devotionals, preparing sermons, and singing for our church services at

Pulaski Heights Baptist Church. I have continued songwriting and have composed hymn descants and choral anthems that have been published. I wrote hymn lyrics for our daughters' weddings. The Covid-19 pandemic has required remote Zoom worship, but it has been great to stay connected. As we resumed in-person worship, I was asked to continue online gatherings with those more comfortable staying home.

Writing about my journey filled with so many wonderful experiences has helped me revisit the many directions God has led me throughout my life. The journey has been meandering, but I am deeply grateful for each step of the journey, the easy ones and the hard ones.

Hearing God's call to ministry through each season of life has been powerful and deeply meaningful, and I look forward to hearing the next call God might whisper to me. Being aware of the Holy Spirit and knowing God is actively working in my life gives me great peace and fulfillment. I expect to enjoy ministry for as long as I live. Blessings and prayers to all on the journey of discernment. What an exciting way to live!

"May the peace that passes all understanding guard your hearts and minds in Christ Jesus" (Philippians 4:7).

Carolyn Yeldell Staley was ordained in 2002 at Briggs Memorial Baptist Church in Bethesda, Maryland, in a dual ordination with Briggs Baptist Church and McLean Baptist Church in McLean, Virginia, both churches she has served. She received a master of theology degree from the John Leland Center for Theological Studies in Arlington, Virginia, and received degrees from Indiana University and Ouachita Baptist University.

Carolyn was acting director and deputy director for the National Institute for Literacy, Washington, DC; state field director for Hands Across America, Little Rock, Arkansas; and director of the Arkansas Arts Center and executive director of the Arkansas Arts Council. She has served congregations in various capacities as pastor, associate pastor, and many iterations of minister of music/organist/minster of worship. She currently serves at Pulaski Heights Baptist Church in Little Rock. Other congregations she has served include Bethlehem United Methodist Church, Lonoke, Arkansas; Briggs Memorial Baptist Church, Bethesda, Maryland; Bethlehem Lutheran Church, Chesterton, Indiana; Sinai Temple, Michigan City, Indiana; Temple Israel, Hot Springs, Arkansas; Columbia Baptist Church, Falls Church, Virginia; McLean Baptist Church, McLean, Virginia; University Baptist Church, Bloomington, Indiana; and Lakeshore Drive Baptist Church, Second Baptist Church, and Temple B'nai Israel, all in Little Rock, Arkansas. Carolyn has taught at Washington Conservatory of Music in Bethesda, Maryland; Valparaiso University; St. Joseph's College, Rensselaer, Indiana; Brescia College in Owensboro, Kentucky; and the University of Arkansas.

As a childhood friend of President Bill Clinton, Carolyn served as chair of the Presidential Inaugural Prayer Services in 1993 and 1997. She also chaired Arkansas governor Bill Clinton's Governor's Inaugural Prayer Service from 1979 through 1990. She was born in Owensboro, Kentucky. She is married to Jerry Staley, a professional photographer and public school teacher. They are the parents of three grown children.

The Fifth Story

Continuing the Legacy of Goodness and Love

Rev. Dr. Anika T. Whitfield

A good name is more desirable than great riches; to be esteemed is better than silver or gold. (Prov 22:1, NIV)

I struggled with choosing a title for this chapter because I recognize there is value in a good name. "Great Grandparents" and "Because of My Ancestors, I Am" were two other titles that I considered before leaning into this one. My life is, and I am, because of the great ancestors and parents who prepared the way and have continued guiding me along my life's journey.

I was blessed to have had three living sets of great-grandparents to physically know and love. They each have an interesting history and legacy of their own that I will not fully share, but I will highlight some of their meaningful and lasting legacies that have directly impacted my life. I'll start with my great-grandparents in Hagerstown, Maryland, "Nana" and "Pop Pop." Nana and Rev. Pop Pop both demonstrated a deep love for God, their family, and the church. Their personalities exuded resilience, determination, love, and strength. I often listened in on some of their adult conversations about their lives and learned that the attributes they had as children were the same attributes I experienced, loved, admired, and respected. Goodness and love characterize some of my most memorable moments with Nana and Pop Pop.

Nana had her own special way of letting you know that she truly saw you. Her smile told me that she was pleased or expecting good things of me. She spoke her mind often and without a filter. We rarely questioned what she thought or believed. Nana's plainspokenness gave us permission to do the same, though most of my generation showed a little more filtering of our expressions. Nevertheless, her liberation of voice stood out and reminded me not only of the importance of my voice but also of the power of how I spoke and what I said.

Some of my fondest memories in childhood while visiting our family "up north" in DC, Maryland, and Virginia were taking turns imitating Pop Pop as preacher while playing church on one of our great-aunt's porches with my cousins. We played until we all had our turn at whatever role we wanted. As well as imitating Pop Pop, at least our interpretation of him, we also imitated pew members, ushers, choir directors, choir members, deaconesses, and deacons as well. Good times, yes, fun times indeed! Our "sermons," though rarely substantive, were quite engaging and dramatic, helping to elicit the call and response that we witnessed while praying and singing during a holiday or during a family gathering prior to enjoying a meal.

Funny thing is, as much as we all loved playing church, none of us that I can remember wanted to be "called" to preach or pastor. If memory serves me correctly, we were quick to stop imitating Pop Pop if someone even hinted that we seemed to have qualities that may lead to a "call" from God to preach.

I also experienced goodness and love with Mama Myrtle, my mother's father's mom. In Mama Myrtle's home, we always felt warm, welcoming love. She had endearing nicknames for us. My nickname was "Peaches," which I experienced as a term of endearment. Mama Myrtle's house was memorable for several reasons, including the way she protected her furniture with plastic coverings and insulated her windows with plastic. The simple artwork and prayers and poems that donned her walls mesmerized me. She had a framed prayer on the wall in her guest bathroom that I memorized:

Now I wake to see the light.
'tis God that brought me through the night.
And now I lift my voice to pray,
that God will keep me through the day. Amen.[1]

That prayer became my common morning prayer throughout childhood and is one that I pray even now with a few addendums. Mama Myrtle also had a sweet smile and embrace that let me know her love was real.

My mother's mother's parents, Big Mama and Grand Daddy, were also full of goodness and love. Big Mama didn't take any mess; she had rules that had rules. On the other hand, Grand Daddy was a gentle, kind, and easygoing person. He would take the time to teach us how to play croquet in their backyard, showing great patience and love. There was something good about Grand Daddy's smile that made everyone feel comfortable and at ease.

Grand Daddy and Big Mama both loved having their yard look and smell beautiful. Their front, side, and back yards were lined with fresh, wonderfully smelling sweet mint. They had beautiful bushes, fruit trees of figs and pears, veggies, and flowers, all providing a sense of intentional attention and love for what they had and were able to share with their family and community.

Big Mama was known for canning and pickling figs, pears, and cucumbers. She cooked delicious things, including some "make you slap yo' mama" peach cobblers using fresh peaches from Mrs. Ward's backyard, directly across the alley. Mrs. Ward and Big Mama would exchange produce and canned products at their back fences.

My great-grandparents, all of them, left an indelible signature on my heart that reminds me of the goodness and love of God. They left a lasting signature by the ways they lived and interacted with us. Now that I have shared a glimpse of my great-grandparents, I must share the next generation, my grandparents—Granny and Paw Paw.

Paw Paw, the king of jokesters in our family, knew how to draw out a good laugh from virtually anyone. He was constantly engaging

---

1. Anonymous, "Little Folded Hands," *Morning Prayers*, 2004, biblehub.com/library/anonymous/little_folded_hands/morning_prayers.htm.

in pranks and jokes, taking you off guard with his unique phrases and actions. Paw Paw's sense of humor and comedy helped to put you at ease in the midst of challenging situations. Paw Paw did not, however, play around when it came to sports, especially baseball. If you wanted to see a different side of Paw Paw, accidentally block his view during a baseball game. Let's just say that you might experience some pretty colorful words that, as children, we should not ever be caught saying out loud to anybody.

Paw Paw, a carpenter by trade, showed me several things that I was made to hold in confidence as a child, our own little secrets. He allowed me at age four to climb up the ladder to a rooftop where he was removing shingles and replacing rotten or damaged boards with fresh wood. Paw Paw taught me that it was better to take your time to do something right than to rush and have to do it again. He taught me to be careful and to try to clean up while I worked so that I would not have more work to do when I finished. Certainly, he emphasized how to keep me from hurting myself on the trash left behind, like roofing nails that should never be stepped on at any time. Paw Paw would let me steer while he was driving. Lessons of goodness and love from him were lessons of living a life without conforming to boundaries set by other people. There was no mention by Paw Paw of my potential limitations because of my age, size, or gender identity. Paw Paw saw my willingness to actively participate in learning and helped me tap into those gifts and desires with confidence and assurance. Priceless lessons.

Granny, wow! Typing her name brings up so many emotions of joy and gratitude. Anyone who truly knows me knows that my Granny was my best friend on this side of glory and remains my best friend in her eternal existence. Granny constantly showed me goodness and love in the way that she cooked, showed up, encouraged me, taught me, kissed me (with her lip-popping kiss on the cheek or forehead), hugged me, and allowed me to rub on her golden-flecked arms that were perfectly scented with sweetness. As you may gather, there was almost nothing about my Granny that was flawed in my eyes, yet in her goodness and love, she even taught me that imperfect people, all of us, were created with goodness and deserve to be loved.

Like Paw Paw, Granny let me do so many things without respect to my age, or size, or any other limiting factor. When Mama told me I was too young to iron, wash dishes, or cook, she was absolutely unaware that Granny had been allowing me to learn all of these things with her gift of patient guidance. There were so many lessons and skills that I learned from Granny, like the importance of paying attention to my environment and acknowledging it in the ways I spoke, acted, showed up, and engaged; the importance of daily gratitude; the importance of having a personal relationship with God; how to not let people define me but to create my own identity; how to use my gifts to bless God, myself, and others; how to appreciate home-cooked meals and carry my weight in preparing and cleaning up afterwards; to invest more time and resources in people and nature rather than in material things; to be ever observant, realizing that the balance of life is often found in the rhythm of music, rest, and relationship building.

There are too many things that I learned from Granny to be able to adequately share in my chapter. However, there are a few specific encounters with her that I think are essential. One begins when I was about five years old and Granny came home from working as a nurse at one of our local hospitals. After settling in her bedroom, she asked me to take off her shoes. She then instructed me to get her foot-care instruments. When I returned to her bedroom, I saw Granny propped up on her pillows in a comfortable position. I brought a towel and her instruments. Granny said she was tired after a long day. She mentioned that the only thing bothering her was her feet. She described and showed me where her discomfort was and then asked me to cut her toenails, corns, and calluses. What seemed like a regular and routine experience of caring for Granny's feet became a transformative and divine moment in my life.

Granny had taught me how to use most of her foot-care instruments—her toenail clippers, corn and callus shavers, metal files, emery boards, etc. But this time, Granny pulled out something I'd only watched her use before. Observing my apparent distress, Granny took my right hand and wrapped it under her right hand. She then proceeded to assist me in picking up the single-edged blade properly. She commenced to talking and physically guiding me through angling and using the blade to shave a corn on the outside of the little toe on her left foot.

I was so nervous but at the same time so confident. I was nervous about messing up, dropping the blade, making a mistake, and mainly about possibly hurting and disappointing Granny. I was also confident because I could feel her warm, loving hand covering and guiding mine as she was giving me a literal hands-on lesson in using her single-edged razor blade properly. I was confident because Granny was with me. I was confident because, clearly, Granny believed that I could do what I didn't realize I was capable of doing.

Granny had been teaching me all along for this moment, but I didn't realize it. She had allowed me to graduate from using a butter knife to cut only so much butter from a stick to using a sharper knife to peel vegetables and fruit. She would remind me that the "meat" of the vegetable or fruit I was peeling was the part we wanted to ensure we had the most of to enjoy. She patiently showed me how not to "cut at" the fruit or vegetable while peeling it. Granny also taught me that the hull had value and purpose. Beyond protecting the vegetables and fruits from bugs, animals, and weather as it was growing and maturing, the hull often also had nutrients that may have more vitamin content than the meat beneath it.

Little did I know that Granny was preparing me for this moment. Together, we successfully removed the corn from the little toe of her left foot. Granny then reclined in her bed on her propped-up pillows. Before I knew it, she was sound asleep! What was I to do? Should I clip her toenails and wait for her to wake up again so she could help me with the calluses on the balls of her feet and heels and the corn on her right little toe, or should I go for it?

This was one of those divine moments where goodness and love showed up with grace, mercy, and favor in my life. As I looked at Granny and saw her beautiful face and peaceful glow as she rested comfortably, I knew I had to step up to the plate, grab the baton that she was passing on to me, and run with it until I crossed the finish line.

Now, don't misunderstand my five-year-old anxiety and insecurities. They were still present, just not as profound or loud as the assurance that Granny taught me by holding my hand through a valley of the shadow of harm. Even now, I sense her calmness and peacefulness. It took me what felt like a full work day to carefully trim her corn and calluses without nipping her, but to my great surprise, I did it. Granny didn't flinch once. It wasn't until I started using the callus file that Granny woke up and started moving. She looked at the bottom of her feet and her right little toe and smiled. I instantly became more confident about the skills my Granny saw in me that I didn't see in myself.

Relevant to my call story, there is one more Granny encounter that I'd like to share with you. After falling down a flight of stairs in her home, my Granny was rushed to the hospital where she worked. Upon arriving at the hospital emergency room with my dad, I asked to see my Granny. Rather than call her Nurse Whitfield, virtually everyone in the ER called her Dr. Whitfield. I asked why they were calling her doctor instead of nurse and was told that Granny often assisted during surgery, not only with her hands but also with surgical advice that had proven time and time again to be more than helpful. After the fanfare of nurses and doctors left her room, providing excellent care and attention to her, I asked Granny about the title they were using for her and how I thought it was odd that her being an excellent nurse was translated as being a doctor instead. I remember telling Granny how much I didn't like pretense, titles, and people feeling like they had the right to demote or promote people's values by titles rather than valuing people for who they are and how they define themselves. I told her that I respected her as a nurse but couldn't see myself being one because I didn't like how doctors often talked down to them or how people in society seemed to see more value in doctors than nurses—the very ones who seemed to work twice as hard and provide care that was often taken for granted or not appreciated. With a bit of righteous indignation, I told Granny how I never wanted to be a doctor because I didn't like how that title seemed to bring out arrogance in people's attitudes and the ways they treated those who weren't doctors. I was about to go on telling

Granny about all the titles and positions that I would commonly hear people aspiring to and why I didn't want to be any one of those things. But Granny stopped my soliloquy and told me, "Baby, you can do or be whoever you choose to be, but be sure you choose it for yourself and are the best at it that you can be."

Granny told me that titles don't make people who they are, but the way people act and treat others and all creation does. "If you choose to be a doctor, it's not the title that will define the kind of doctor you are; it will be the way you treat and take care of your patients and staff that will determine it. You are defined by yourself, not by your title or your position. Always keep that in mind."

Granny's pearls of wisdom continue to resonate in my life today. I have so many Granny stories to share that relate to my call story, but I must share the next generation that helped influence me. Mama taught me that being a Christian and living as a child of God did not require the traditional limitation of pretenses and protocols often prescribed in popular culture. Most of my formative years, I remember my mom's attendance at the traditional services inside of the church building being rather limited. She has a beautiful alto singing voice, and I remember enjoying joining her occasionally in choir rehearsals as she blended her sweet sounds with those of other choir members of the Sanctuary Choir at Union AME Church. Mama was not keen on people walking and operating in hypocrisy and judgment. And she absolutely did not condone gossip or demeaning people because they didn't fit into normatives or standards set by others who often didn't live up to them themselves. "Church folk" seemed to be people my mom was not enthusiastic about spending time with regularly. She would spend a lot of her time with people committed to being in loving fellowship and relationship with one another, seeking to connect with more people in need of love and support. Ironically, the spaces and places where Mama was able to enjoy these healthy relationships were usually outside the traditional church walls. As a child, I didn't always understand why Mama didn't feel like coming to "church" and shining her light, but once I became an adult, I better appreciated her value of being the church without walls.

Daddy is and has always been a comfortably unique individual with a heart for community. Growing up, Daddy was "Uncle Bob" to virtually everyone in our neighborhood, community, and church. He rarely met a stranger. His bubbly, welcoming, and joyful personality was engaging but sometimes over the top for people. Daddy, like Mama, embodies love in the person he is. Daddy, like Mama, is the church without walls, and by the way he lived he showed my brother and me how to be. Daddy also valued the importance of being the change he wanted to see in the "formalized" church. I remember him being our church van driver and hearing adults in our church building talk under their breath about him being "crazy," as if we couldn't hear their criticisms and judgments. It never seemed to bother my dad, but it certainly got under my skin. Daddy would often tell me, "Baby, the church folk talked about Jesus, so we know they will talk about people trying to live like him. Don't let that bother you, Puddin'. Just keep your eyes on the prize and hold on!" I would get frustrated with Daddy because I wanted him to tell some of those people off, especially the hypocrites who would smile in his face and offer him compliments while talking about him behind his back or even in his presence with cutting and hurtful sarcasm.

Many Sunday mornings for Sunday school and Sunday worship service, Daddy would dress in jeans, a casual shirt, and tennis shoes. Talk about being the hot topic! I couldn't understand, on one hand, why Daddy wouldn't wear one of the many suits, slacks, or dress shoes he had in his closet. But on the other hand, I couldn't understand why what he wore mattered so much to these church folk. So, being the person I am, I asked Daddy and I asked them. Daddy told me that there were children and families that he picked up in the church van who couldn't afford to wear typical Sunday attire, and he wanted them to know that they were just as welcome to come as the people who chose to wear dressier clothes. The church folk told me that it was inappropriate for people to come into the house of the Lord in plain clothes for Sunday worship. They explained that we should always wear our best to church. I then asked, "What if your best is jeans, a t-shirt, and tennis shoes?" To that I got frustrated stares or "Girl, you act just like your crazy daddy."

Daddy and Mama taught me that we are the church. Our bodies are the temples, not the brick and mortar. How we love, treat, see, interact with, and are present with people is who we are as the church. They taught me that we are often the only Bible people read. The pages of our daily lives are being read by people we don't even realize are reading our testimonies and witness about who God is.

After years of reading, searching, seeking, praying, volunteering, and serving in the church and community, I realized that God had called me to be a podiatrist. I always thought my calling was in acting, writing, and producing plays, and in performance (I was also a flautist). Then, in May 1990 when my Granny committed her Spirit to God in Glory, I thought I couldn't breathe or live without her. I searched for peace, joy, and someone I could trust and confide in like my Granny. I needed someone who valued my quirkiness and who loved my heart like I knew she did. I challenged, questioned, and even expressed my anger with God for taking Granny away from me. An all-knowing God had to know that I was not alright, and not going to be alright, without her physical presence in my life.

The summer of 1990, while I was attending Governor's School at Hendrix College in Conway, Arkansas, I had an epiphany. As much as I loved acting, writing, directing, and producing, I loved my Granny even more and needed a divine connection with her on earth. What connected me with my Granny was the way she connected with me—nurturing and caring for me with love. She was my nurse who took care of so many of my health and wellness needs. I realized that the best way for me to honor her and God was to honor the gift she had stirred up in me—podiatry. This was my first call. Everything about being a podiatrist reminded me of Granny's goodness and love that she so freely and generously gave to me.

In 2004, after I completed my second podiatry residency program in Maine, I returned home on fire for teaching and serving in the community and church. Not long after I returned home, I learned that one of my childhood friends had been hospitalized with a rare cancer. My heart and soul were drawn to pray with and for him and his family. After receiving permission from his family to visit him in the intensive care unit, I was led to pray with him, placing my hands on his feet. I invited the medical staff to stay and join me in prayer. While I was praying, something miraculous happened—his vital signs started regulating, his temperature went down, and he became a lot more peaceful. The doctors and nurses commented on the immediate transformation and expressed gratitude for the prayer. I told them that God was working and I was simply a willing vessel.

That evening, I went home and reflected on the events of the day and thought about the many ways God speaks in us and through us. I am normally someone who can rest soundly if I am still for a few minutes, but this night I could not seem to quiet my mind. No matter what I tried to help me rest—being still, lying down, listening to music, reading—nothing seemed to help. So I got up and went to the restroom, and while washing my hands I noticed a strange condensation on my bathroom mirror. It was an image of a fish. I laughed at this fish on the mirror and reminded God that I had fed some of my church family at a house warming at my home and was planning another dinner soon for the choir and Sunday school class, but I did not feel that God was talking to me about feeding people food. So I went to my bed and opened my Granny's Bible. As I read, I came across the Exodus passage where Moses asks God, "Who do I say sent me?" Immediately, I said out loud in my own comedic mode, "I'm not Mosetta, God." I quickly turned to the passage where Elijah is trying to hear God's voice, and I said, "God, I'm not Elijetta." Turning the pages to another passage that surely related to me, I made it to Job where God starts reminding Job who God is. You got it by now; my response was, "I'm not Jobetta, God."

So I decided to put on a video to watch. I picked out one from my Trinity United Church of Christ collection. Of all the videos I could have chosen, I managed to put in the one about Pastor Jeremiah A. Wright Jr. and his call story. I had not seen this one before. At this point I was a bit frustrated with God. I kept reminding God who I wasn't, not realizing that God was showing me who I am.

I finally gave up and prayed, "God whatever it is that you are calling me to do, I will do it. Just please let me go to sleep." The next thing I knew, I was waking up about four hours later fully rested and clear about what I had said to God just before getting that restorative rest.

Before I could argue or take back my word to God, I felt in my spirit that my friend had committed his spirit to God. I looked for my cell phone to text my friend's sister, and before I could text her she sent me a text, confirming what I felt. I asked God why I was sent to pray with him at all. I didn't want people to think of me as a death angel. In the past, I had similar experiences of being called to pray for people and their families while they were in critical care units, and more often than not the people I was praying for died at some point during their hospitalization. I was truly concerned that I would have a negative stigma attached to my presence, but God reminded me of the book of Ecclesiastes and Jesus' final words on the cross, Scripture passages that gave me great comfort.

I finally connected the dots by the time I made it back to my bathroom. The fish condensation was no longer on the mirror, but it was in my heart. I realized that God was calling me to preach, and I had answered, "I'll go, Lord. Send me."

After being hazed in the AME Church, as a young woman and a doctor, I realized that my gifts were creating sacred space for me but were not appreciated or received by the people I had come home to honor and bless. I was devastated by some of the constraints placed on me and by the accusations and challenges to my integrity that came not only from the minister who first licensed me but also from the church family I had known all my life. They stood in malicious judgment of me because I was a radical Christian who believes that the church is not an institution filled with rules of "dos" and "don'ts" that constrain our abilities to connect, reach, and grow with creation. I was challenged because I did not ascribe to patriarchy, sexism, homophobia, ageism, or any systems that "other" people or creation.

I have to give credit where credit is due. During one of the most challenging times in the infancy of my acceptance to my call in ministry, I experienced a meeting with our Stewards' Board and Pastor. With pages of the AME Discipline in hand with highlighted sections, I was questioned time and time again about my loyalty to the pastor, to the discipline, and to the doctrine of the AME Church.

Surprised by the questions about my integrity and my commitment to a discipline and doctrine, rather than an opportunity to acknowledge my gifts and to offer support as I used them, I found myself repetitively asking how any of these questions lined up with God's word or with God's specific calling in my life.

Before I left the meeting defeated, God heard my cries and answered. One of the most reserved Stewards in our church family raised his hand and said this:

> Pastor, I'm sorry. I just can't keep quiet anymore. I cannot believe we are spending so much time questioning Anika about her loyalty to the church, to the discipline, and to authority in the church. We know Anika. Her works speak for her calling. I have been waiting a long time for her to answer her call. We all saw it in her when she was a child. We watched her attend to seniors and children younger than her with tender loving care. We saw her praying with teenagers and adults in the parking lot of the church as a mighty prayer warrior. And my wife and I can testify that when our son died, Anika called and prayed with me and my wife and daughter almost every day for a month while she was living in Chicago at the time. She had words that lifted us and was more present for us than some people who were right here in town. She treated our son and daughter like her little sister and brother. They loved her and felt comfortable confiding in her and spending time with her. We should be lifting her up rather than tearing her down. We should be asking her how we can help her with seminary and offer to pay for books that she might need or offer her help starting up her podiatry practice. We know her. She is not a stranger to us. She has already proven her love and devotion to God. I am ashamed of this board and I don't want to have anything to do with what has been going on today. I am not only voting for her to receive her license to preach; I think we should offer her an apology and beg her not to leave this church because we need her.

I cannot explain how much his words meant to me at that moment. He rarely says much at all, but his words seemed almost unending. He apologized to me for being quiet for so long during that meeting and thanked me for all the ways I had been a blessing in his family's life and in the lives of our church family and community. I cried and witnessed a tear roll down his cheek while he spoke. I hope to never forget his words and the radical way he expressed love—disrupting an evil system of harm and destruction that was considered "normalcy" by virtually everyone in the room save me and this good steward.

I found myself looking for a place where I could serve and be myself in ministry. It was hard to find. I served in the Christian Methodist Church, the United Methodist Church, and the African Methodist Church. Ultimately, I found my way to a church affiliated with the Cooperative Baptist Fellowship and the Progressive National Baptist Convention. In that church I was ordained. At the end of March 2013, the ordination council that my then pastor had organized approved my ordination, and in April 2013, Pastor Jeremiah A. Wright Jr., my former pastor, agreed to preach my ordination at New Millennium Baptist Church in Little Rock. As with all of my previous ministerial assignments, I accepted the responsibility of serving as minister to the children and youth. One of my godchildren, who was living with me at the time, was the only child who regularly attended our church. We had two teens that I enjoyed working with as well. After realizing that I couldn't afford to attend seminary and run my private podiatry practice, my tenure at New Millennium seemed to have an expiration plan in place.

After the many heartaches, attacks, and disappointments of the limitations I felt placed on my calling in ministry in all of these places, I realized that what I had learned from Mama's years of not attending formalized church services regularly had a lot to do with her resisting being placed in a box of "abnormalcy" for the sake of checking off a weekly box of attending worship in a building with people who may or may not have love, respect, or support for one another. In her viewpoint, this wasn't God's church; it was a social club that spent a lot of time focusing on things that are of the world and not of God—popularity, money, clothes/fashion, and appearances. I didn't understand her viewpoint growing up, but as an adult ordained woman preacher, I fully understood her experiences and her sentiments. I was learning through firsthand experience that even congregations that professed to be inclusive and nonjudgmental were sometimes blind to their patriarchal, exclusionary, and line-drawing judgmental beliefs and practices.

My story about goodness and love doesn't end with sadness, resentment, or defeat. It isn't over but is recharging and still creating. For the past seven years, I have been the "church without walls"—preaching, teaching, healing, encouraging, learning, and growing outside the brick and mortar of a formalized church. And last year I formally became a member of a church community called The Church Without Walls Global Reach Ministries, Inc. (CWOW) that truly lives up to its name. This year, we agreed that The CWOW was ready to become an even more radical faith community that ministers and serves without a hierarchical structure. We are all ministers called to be the church in the world, wherever we are. We are seeking to be a contemplative and interactive faith community that wishes to "uphold justice; love mercy, and walk humbly with our Creator" (Mic 6:8) as an intentional social justice ministry.

I now live in my sacred place of call, preaching and teaching, caring and loving, creating beloved community, and working for social justice. My ministry has led me to organize Save Our Schools, a community advocacy organization working to prevent the closure of more public schools and prevent the resegregation of education through the privatization of public education. It has led me to serve as a founding member of Grassroots Arkansas, another advocacy organization whose mission is to realize equity and liberation from state control of our public schools while seeking to create world-class public schools that are inclusive and sustainable. My ministry has led me to the city streets, walking and marching for justice; to board rooms where decisions are made; to the halls of our state capitol, standing with beloved community for equity and righteousness; and to our nation's capitol as a part of the Poor People's Campaign: A National Call for Moral Revival movement working toward ending systemic poverty, systemic racism, the war economy, ecological devastation, and distorted white nationalism narratives that have been used to divide us.

To the generations to come, my sage advice focuses back to the goodness and love that marked my way. I encourage both young and seasoned women to embrace through intentional love the person God created you to be; believe and walk confidently in your sacred worth; mute the voices that attempt to bring you to your knees; listen intently to the voice of God who created you and called you by name; draw close to and appreciate the people in your life who hold you in goodness and love while intentionally avoiding those who do not.

The ideals of goodness and love encapsulate the stories of my call as the common thread that was sown into my life and my name long before I existed. It continues to be my truth even as I am becoming who I know myself to be. My parents, because of their relationship and connections with their parents and grandparents, raised me to live up to my name Anika (Goodness) Tené (Love). It is because of goodness and love that I didn't give up on my call. It is because of my ancestors that I am who I am. I am grateful for the call and even more grateful for the journey!

Anika T. Whitfield accepted her call to preach and was licensed in the AME Church in 2003. Nine years later, Anika was ordained at New Millennium Baptist Church, Little Rock, Arkansas, in 2012 as a preacher and minister to youth. She now serves as assistant minister and minister to youth at The Church Without Walls Global Reach Ministries (Mt. Rainier, Maryland).

Anika is also a family care provider, a community organizer and activist, a justice warrior, and a podiatrist. In her ministry as a grassroots organizer, she is one of the founding organizers of Grassroots Arkansas, an organization led by parents, students, educators, and community organizers and allies working to realize equity, liberation, and sustainable community schools. As co-chair of the Arkansas Poor People's Campaign: A National Call for Moral Revival, Anika works to unite people across Arkansas to challenge the evils of systemic racism, poverty, ecological devastation, and religious nationalism. She received the 2019 Activist of the Year Award from the Arkansas Coalition for Peace and Justice for her tireless activism and advocacy.

Anika grew up as an active youth leader at Union AME Church in Little Rock, Arkansas. She is a native of Little Rock. She is the daughter of R. L. and Constance Whitfield; sister of Jawanza Whitfield; auntie of Levi, Aaron, Samone, Merissa, and Karmen; and godmother of twelve. She enjoys many things but especially gardening, live music, swimming, cooking, and spending quality time with her family and friends.

The Sixth Story

If God Can Speak through a Donkey

Rev. Dr. Rhonda Abbott Blevins

It was a rare opportunity for me to preach. In the Baptist Student Union (BSU) at the University of Georgia where I served as campus minister, the three campus ministers preached only a couple of times per year. I can't recall what my sermon was about that evening or what biblical text I preached from, but I do remember a conversation that followed:

"Rhonda, can I come see you tomorrow?" asked James (not his real name), an earnest college student I had known for a while.

"Of course!" I said.

We scheduled a meeting in my office for the next day. James was a quiet young man, serious about his faith. I liked him, although I didn't know him well. We hadn't had many one-on-one conversations, so I was curious why he suddenly wanted a meeting. I would find out the next day when James showed up in my office, right on time.

"Rhonda, I wasn't happy about you preaching last night," James began. I nodded, not surprised that James would object to a woman preaching. "But you did a pretty good job," he said to his own amazement.

"Thanks!" I said with raised brow, appreciating the hard-won compliment.

James continued, "I was talking about you with my roommates last night. Rhonda, do you remember the Old Testament story about Balaam?"

Not sure where this was going, I said, "Sure! The story in which God spoke to Balaam through a donkey?"

"That's right," James acknowledged. "My roommates and I decided that if God can speak through a donkey, then God can speak through a woman."

After I picked my jaw up off the floor, I affirmed James in his conclusion, recognizing that it went against everything he was taught in the Southern Baptist church of his upbringing. For my part, if being compared to a donkey helped move the needle a little for women preachers in Baptist life, then hee-haw! I was happy to be an ass for the Lord!

As I reflect on my journey as a woman called to vocational ministry from within the Southern Baptist tradition, I compare it to a winding road. While my male contemporaries seemed to have a straight shot, my way has been circuitous just like walking a labyrinth requires many twists and turns before arriving at center. I don't regret the journey, and most days I hold no grudges against those who attempted to stand between me and my calling (although my husband likes to quip that if you give me a couple of glasses of wine and bring up Southern Baptists, you might hear a few expletives).

Letting go of grudges has been a conscious choice for me—a choice I made years ago.

When I was a college student contemplating vocational ministry, I attended a conference at the Southern Baptist Theological Seminary in Louisville, Kentucky. This was in the early 1990s, before the conservative takeover of the seminary. One of the breakout sessions was about women in ministry. I was thrilled that there was such a session. With great zeal I sat among other young women who were considering vocational ministry. The presenter was a female military chaplain. I can't remember anything she said, but what I do remember is that she was angry—livid, really—at the years of misogyny she had experienced throughout her vocational journey. The excitement I had going into the breakout session was doused with her bitterness.

It was . . . sad. I decided that day that if I was going to pursue vocational ministry, I would not give myself to that kind of rage.

Looking back on that experience, I see that I judged her harshly. Letting go of resentments isn't always easy, and shadow work[1] continually reveals hidden layers of latent ire. Years and experience have helped me appreciate that sister and her journey. Her generation smoothed the way for my generation. And while my path remained circuitous, there have surely been fewer obstacles because of that chaplain and other trailblazers.

Those college years were formative in my vocational journey. The Baptist Student Union (BSU) at Tennessee Tech was my home away from home. That is where I heard about summer missions. My first entry point into ministry was serving as a volunteer summer missionary in Charleston, South Carolina. Returning to campus after that summer, I was ready for more. I became the youth director at a small Southern Baptist church just outside my college town. This was my first paid ministry position; I made a whopping $30 per week—just enough to pay for gas. I loved those sweet people, and they loved me. The next three summers I worked at the Tennessee Baptist Convention Girls in Action camp.

My fifth year on the college campus (why do in four years what you can do in five?) I was asked to be the intern at the BSU. What bliss! "You want to pay me to do what I love to do?" Somewhere along the way I found my calling. No, women couldn't be pastors (in my experience), but women could be campus ministers. I would become a Baptist campus minister. Off to seminary I went.

I drove to Fort Worth, Texas, in the middle of August, bound for Southwestern Baptist Theological Seminary. Little did I know that the flat, dry barrenness of the Texas landscape in August would mirror my own spiritual journey during my three years at Southwestern. During my first year there, the president was fired—one of many casualties in the conservative takeover of the denomination. The mood on campus was dour. Students found themselves divided in camps either supporting or opposing the termination. I

---

1. D. Gill, "What Is Shadow Work?" *Go Within Spiritual Coaching*, June 1, 2020, gowithinspiritualcoaching.com/what-is-shadow-work/.

was among the infuriated. A few like-minded classmates left for new Baptist seminaries that had not yet achieved accreditation. I decided to stick it out.

A large part of the reason I decided to stay was that I had landed a sweet internship at a Baptist Student Union about an hour away from the seminary. This internship was perfect—complete with a real-life female campus minister.

Carrie Beaird was the campus minister for the BSU at Texas Woman's University. When she interviewed me for the position, she asked, "What is your vocational goal?" I said jokingly, "I want your job!" Carrie and I became fast friends. We worked hard; we played hard. Watching Carrie navigate campus ministry as a woman in Texas Baptist life was eye-opening. It wasn't easy for her. A skilled minister, Carrie was passed over for more prestigious campus ministry positions in favor of men with less skill and experience. I was fortunate that Carrie remained in her role and that I got to be her intern throughout my three years in seminary. Not too long after I graduated from Southwestern, Carrie would take a different vocational path, becoming a licensed professional counselor. There were fewer barricades in that field than she encountered as a woman in Texas Baptist life.

I fell in love in seminary—my first true love. He was a classmate. I fell hard and I fell fast. He was also interested in campus ministry, but he had talent in so many areas. He could be a minister of music, or he could serve bi-vocationally—his skills as a computer engineer could pay the bills. We dated for two years and planned to get married. He was a couple years older than me but in the class behind me at Southwestern. After I graduated, I spent the summer working at a Lifeway Centrifuge camp. While at camp, I was offered a position as a full-time campus minister at a Baptist Student Union in Mississippi. I had finally landed my dream job! My boyfriend, however, didn't want me to take the position. He wanted me back in Fort Worth with him as he completed his final year in seminary. Through many tears, I turned down the job, doubtful I would ever again be offered a full-time campus ministry position. When the summer was over, I headed back to Fort Worth with nothing but a few dollars in my pocket and plans to marry this boy.

I have never shared this publicly before, but when I arrived back in Fort Worth, I didn't have a place to live. I was no longer a student, so student housing was not an option for me. I couldn't live with my boyfriend because, well, seminary. I slept on friends' couches. When I wore out my welcome, I slept in hotel rooms. When I spent all my money, I slept in my car. I was . . . homeless.

Eventually I got a part-time job as a college minister at a large Baptist church outside Dallas. With another (non-ministry) part-time job, I was able to afford a small apartment. But the cat was out of the bag in my relationship—the one I gave up my dream job for, the one I went back to Texas for, the one I became homeless for. I discovered he wasn't willing to join me where my vocational calling might lead. I guess I had imagined we'd follow my ministry first, since I was first to graduate seminary, and then maybe we'd follow his ministry. It would be his turn, after all.

Maybe I hadn't thought it out at all because I was in love. I discovered that he was complementarian-lite. In his view, women could be ministers, but men were the head of the household. Somehow, I had missed this with his winsome, easygoing, women-in-ministry-affirming personality. Could I be one of those women who smiled and winked while saying, "Men are the head of the household, but women are the neck?" The first time I heard a woman say that, I threw up in my mouth a little bit. Could I do that? For love?

That year—that homeless, rudderless, tumultuous year—would make me choose between my theology and the love of my life.

If he loved me, I wondered, how could he not want me to flourish? I had given up my dream job for him, possibly my only shot at becoming a campus minister, but he wanted me to wait around until he landed *his* dream job.

Eventually I had to break it off. I loved him deeply, but I could not cede my calling for him. When I was offered a campus ministry position at the University of Georgia—the *University of Georgia!*—my excitement was tempered, knowing that it would mean the end of my relationship. I said goodbye to my love. My heart was officially broken. The next day, I drove a U-Haul from Texas to Georgia. I cried for 853.4 miles—all the way to Athens.

Athens, Georgia, is the perfect college town. It is beautiful, it is eclectic, and it buzzes with the energy of tens of thousands of college students when they pour into town each fall. My first few months in Athens were marked by excitement to finally be living my calling as a campus minister during the day and by tears borne of heartbreak during the night. I was the third of three campus ministers at the Baptist Student Union—the youngest and only female. I was pleased to learn that my colleagues were among the open-minded variety of Baptist clergy (a hallmark of those serving in campus ministry). I poured myself into ministry, I enjoyed my work, and I was good at it.

Baptist campus ministers are required to join a Baptist church, and I found the perfect little church to join. Milledge Avenue Baptist Church (MABC) was a dually aligned congregation—at that time, it supported the Southern Baptist Convention and its state counterpart, the Georgia Baptist Convention, my employer. It also supported the Cooperative Baptist Fellowship (CBF), which formed as a reaction against the conservative takeover of the Southern Baptist Convention. At first, I felt lonely as a single adult sitting alone in the pews on Sunday mornings. But I stuck it out, got involved, and eventually MABC became home for me.

Back at the BSU, things were going well, and I loved my ministry with college students. There were occasional skirmishes from local pastors who thought we, the campus ministers, were too "liberal." I enjoyed watching the good ole boys squirm when I showed up, the only woman, to the Baptist Association clergy meeting. I felt much more at home in the meetings of the interfaith Campus Ministers Association alongside conservative Protestants, progressive Protestants, Catholics, Jews—I discovered I had a heart for ecumenism and interfaith work.

For about five years, things went well for me at UGA. That is, until an edict came down from the Georgia Baptist Convention that employees who were members of dually aligned churches had to join congregations aligned solely with the SBC . . . or else. Most of my colleagues acquiesced. Could I be one of those ministers who smiled and winked as I joined a church that did not affirm my calling as a woman? Could I join a church that offered fealty to the *Baptist Faith and Message 2000*[2] with its assertion that "the office of pastor is limited to men" and "a wife is to submit herself graciously to the servant leadership of her husband"? When that revision was made to the *Baptist Faith and Message*, my Baptist blood boiled. Could I do that? For employment?

I could not. I kept my membership at Milledge Avenue Baptist Church, come what may. The next couple of years were challenging as it became apparent that my supervisor at the Georgia Baptist Convention was looking for reasons to "write me up" in order to build a case for my termination. My "writeups" were often over matters of paperwork, not my forte, to be fair. The final straw was something that happened at a meeting of the interfaith Campus Ministers Association. The new pastor of the Metropolitan Community Church applied for membership. I was told, in hushed tones, that this new pastor was a lesbian. An ordained, seminary-educated clergy person, this new pastor met all the criteria for membership in the association —nowhere in the bylaws was heterosexuality a requirement for membership. We cast our votes; her acceptance narrowly passed. You could say that my vote was the deciding factor in her acceptance. Word got out about my vote, traveling all the way to Atlanta and landing on my supervisor's desk. He hightailed it to Athens for a disciplinary meeting in which he told me that the situation for my employment was "very grave." In other words, I was going to be fired. He just had to run it up the chain of command. In the meantime, I resigned. My dream job was over. Though I offered a two-week notice, I was given twenty-four hours to vacate my office. I packed up my growing theological library and closed the door behind me. I would never again serve as a campus minister. A few months later, however, Milledge Avenue Baptist Church would ordain me to the ministry, something I had been forbidden from as a female campus minister with the Georgia Baptist Convention.

On a couple of occasions during my time in Athens, I went rogue (cue the *Mission Impossible* theme song). Knowing I would be

---

2. Southern Baptist Convention, *Baptist Faith and Message 2000*, bfm.sbc.net.

fired if my superiors at the Georgia Baptist Convention found out, I snuck into gatherings of the Cooperative Baptist Fellowship. This was before smartphones were ubiquitous, so I watched carefully for anyone pulling out a camera. If I saw a camera, I would hide behind a column or a large plant. Notwithstanding my fear of photography, I felt tremendous freedom at those CBF meetings. It seemed I had found "my people."

As my time with the Georgia Baptist Convention was coming to an ugly end, my resume landed in a state CBF office in Louisville, Kentucky. The Kentucky Baptist Fellowship (now CBF Kentucky) was looking for an "associate coordinator for missions." I had set an intention that one day I would work for CBF in some capacity, so this was my big break. I remember the interview process as them asking questions to determine "is she really one of us," and me answering questions to convince them "I really am one of you." (As it turned out, my rogue CBF escapades helped seal the deal.) When the coordinating council met to lend a final stamp of approval, one of the council members drilled down into why I left my campus ministry job just as the fall semester began. I was terrified of my answer—that I had voted for a lesbian to become a part of the interfaith Campus Ministers Association. I took a deep breath and spilled the beans. I winced, wondering if my honest answer would lose me this job I had firmly in my reach. I looked around and saw most heads nodding in approval. "They're like me!" I thought to myself. "I'm home!"

I packed my bags and headed to the Bluegrass State.

Part of my charge in Kentucky was to lead the Kentucky expression of CBF's rural poverty initiative, Together for Hope. With little poverty-related work in my background, I would have a steep learning curve. I recognized that I had skills in mobilizing people toward a common task; I also knew that I lacked training in effective methods for transforming poverty-stricken communities. I set out to learn asset-based community development techniques. It seemed there were competing charges in my job description: first, I had to build programs and create projects in keeping with the goals of community development, and second, I was expected to engage people in CBF churches in that work.

Housing seemed to be the unifying answer. If a child has adequate housing, that child's life trajectory is far more promising than the life trajectory of a child who grows up in insecure housing. That is systemic change! How could I engage a large number of CBF individuals in sustainable housing solutions in one of the focal counties for the CBF rural poverty initiative? I discovered the idea of a "quick build" in which dozens of people come together to build a house in a week. There were organizations already doing that in Eastern Kentucky. Could we, CBF churches and Christians in Kentucky, pull this off? Believing we could, I set out to bring others into this dream. Kentucky Baptist Fellowship built the first "Extreme Build" house in 2006. With a couple of exceptions, that program continues to build a house each year in one of the poorest counties in the nation.

As it turns out, I was in a "building" phase of my life during that time in Kentucky, professionally and personally. Eight years after my big heartbreak, I wondered if I would know love again, especially of the egalitarian kind I so desired. I met a man who would help me answer that question. His name was Terry Blevins. E-Harmony decided we were a "match," and he met my criteria for an in-person meetup (namely that he wasn't reading the *Left Behind* series that was so popular at the time). We met, and the rest is history (and herstory). I was thirty-five years old; Terry was four years older. Our romance was of the whirlwind variety. We met online in June, we met in person in July, by August we were engaged, and we married in December that same year. Terry affirmed my calling and joined me in my desire for an egalitarian marriage. Maybe it helped that he wasn't Southern Baptist. Our first child, Jake, would come along seventeen months after we were married. What we had in love we lacked in financial resources. Even though I enjoyed my work with the Kentucky Baptist Fellowship, my entry-level salary was no longer sufficient. Additionally, having a baby made me want to be closer to my family. My growing family and I left Kentucky just shy of my three-year mark when I accepted an associate pastor position with an interdenominational congregation in Loudon, Tennessee.

I wasn't sure what to think about an interdenominational church at first. How does baptism work, for instance? "Baptize babies? Can

I do that?" Answer: yes I can, yes I have, yes I will. As it turned out, the interdenominational setting was a breath of fresh air. Everywhere in CBF life, people seemed angry about doctrine and what was lost in the conservative takeover of the SBC. In the interdenominational church, people didn't carry that baggage. They were happy to "do church" together without splitting doctrinal hairs and waging anachronistic wars over inerrancy or women or Calvinism or whatever battle du jour the Baptists conjured up.

Being an associate pastor has its perks. There's plenty of work to do and niches to fill without the responsibility of being the "buck stops here" person. I leveraged that freedom to ramp up my education. I received coach training and launched a ministry to clergy through Pinnacle Leadership Associates. I also earned my terminal degree in ministry. Thinking it might benefit me down the road to keep my moderate Baptist network fresh and missing out on the opportunity to attend a moderate Baptist seminary for my master of divinity, I enrolled in the doctor of ministry program at Mercer University's McAfee School of Theology. What fun!

If Southwestern Seminary was a spiritual desert for me, McAfee was a land flowing with milk and honey. I devoured the books assigned and relished the challenge of scholarly study. The professors became friends, and many classmates were kindred spirits. The only wrinkle I experienced was that I found myself pregnant with our second child during my final year of the program. By the time I defended my thesis, baby boy Rhys was in tow on my round-trip excursion to Atlanta. I nursed him before my oral defense, and he slept in the office at McAfee School of Theology while his mother defended her thesis. That is the day I became Dr. Mom.

Back in Tennessee at Tellico Village Community Church, my doubts about being a minister and having a family were assuaged. We were making it work. I found ways to use my unique skill set in ministry at the church. One of the gifts of that time was that the senior pastor, Marty Singley, was generous with the pulpit. Marty gave us associate pastors ample opportunities to preach on Sundays and for our weekly "Wednesday Church." I had freedom to preach some experimental sermons, and over the course of my nearly eight years there, I found my "preaching voice." Church members and Marty alike were generous in their praise of my preaching. When Marty had to be out for several weeks after open-heart surgery, he appointed me as the primary pulpiteer.

When Marty announced his retirement, it seemed the next step would be for me to throw my hat in the ring to become the next senior pastor of the church. I was ready. At forty-five years old, I had been in vocational ministry for over twenty years. I knew how to lead a funeral and officiate a wedding. I knew how to work with a church board and read the profit and loss statement. I knew when to speak and when to remain silent (not perfectly, but hey, everyone has growth edges). I knew how to inspire and mobilize people. Not only did I know how to pastor, but I was already *their* pastor. Just not their *senior* pastor.

They broke my heart when they said, "No thanks." I don't know why exactly. The search committee said I lacked sufficient "experience." I never quite bought that. Maybe it was because, as the interim senior pastor said, I had been there "long enough to step on a few landmines." I will go to my grave, however, suspecting that at least a majority of the search team members couldn't bring themselves to call a woman as senior pastor. Recognizing that my impact at the church had peaked, I knew I needed to move along and give the new senior pastor freedom to build the staff he wanted. I would not be part of the future story at the church. I got my resume together and circled back around to some old Baptist networks.

It just so happened that Kentucky Baptist Fellowship needed a new coordinator. My time as an associate coordinator had been a rousing success. The "Extreme Build" project I started was still going strong. People in the organization knew me, and they respected my work. Furthermore, I was roughly eight years older, old enough to command a bit of gravitas I lacked when I worked for them in my thirties. I took the job as coordinator, despite the red flags.

"Don't paint your red flags green," a pastor friend once told me. Advice I failed to heed.

This is where the story gets tricky. It is tricky, in part, because I probably need more therapy around this; there are parts of the story that are still quite raw for me. If I fail to be completely forthcoming here, I hope it is less about self-preservation and more about treating those who hurt me respectfully. Here we go . . .

Before my arrival back on the scene at Kentucky Baptist Fellowship, there had been a major staff disruption. Two key staff members left the organization. The two remaining employees didn't get along and everyone knew it. When one of those individuals resigned within a couple of weeks of my arrival, I thought it was for the best—that the conflict was taking care of itself with that departure. Boy, was I wrong.

My husband tells me I didn't have much of a chance to succeed in that position with someone constantly undermining me. That is probably enough said there. At one point I had a choice: I could escalate and face unknown challenges, or I could go quietly into the night and leave the problem for the next coordinator. If you've read my story to this point, you can probably guess which path I chose. I escalated, believing that escalation was ultimately in the best interest of the organization. I paid the price for that escalation. What I have found so painful about this chapter is the betrayal. I discovered how easy it is for a set of lies to quickly destroy a reputation built over decades.

Friends familiar with the situation, both men and women, suggested that things would have been different had I been male. It is difficult to know. Would a male executive have been given the benefit of the doubt? Would the undermining have been seen as such instead of the "catfight" it was labeled? It's hard to say. Among the lessons learned in this dark chapter of my vocational journey is a lesson in forgiveness. There was never a moment when I didn't forgive the central player in my downfall. I recognized all along that this person was acting out of a deep, visceral woundedness. Though it felt personal in the moment, I know it wasn't personal at all. There was never a moment that I didn't forgive the many others dragged into the mess. They were all doing their best.

There are times in vocational ministry when you must "shake the dust off your feet" and move along. I haven't been back to Kentucky since I left, even though we have family there. At the time of this writing, it's been just over four years. I've shaken most of the dust off, but lessons remain. I am a better minister, and a better person, today because of what Father Richard Rohr calls the "necessary suffering" requisite for growth. Godspeed to CBF Kentucky and everyone involved in those tumultuous days.

Four years later, I can say that I've landed well. An interdenominational church in Clearwater Beach, Florida, called me as pastor in July 2017. Chapel by the Sea is a warm-hearted, fun-loving group of people in a beach town—they don't get too worked up about doctrine or the religious battles of the day. My four years as their pastor have been challenging years in the larger world, with national politics and a global pandemic wreaking havoc on churches everywhere. We have weathered these storms well, remaining positive and fixing our eyes to the future. I have been able to maintain my ministry to clergy through Pinnacle Leadership Associates, which continually sharpens my pastoral skills.

During my first year at Chapel by the Sea, I dipped a toe in Baptist life. As time went on, however, I grew more comfortable saying, "I *used to be* Baptist." I can't imagine I'll ever serve a Baptist organization again. As I reflect on my life's work as a woman in ministry, I recognize that there were times I was filled with self-doubt and times marked by self-importance. Occasionally my faith has soared; at other times, I could barely believe. It has all been a part of the journey. There are many gifts I acknowledge from my Baptist pilgrimage:

The Southern Baptist church was a spiritual "mother" to me, giving me birth, nurturing me through my early years.

The Cooperative Baptist Fellowship was a spiritual "home" to me, a soft place to land when I had to leave the home of my birth.

The Kentucky Baptist Fellowship was the first group of Baptists, or Christians for that matter, who saw my "executive" potential and gave me a chance.

For the desert I experienced at Southwestern Baptist Theological Seminary and for the richness of my experience at McAfee School of Theology, I give thanks. Every step of my Baptist journey brought me to where I am today: living into the fullness of my calling as a minister of the good news of Jesus Christ. Most days, I absolutely love being a pastor.

I no longer consider myself Baptist, but my Baptist faith formed me: Baptist is my native tongue, Baptist is my homeland. And like any homeland, you can take the girl out of the Baptists, but you can't take the Baptist out of the girl.

Rhonda Abbott Blevins is the pastor of Chapel by the Sea, an interdenominational congregation in Clearwater Beach, Florida. Rhonda is an East Tennessee native and a graduate of Tennessee Tech University with a degree in secondary education. She earned her doctor of ministry from McAfee School of Theology and her master of divinity at Southwestern Baptist Theological Seminary.

Theologically progressive, ecumenically minded, spiritually impassioned and relationship oriented, Rhonda seeks to minister in a way that promotes a thoughtful, compelling, and life-giving faith that manifests through love in action. In more than twenty-five years in ministry, Rhonda has served as a campus minister, associate pastor, and denominational leader. A trained life coach, she practices clergy coaching through Pinnacle Leadership Associates in Chapin, South Carolina. Through Pinnacle, Rhonda co-hosts a podcast for clergy called *Pastor Life*. Rhonda and her husband, Terry, have two sons, Jake and Rhys. She enjoys camping, kayaking, exploring new places, and singing along with the *Hamilton* soundtrack.

The Seventh Story

Holy Whispers

Rev. Kathy Manis Findley

I love hearing whispers—secrets for my ears only, messages so extraordinary they cannot be spoken out loud. I love the whispers I have heard in my life that I could not explain, like God-whispers coming on the wind of the Spirit from a place too holy to define.

I heard that kind of holy whisper, softly calling my name, in an unusual time and in an unlikely place. I was twelve years old, a little lost girl whose heart was shattered by abusive life circumstances, but still full of stirrings and longings (a likely candidate for hearing holy whispers). I was one hundred percent a Greek girl, raised by immigrant parents and an inescapably obtrusive Greek yiayiá (grandmother). Being a Greek girl through and through means you are all-in religiously, spiritually, and socially. And yes, I have attended hundreds of "big fat Greek weddings," including my own! In a Baptist church!

I should explain the holy whisper I heard sixty years ago. I still remember it as if it were yesterday. It happened on an afternoon while I was in my Greek Orthodox Church's Greek School. That's when you ride the bus to the church every afternoon after American school and stay there until 6:00 p.m. Every weekday, Monday through Friday. And the purpose of Greek School? Well, Greek School's "divine" purpose is to teach Greek children how to read, write, and speak Greek as if they had just stepped off a boat from the old country.

At least we had recess! Everyone would run from the schoolroom to play kickball in the church yard. Not me, though, I walked past the kickball game to the church door. I opened the huge wooden doors and reverently walked in, making the sign of the cross, lighting a candle in the vestibule, and heading to a pew in front of a daunting life-sized icon of St. Michael the Archangel. I sat for a few minutes, taking in the sacred aroma of burning candles and incense. It was so completely silent that the only sound I heard was my own breath. Until the whisper!

From nowhere and everywhere I heard it, not audibly like a real voice but deeply in my spirit. How can a voice be so clear and unmistakable when it doesn't come from a real person's vocal cords? How could I hear an almost silent whisper? I could not answer the questions that formed in my mind, but I could clearly hear and understand the whisper I heard in my soul.

She whispered one word: *Kalliope*, the name given to me at birth and affirmed in the waters of holy baptism where folks say I screamed the entire holy time. *Kalliope!* I don't know how a twelve-year-old would interpret that, but I believed at the time that this female voice was a Spirit whisper from God, who called my name as if it were a sacred word in the Divine Liturgy.

To buy all of this, one has to understand that I had always been a religious little girl. With my yiayiá's constant tutelage, I memorized the Lord's Prayer, the Nicene Creed, a variety of Scripture passages about God, Jesus, and the Holy Spirit, plus Yiayiá's entire repertoire of poetry—in Greek. To prove the devotion to church and the ethnicity of a Greek family, the children, especially the firstborn child, were expected to recite for company. We dutifully recited it all—prayers, creeds, poems, and long passages of Scripture—and with a good attitude. Not insignificant was the painful reality that Yiayiá forced me to recite all of these memorized offerings every time company came over. Every time! All in Greek.

As for the holy whisper, I understood it years later as God's first call on my life. As a twelve-year-old, I had no idea what it meant. Yet I knew with complete certainty that the holy whisper that called out *Kalliope* meant I had just been named God's beloved daughter. As the years passed, I would more fully understand that holy whisper as a call to embark on a journey led by Spirit winds to places near and far, to people who needed to hear whispers of their own. The first line of a beautiful hymn speaks to me about the meaning and mystery of calling: "God is calling through the whisper of the Spirit's deepest sighs."[1] How well the hymn describes what I experienced!

I ask myself often if I can remember a single transformative moment in my journey of call. Does any single moment rise up in my memory as the most extraordinary moment? I've given this some thought. No, there wasn't one single moment. There were *many* moments along the journey that transformed me in unmistakable, beyond-any-doubt ways. Other moments, the most sacred ones, transformed me in ways imperceptible. One might say that those most sacred moments were moments of spirit transformation, when something reached down into the depths of my soul to mold me and change me.

The years ahead held extravagant surprises that lifted my spirit to higher ground. The years also brought obstacles, rough and rocky pathways, times of loneliness, heartbreaking moments, and assaults on the call from God that I was so sure of. But let me skip from age twelve to age seventeen, when this thoroughly Greek Orthodox girl found herself in a Baptist church.

Quite unexpectedly, my family moved to a small Alabama town, and there I got my first glimpse of being Baptist. The move was a twist that changed my life in many ways. The tiny town of a thousand residents had no Greek Orthodox Church, so I went to the church where all my friends went, First Baptist Church in Reform, Alabama. Where in the world was Reform, Alabama, anyway? I was a city girl, raised in Birmingham, so Reform was a strange kind of town. My perky personality fit right in at Reform FBC, and almost immediately I was "active."

"Baptist activeness" means going to church every Sunday morning and every Sunday night, plus Sunday school, Training Union (a rather dreaded session of reciting "parts" that took place

---

1. Text: Mary Louise Bringle, 2003; music: Polish carol; harm. Wilbur Lee, 1958 (public domain). Text © 2006 GIA Publications, Inc. Music Harm. © 1958 Broadman Press.

before Sunday night worship), Wednesday night prayer meeting, Young Women's Auxiliary, and, if you can sing at all, choir practice. In other words, being active in a Baptist church means being there every time the church doors open.

This was, to say the least, an unlikely place for a Greek girl to be. But oh, how I loved the Baptist church—singing hymns of joy and blessed assurance, hymns of rebirth and resurrection, hymns of devotion, hymns of revival! I loved the fervent preaching and the impassioned invitation to commitment that followed. I loved singing in the choir, going to Sunday school and Vacation Bible School, and learning about missionaries serving all over the world. I loved the stories of Lottie Moon.[2] I loved singing "We've a Story to Tell to the Nations"[3] and imagining that one day I would become a missionary. I even loved Training Union on Sunday nights, after which I would go to Sunday night church and sit on the back pew holding hands with my boyfriend. All of it was so very Baptist, and I was a quick study on what being Baptist was like.

One day, as my friends and I were decorating for the church's Valentine's Day banquet, my pastor dropped in and asked me to come to his study for a chat. From the "big pastor's chair" in his study, he asked me if I was a Christian, to which I responded, "Of course!" He went on to explain. "I mean have you ever accepted Jesus Christ as your personal Savior?" I thought about that for several seconds.

"I guess I have not *actually* done that, but I *have* been baptized," I responded. The conversation continued with lots of Baptist information I didn't know about. I think he called it the "Four Spiritual Laws." After listening to the "laws" and suddenly becoming terrified about going to hell, I made a profession of faith. I declared that I would accept Jesus Christ as my "personal Lord and Savior" and be baptized. Still, I thought about that conversation over the next few days and concluded that I had done all of that already, just not in the

---

2. See "Lottie Moon," *Wikipedia*, en.wikipedia.org/wiki/Lottie_Moon.

3. H. Ernest Nichol, "We've a Story to Tell to the Nations," *Hymnary.org* (Baptist Hymnal 1991, 2007), hymnary.org/text/weve_a_story_to_tell_to_the_nations.

prescribed Baptist way, a way that would cause my Greek Orthodox family to denounce me in dramatic fits of weeping and wailing.

Are you ready for it? My baptism was a county-wide youth rally! After all, a tiny church in a tiny town doesn't convert someone from Greek Orthodoxy every day. It seemed that my baptism, complete with my testimony, was going to be a big "happening." And so it was, with stirring revival hymns, the excitement of an honest-to-goodness Christian conversion, my spirited dunking in the baptistry, and, in the fullness of time, my testimony given with wet hair. I don't remember much of what I said, only that it was long and quite preachy. Maybe a glimpse of things to come?

My father, who had declared the day before that I was dead to him, came and stood in the back of the church, probably drunk. I felt the familiar panic of being embarrassed by him. As my anxiety built, I heard something. Well, I knew I didn't *actually* hear anything, but I "heard" another holy whisper saying, "You've got this! You are my beloved daughter."

I did not plan for my testimony to address my father's vehement diatribe of disowning me, nor the slap to my face he delivered with the power of a mobster wearing a heavy gold ring. Yet, with his ring's indentation still visible on my face, I looked to the back of the sanctuary and said, "My profession of faith has nothing to do with being Greek Orthodox or Baptist. It has nothing to do with dishonoring my family. Professing Christ as my Savior has everything to do with my heart."

An understanding of "call" was beginning to claim its space in me. As I reflect on that season of my life, I remember it as being charged with some indefinable power, almost like a series of electric shocks, or the electric atmosphere of a youth rally in a small county in west Alabama, or maybe even Spirit fire. Even now, I don't have words to describe it.

I left the youth rally that was planned for the entire county to witness "my miraculous conversion" with only one intention: to find a minister to marry. Back then, we called them "preacher boys." For a woman, God's call meant finding some holy coattails to latch on to. Two years later, I grabbed the coattails of Fred Findley and held on for the ride. And what a ride it was! We were both in college at the University of Alabama when we first entertained the idea of dating. An unlikely match, we were! Our friends laughed at the pairing. On our second date, I shared with Fred some inside information from God: "God told me we are going to get married."

Fred replied that God had not told him any such thing. Ten months later, we were married, and I had my "big fat Greek wedding" in a small-town Baptist church. I had achieved my goal of marrying a minister because that was the *only way* out of no way. These were my conservative years, the years of revivals, conversions, and being anxious about the Second Coming of Jesus. These were the years when I gave my two brothers Bibles and a paperback copy of Nicky Cruz's book *Run Baby Run*[4] and made sure at least one of them got saved. It worked with my brother Andrew. Later, I was compelled to convert that same brother from Methodism, insisting that being Baptist was the only path to saving grace. By the way, he did become a Baptist.

I eventually eased out of my conservatism, but not before knocking on the doors of strangers, witnessing to people walking around the Iowa State Capitol, and performing at churches and revivals all over the place with my husband. We were posing as traveling music evangelists. You should have seen our matching outfits! Our years of high-octane evangelistic fervor passed, and we settled into the sacred calling of ministry that has a fervor all its own.

Fred was a remarkable minister, gifted in so many ways. As a choral conductor, he magically pulled out incredible sound and melody from even the smallest choirs. His pastoral care was full of caring, and his comforting presence calmed many struggling congregants. For the next many years, every church Fred served had both of us, the proverbial "two for the price of one" deal churches love.

We both found deep fulfillment in serving the church . . . until we didn't. When we didn't, we accidentally made a wise and life-altering decision to attend Southern Baptist Theological Seminary. We were visiting with my brother Andrew, who was scheduled to

---

4. The best-selling classic *Run, Baby, Run* was written by Nicky Cruz with Jamie Buckingham (United Kingdom: Hodder and Stoughton, 1969).

move to Southern Seminary in few days. Out of the blue, he said, "Why don't y'all just come on to seminary with us?" This was the same brother who received my gift of the Nicky Cruz book about New York gangs being miraculously saved.

On the ride back home, Fred and I laughed about my brother's serendipitous question. Then we looked at each other and said (almost in unison), "Why don't we?" Instead of going back home, we headed straight to Louisville, about a five-hundred-mile trip. When we got there, we looked around the seminary campus and the nearby neighborhoods, Fred filled out his application, and we rented an apartment. Then we drove back home and started packing.

Southern Seminary, the seminary that it was in the late 1970s, rearranged my life in ways I can barely explain. I attended classes at night and worked a few campus jobs: Grounds crew—too sweaty. Mopping the professors' offices—mop was too heavy! My third and final job was in the seminary development office. The day that turned my life upside down was a Wednesday, chapel day, when students, professors, and staff alike gathered. I do not remember any of the chapel services I attended except this one on the day that changed my life.

Dr. Paul Simmons delivered the address. I was not hanging on his every word. I was almost dozing, listening but not truly hearing words. I heard the sound of Dr. Simmons speaking loudly at times, and then medium-loud in a conversational tone. I had no idea what he had said until he whispered—a preaching whisper one can hear, but still a whisper.

"Is what you're doing worth giving your life for?" That's what he whispered that day *to me*. A holy whisper, a holy question that landed deeply in my spirit. When I returned to my office, I resigned my job, enrolled in seminary, and dove into my studies as if the whole world depended on me. I drank fresh water from the well of theology, history, homiletics, etc., like someone dying of thirst. I learned, and I grew, and I devoured everything around me. I knew many women seminarians, and I often wondered why they were there. I even heard that some of them were planning to be pastors.

My professors opened my mind and heart to what I can only describe as theological wonders. They challenged and encouraged me, constantly enhancing my faith. I was captivated by the liberation theologies of James H. Cone and Gustavo Gutiérrez, and to this day my passion for liberation has never waned.

I cannot leave this part of my story without recalling the enlightening impact of my seminary education—the New Testament opened to me in new ways by Frank Stagg; the challenging thought and contemplative spirit of Glenn Hinson; the grounding in church history from Bill Leonard and Walter Shurden; the depth and breadth of preaching exemplified by David Buttrick and our on-site evangelist, Lewis Drummond; the challenging theological thought of Wayne Ward and Dale Moody; the perfect Greek pronunciation expected from me by David Garland, who made me read from the Greek New Testament in every class because Greek was my first language; and finally, the visionary before his time, Findley Edge, who dreamed of the "greening of the church"[5] and inspired me to long for the greening, too. For you see, the greening of the church is what I imagined and longed for—being a part of a congregation of people who were renewed to create a church where all were welcomed, where all became a part of a loving community, where all members were ministers in their own right—and from that the church would experience a sacred greening, the sprouting of new buds of incomparable growth. The greening of the church was a movement of renewal, and I envisioned my life and ministry in the center of that renewal. And so, the profound work of Findley Edge became my freedom in ministry. The church did not have to fall into stale and rigid practices and ministries. Instead, the church can move by Spirit winds to a place of freedom in ministry. Dr. Edge was my hero, and for him, I was "daughter," the name he called me until he died.

The story of the protracted and painful schism of the Southern Baptist Convention (SBC) beginning in 1979 resulted in the loss of our six seminaries. We were witnesses of the persecution of our professors, watching them leave or be forced to leave one after another. This was an excruciating and unforgettable moment in time for Baptists,

---

5. Findley B. Edge, *The Greening of the Church* (Waco: Word Books, 1977).

a time in which the role of women landed, as always, in the center of the controversy.

In the next few years, the document we had long known as the *Baptist Faith and Message* (BFM) would be cited again and again to justify limiting the role of women in the church. A revision in the year 2000 cemented the resistance of church leadership for women and, stunningly, also marked out boundaries for a woman's role in the home. The two articles in the BFM 2000 revision—"The Church" and "The Family"—were adopted to cement Baptist thought regarding the roles women were allowed to fill. "The Church" stated, "While both men and women are gifted for service in the church, the office of pastor is limited to men as qualified by Scripture."[6] "The Family" reaffirmed Baptist thought on what they had long referred to as gracious submission: "A wife is to submit herself graciously to the servant leadership of her husband even as the church willingly submits to the headship of Christ. She, being in the image of God as is her husband and thus equal to him, has the God-given responsibility to respect her husband and to serve as his helper in managing the household and nurturing the next generation."[7]

Such is the description of an unforgettable and life-changing seminary experience, punctuated by the chaos of a denomination in chaos. While in seminary, Fred and I felt a strong pull to the mission field, wanting to go where the need was great and also wanting to escape the church and denomination in America. We entered the appointment process of what was then the SBC Foreign Mission Board, naively believing that the SBC schism could not reach us on the mission field. We were wrong. Fred would be appointed as a "church planter," while my appointment would be named "church and home," as if I was forbidden to go anywhere that wasn't church or home. I was strongly advised by our Foreign Mission Board (FMB) seminary liaison to apply as a "church and home" missionary. If I balked, he told me, I would put our appointment at risk.

In August 1979, we were appointed by the Southern Baptist Convention Foreign Mission Board in a moving worship service in

---

6. Southern Baptist Convention, *Baptist Faith and Message 2000*, bfm.sbc.net.
7. Ibid.

Glorieta, New Mexico. Even the breathtaking beauty of Glorieta was overshadowed by the feeling of having reached what I believed to be the highest pinnacle of Baptist ministry. After seventeen weeks of missionary orientation, we ended up in Uganda, East Africa.[8] I marveled that God had allowed me to reach what I considered the loftiest place of ministry before ministering anywhere else, and before I had to learn the agony of a holy call that my denomination did not recognize, much less affirm.

We arrived in Uganda immediately after the fall of the evil dictator Idi Amin. The country was decimated during Amin's reign of terror that lasted from 1971 to 1979. Considered one of the most brutal despots in world history, Idi Amin had a taste for genocide. During his reign, an estimated 500,000 Ugandans were killed.[9] When we crossed the border from Kenya to Uganda, we immediately saw the massive destruction—demolished roads, burned churches and schools, decaying animal carcasses, and mass graves. The most heartrending sight of all was the people walking about aimlessly, in shock, harrowing expressions on their faces. Uganda had become a country of widows and orphans.

Uganda was most certainly the right place for someone like me who had come to see the grace of God through the lens of liberation. I knew that the God who called me did not measure me by my gender. Spirit wind was blowing through my life. Still, the work was arduous—in-the-trenches work in the black mud of Uganda. Our ministry was with a people in desperation. From village to village we traveled, taking seeds, shovels and hoes, blankets and food, and formula for babies near death.

I felt as if our work was saying to them, "The gospel good news is a liberating gospel. You will dig water wells in your own villages so that your women and girls will be liberated from carrying heavy jugs of water for miles. You will grow your own food and be liberated

---

8. Editor's note: One of our writers, Melody Carroll Harrell, is the daughter of Uganda missionaries who became our dearest colleagues, so Melody was our missionary family "niece."

9. W. Stanley Mooneyham, "Uganda Genocide: A Nightmare Finally Comes to an End," *World Vision: Voices*, January 9, 2014, worldvision.org/disaster-relief-news-stories/uganda-genocide-nightmare-finally-end.

from hunger. Your despairing hearts will be liberated to once again to know joy." I believed with all my heart that God was whispering to me again, "Let the oppressed go free."[10]

While leading a weekly support group for teenage Ugandan girls, I heard their grief and saw their tears flow freely. Sitting in a circle of mutual mourning, I kept vigil with them in their heartbreak. Yet, in the same beautiful way Ugandan people expressed their emotions, these precious girls wept in one moment and laughed in the next. The sorrow in them coexisted with joy and faithful hope.

"I am lost," Tabaganyizi said, "lost because my family is gone, my home is no longer in the shade of the banana tree, my school is finished, my church is only ashes. But I am free because I have my God."

"Let the oppressed go free!"

I heard the holy whisper again in my soul. In those moments when the girls shared their stories of heartbreak, I received their stories as gifts. I will forever remember bearing witness to Tabaganyizi's story that was for me a cherished grace.

It was in Uganda that we received a long-anticipated message from an adoption organization in Kentucky that a child was available. It was a miracle we thought impossible when we applied, so we had barely thought about it as our life and work in Uganda began to consume us. One late afternoon, we heard a car horn in our driveway. Betty Carroll, a missionary colleague, had driven eight hours on jarring dirt roads because we had no phone service. She brought us news that could not wait: "The adoption agency called! They have a baby for you!"

Back to the States we went. We traveled to Louisville, Kentucky, to get Jonathan, our four-month-old bundle of joy. As we left the adoption agency, receiving our child, we lingered for a few minutes in the parking lot. Fred held Jonathan close, I could not keep my eyes off him, and both of us wept—tears of joy for this precious boy and tears of relief that followed eleven hard years of infertility. Eventually, we were able to drive to the special home that first received Jonathan, the home of our dearest friends, Findley and Louvenia Edge.

---

10. Isaiah 58:6, NRSV.

After three months of being detained in the United States because of increased danger in Uganda, we took our six-month-old gift to his home in Uganda. In the next several months, having a new baby in a country still under the dangers of military occupation began to weigh on us. We had never feared for our own safety, but now we feared for his. I was taken aback by this unexpected reaction in myself—this switch from being a fearless and adventurous person to being a protective mommy.

And Fred and I were both taken aback by new requirements that came to us from the FMB. We first noticed this on an application for world hunger funding: "All hunger-related ministries must be tied to new baptisms and the planting of new churches. Please indicate the number of new baptisms/new churches you anticipate through the granting of hunger funds." We were shocked and worried. What was reported in the Associated Baptist Press in 2003 was already upon us as early as 1981:

> All of the SBC agencies, including the mission boards, asked employees to sign the new BFM 2000, which prompted a number of overseas missionaries to resign their positions rather than be forced into stating agreement with the new confession. Others refused to sign and were terminated.[11]

With the new Foreign Mission Board actions looming over us, the next turn of events seemed to be the proverbial "last straw." When all three of us developed a debilitating eye disease, we gave in and made the hard decision to return to the United States, back to a denomination in shambles, back to the broken churches we had tried to run away from.

We deeply grieved leaving Uganda and leaving the special relationships we enjoyed with our Ugandan family and our missionary family. For months I nursed despondency and despair, a depth of heartache that wouldn't let me go. Fred was called as pastor of a church in Little Rock, Arkansas, a life-saving focus for him that helped with the feelings of loss. I was called to nothing. The place

---

11. Mark Wingfield, "Missionaries Told They Can't Return to Field without Signing Statement," January 24, 2003, Associated Baptist Press, vol. 03-06.

of nothingness in which I found myself was almost unbearable. As I learned just how conservative our church was, I realized how difficult life would be for me. I never uttered a word about being called to ministry to anyone in that church.

Fortunately, I found a group of friends outside the church who would hear me and weep with me. One of those friends, an eighty-year-old delight of a man, became my mentor. He was a former hospital chaplain, one of those people who believe *every* minister should be a hospital chaplain! I was not amused the day he told me that *I* should be a hospital chaplain. Nevertheless, he persisted!

He persuaded me to make an appointment with the director of pastoral care at Little Rock's Baptist Medical Center. Truth is, I made the appointment just to get him off my case. This was my prayer the night before the appointment: "God, if this is your doing, do you remember that I promised to go anywhere you lead me, with one exception? *Not* a hospital chaplain! Ever!"

"Are you interested in joining our chaplain residency program?" the director of pastoral care asked. I definitively answered, "No!" He then told me that they did not currently have an open slot. *Good*, I thought, since I was not even a smidgen interested. Still, he asked me to pray about it for a few days and then to get back to him. I did not intend to pray about it, but in the interest of collegiality, I *would* call him back.

The prayer—the one I said I would not pray—rose up in me for two full days. I kept pushing it away to no avail. When I called him back, his first statement was, "I am going to send you a formal invitation to join our residency program. Pray about it and let me know."

There he goes with the prayers again! What part of "I am not interested" did he fail to understand?

You have probably guessed the rest of this story. Serving as a chaplain was a heartbreaking, grueling, gut-wrenching, life-giving four years. As for the patients—suddenly being hospitalized, being rushed to the emergency room, hearing the news that they were dying, unexpectedly losing a child, suffering from psychosis in a locked unit—in all of it, they longed for liberation. Sometimes they experienced a little of it when a chaplain cared for them.

By this time, Fred had resigned from the church in order to avoid the constant liberal/conservative/fundamentalist fights that consumed his ministry there. I will never forget the words of the resignation letter he read to the church: "I have a limited number of fights in me. This is not one of them." We joined a nearby church, one that over the years was known as the liberal Baptist church in Arkansas. Fred served as their minister of music while I continued my ministry at the hospital.

At the end of my fourth residency year, I interviewed for several chaplaincy positions and learned that ordination was a prerequisite. So I naively approached my pastor and asked that the church enter with me into the process of ordination. I never anticipated my pastor's response: "This is not the right time for the church." My heart sank as I recalled the patriarchal pronouncements I had heard so many times before: a woman must stay in her rightful place in God's hierarchy.

Without any trace of timidity, I asked to meet with the deacons. Their overwhelming response was an unequivocal "no." In the next six months, I was dismissed, disrespected, shouted at, and even threatened. The machinations at *every* business conference, *every* month, were enormously hurtful to everyone. So I informed my pastor that I would share my story of call at the next business meeting and end the harrowing process.

I was drained, empty, inconsolable. The rejection had lodged into the depths of my soul. People who loved me had abandoned me, denying the legitimacy of my call. On the Wednesday afternoon of the business meeting, an Arkansas Baptist State Convention executive called to let me know that what I was doing was "an abomination," that a woman could not be a pastor and that I would destroy my church. I was wounded by his harsh verbal rebuke. "You must not speak at the church's business meeting tonight," he said. "If I had the power, I would stop you!"

My very being went into overdrive. *What?* I thought. *What did he just say about his power to stop me?* I gathered myself before I replied to his ridiculous statement, and somehow I was able to call up my "good girl" voice. I politely explained that my call to ministry was real, that it had been tested in missionary work and in four years of hospital chaplaincy, and that I did not intend to serve as a pastor. He responded that my impudent behavior should disqualify me from *any* ministry.

"Nevertheless, I will speak to my church tonight," I said, "and God will be the judge of my behavior, my presumptuousness, and my qualifications for ministry!"

I said that. And then I got off the phone and cried for the next hour.

I spoke that night without a trace of ill will. Then my mentor, Rev. Wilson Deese, a highly respected retired minister, spoke pleadingly on my behalf. He was shouted down by three people who literally got in his face. He fainted. We tended to him, and then twenty people walked out of the meeting and out of the church.

Fred was angry about the treatment I had received and the end of yet another ministry. He resigned, again. In the next month, the people who supported me and left the church they had loved for so many years formed a house church. I just mourned.

One Sunday night, the phone rang. The caller introduced himself as Dr. Charles Ashcraft, pastor of North View Baptist Chapel in El Paso, Texas, and former executive director of the Arkansas Baptist State Convention. I didn't know him except by reputation, so I didn't understand why he would call me.

"I learned about your ordination fiasco from our mutual friend, Wilson Deese," he said, "and our church voted tonight to ordain you." In complete shock, I responded, "But you don't even know me!"

"We know you were a chaplain at our Baptist hospital and a missionary. If you went through Foreign Mission Board appointment, you are good enough for us."

I promised to think about it. The whole idea felt strange to me. I didn't want to be ordained by a congregation that didn't know me. I prayed for several days, consulted with colleagues, and decided to send him my biographical information. If this church was going to ordain me, I needed them to know me.

Dr. Ashcraft called after reading the biographical information. "I read it but didn't need to," he said. "Now let's schedule this ordination service!" And we did. Twenty-five beloved friends traveled to El Paso for my inspiring, affirming ordination service. My Little Rock friends, friends from many states, and the congregation of North View Baptist Chapel blessed me by gently laying their hands on me and whispering sacred words.

When I walked into the church on the night of the ordination, I sat down in a pew and looked over the worship bulletin. On the cover, I saw a prayer written by a friend and colleague, a wonderful Methodist minister in Little Rock. When I opened the bulletin, I saw that Dr. Ashcraft would deliver the introductory remarks. He had used this title: "Our Finest Hour." That describes exactly what my ordination meant to this congregation I would come to know and love. When they promised that their prayers for me would continue throughout the years of my ministry, I believed them. I have sensed those promised prayers many times over the years when I most needed them.

I was overcome with emotion when Fred and our closest friend, Marvin, sang the hymn that had long been my inspiration.

> I, the Lord of sea and sky, I have heard My people cry.
> All who dwell in dark and sin, My hand will save.
> I who made the stars of night, I will make their darkness bright.
> Who will bear My light to them? Whom shall I send?
> Here I am Lord, Is it I Lord? I have heard You calling in the night.
> I will go Lord, if You lead me. I will hold Your people in my heart.[12]

My dear friend, Nancy Hastings Sehested, sent words of calling to be read in the service. She had been such a steady emotional support to me during the time of my ordination struggle, and I consider her a midwife who helped birth my ministry. The words she sent still resonate in me when I think of that day, March 29, 1992. I felt her words in my heart even in her absence, especially these: "My sister, today you are being handed a towel of servanthood with your name on it."

By this time, my friends who left our former church were getting weary of "house church." So they consulted with Dr. Ashcraft on

---

12. Daniel L. Schutte, "Here I Am, Lord," *Hymnary.org*, OCP Publications, 1981, hymnary.org/text/i_the_lord_of_sea_and_sky. Based on Isaiah 6:8; 1 Samuel 3:4.

next steps. On our final day in El Paso, we gathered to say our goodbyes to the North View church members. In that farewell gathering, the "house church" folk asked a few more questions about forming a church. Dr. Ashcraft answered their questions and ended with this statement as he pointed to me: "You've already got your pastor right here!"

And so it was that I had to go nearly to Mexico just to be ordained. This is the story of how I became the pastor I never intended to be, the first female Baptist pastor in the state of Arkansas. My serendipitous ordination was officiated by the former executive director of the Arkansas Baptist State Convention. Doesn't God have a sense of humor? Doesn't Spirit blow every way she wills and almost never in the ways we expect?

I ministered with a vibrant, authentically Baptist congregation for nine joy-filled years. The Providence Baptist Church of Little Rock—an open, inclusive, committed, and ecumenical people—worshiped in a Catholic monastery. In the chapel of Carmel of St. Teresa of Jesus, we were occasionally joined in worship by the thirteen Discalced Carmelite Sisters of the Carmel. What an indescribable gift we received from them for nine years!

Fred was just as dedicated to our church as I was and did everything but preach. His trek with me through the woods to find dogwood blossoms or thorn bushes was a true act of resigned but good-natured help. I counted on him, on his strength and on his support. The only way I can describe the new relationship that had swapped our roles is to say that Fred has always been my muse and my most faithful champion.

As for the minister/mommy role, Jonathan and I played our parts admirably. It mostly worked, except on the many occasions when he hung on stubbornly to the hem of my robe right before worship. My little boy clinging to the hem of my garment was always a powerful symbol of being torn and wondering how I could manage being a mother and a minister. The years ahead would test my resolve and sometimes leave me in a space of hard discernment and decision. I will never tell any woman who is a minister and a mother that she will walk an easy path. Both calls weigh so deeply in a mother's heart. Both calls—minister and mommy—come from the same holy whispers.

My years as pastor hold my most cherished memories. I learned to see myself as a pastor who was privileged to keep vigil with a parishioner in mourning; as a pastor led by Spirit to create powerful worship experiences every Sunday; as a pastor entering baptismal waters with a child; as a pastor lovingly dedicating a baby who would one day hear her own call to ministry.[13]

There's that phrase again, "call to ministry," words I can never escape. Fortunately, I never wanted to escape from my call, no matter how thorny the path became. "Call to ministry"—words that codify my long journey and buttress the story of my call. Yet, how can I end a story that has not yet ended? When I left Providence, I returned to my unrelenting call to liberate people who are oppressed, accepting a position in a behavioral health organization as sexual assault center director. A few years later, I founded an organization that would provide compassionate care to all people victimized by violence and abuse—The Center for Healing and Hope, later to become Safe Places, the name that came to me as I helped young girls and remembered that when I was a girl, I had no safe place.

For the next ten years, I worked with my staff to offer advocacy, compassion, healing, and liberation. In a typical week, we might find ourselves counseling a sexually abused child, sitting in an emergency room with a young girl who had been raped, liberating a child from the terrors of child sex trafficking, freeing a woman from an abusive spouse, leading a support group at the prison or at the juvenile detention center, advocating in a difficult juvenile court hearing, standing unflinchingly before the principalities and powers that constantly victimize and oppress people. I never once considered victim advocacy to be secular work. This work was ministry that reached long and deep and wide to touch people in desperate, horrific circumstances. In fact, in every setting my "clients" considered me to be a minister. For instance, I remember one occasion when I had to miss my weekly trauma-informed spiritual care group for incarcerated women. When I returned the next week, I noticed that they were

---

13. Rev. Jenna Sullivan, one of the contributors to this book, was that baby.

already seated and waiting. When I opened the door, greetings came from all over the room: "Reverend Kathy, where were you last week?" "Pastor Kathy, we missed you." "Reverend Kathy, we're glad you're back." The discussion that followed—a discussion that revealed fear and traumatization and regret and deep pain—was not secular work. It was soul work. This advocacy with victims of violence compelled me to courageously uphold equity, justice, liberation, righteousness, soul freedom, compassionate care, and gospel truth.

Yes, early on, theologies of liberation captured my heart. No, I never had the giftedness or the theological prowess of a James Cone or a Gustavo Gutiérrez. Instead, I was led by God's whispers and Spirit wind to people in despair—in crisis, in mourning, in prison, in violence, in abuse, in detention, in all the places that held them captive. I was a "liberation theologian" to many wounded people in trauma rooms, and it was my honor to show them even small glimpses of freedom from oppression.

In 2013, I joined Little Rock's New Millennium Church as minister of worship. This congregation was a light to my spirit. The way they studied and learned, the way they worked for social justice, the extraordinary way they worshiped God enriched my ministry. If I ever thought I understood liberation from injustice, the New Millennium people would teach me a more full and complete vision of it. Most of all, I delighted in the way they fully accepted me—a White female minister in a predominantly Black church—and lovingly called me "Rev. Kathy." New Millennium was my church when I was diagnosed with end-stage kidney disease. Abruptly, illness ended that season of ministry for me. I spent much of 2014 hospitalized and was placed on dialysis. I spent the remainder slowly recovering at home. I had a long journey of restoring my health to something near normal, of learning how to write and walk and think as I used to.

End-stage kidney disease and the many complications that came as a result—sepsis, viral encephalitis, sudden spells of my blood pressure bottoming out, a bleed following a kidney biopsy, days of semi-consciousness, confusion, memory loss, pain, loss of function, dangerously high fevers, loss of physical skills, the inability to even to write my name, and three brushes with death—all of it was a loss of the person I had been. Emotionally and spiritually, kidney disease ravaged my heart for a long time. Who was I now? What could I still do? Was my ministry over? Was my life over, at least my life as I knew it? I was very sick for almost three years, and I mourned that loss. I was not angry; I was hurt about having my life and ministry stolen from me so suddenly and so forcefully. I spent the next few months watching my kidneys continue to fail regardless of the high doses of prednisone and the daily dialysis. But so often I am overwhelmed by a sweet memory of that time, that all the while, I was cared for by the gracious congregation called New Millennium Church.

In 2015, while I was still very ill, Fred and I moved to Macon at the insistence of my Georgia family. The decision to leave our home of over thirty-two years was difficult. The reality of moving far away from my son and grandchildren was pure agony. I had been so ill, and with Fred exhausted from caring for me, everyone who was making family decisions at the time made this one. Whether it was the right decision, my heart says "no" and my brain says "maybe." Nevertheless, I have grieved the consequences of that decision for almost seven years.

With these life tales well positioned in my rearview mirror, I can objectively analyze this most recent turn in my journey. I can finally acknowledge that end-stage kidney disease came upon me like a fast-moving freight train and rearranged my life. I can finally own the stark reality that kidney disease forced me to retire.

So I search every day to learn what ministry means for me in this stage of my life. I am beginning to redefine my ministry after the losses I experienced, the reality of daily dialysis, and, in 2019, a kidney transplant and all the difficulty that comes with it. I'm getting there. I have come a long way since I left the hospital in 2014, having painstakingly relearned the alphabet, counting to twenty, identifying colors, and finally being able to write my name again.

Kidney disease took over my life unexpectedly and suddenly. It ruthlessly changed me and forced me to retire, but it is impossible to retire from a calling. Being so ill also forced me to pause for a few years and find sacred space for listening to the holy whispers that would lead me to other ways of living out my call. As always, God's whispers and Spirit wind showed up again to open my soul to writing and creating art, counseling and teaching.

As I have mended over the last two years from my kidney transplant, I finally made peace with my *retirement* calling. I can now delight in new calls as I work for racial justice with the Alliance of Baptists, as I teach a special Sunday school class, as I continue providing pastoral care, trauma counseling, and spiritual direction. I serve my new church—First Baptist Church of Christ in Macon, Georgia—in various ways. I am writing more than I ever have—essays, prayers, liturgy, hymn texts, opinion articles, and blog posts. I picked up a watercolor brush for the first time, and I paint my dreams, my longings, and everything that is moving inside my soul.

Holy whispers spoke of new things, new passions, and new calls. I listened, and although it took me a while, I finally heard Spirit wind again and felt it rustling around me.

How true it is that my journey has not followed a straight path! I followed a path that often seemed like an ethereal labyrinth with Spirit Winds moving in circles around me. Not leading me on a path really, but more like gentle winds moving me. I never got lost because the journey moved toward a sacred center where I could linger, find my soul's deepest longings, find the sacred path God places before me. The labyrinth, genuine and unwavering, somehow has always led me well.

As I bore witness to the authenticity of new and captivating calls, I heard another holy whisper, a most captivating new call that rose up in me after the death of George Floyd. Like most of the world, I responded to that season with profound grief. Out of my lament arose a creative response to racial injustice as I birthed a new thing, a series of five paintings that inspired a curriculum I call "Transforming Injustice!"

I was midwife to "Transforming Injustice!"—to the paintings, the narrative, the video, the guided meditation, the prayer and the lament that opens the learner's heart to the reality of injustice and oppression. "Transforming Injustice!" is all about living into the liberating tradition of Jesus, and that means struggling against injustice with and for *all* marginalized people. I cannot help but recall the inspiring words spoken by one of our foremothers, Rev. Prathia Hall, who said out of the urgency of oppression, "Out there in the brush arbors, the wilderness and the woods, the God of our ancestors, the God we had known on the other side of the waters met us and whispered words in our ears, and stirred a song in our souls. . . ."[14]

So it was with me in some very real ways, often finding myself "in the wilderness and the woods," listening for whispered words and waiting for a new song to stir in my soul, a new response to the God who whispered my name:

> Here I am, Lord;
> It is I, Lord.
> I have heard you calling in the night.
> I will go, Lord, if you lead me; I will hold your people in my heart.[15]

Even now—retired, aging, and with compromised health—I will still go. If God calls out my name again, I will go, because people are still oppressed, downcast and in need of liberation.

"Let the oppressed go free." That is a lifetime calling. There will never come a time when we will see every oppressed person freed. And so the call continues.

Underneath it all, I still believe that liberating oppressed people is my ultimate calling. In some discernible ways, creating "Transforming Injustice!" tied together the threads and strings and scraps of my ministry, weaving them together to create a rich tapestry that portrays the story of my calling. The tapestry hangs in my imagination, its timeless beauty beyond measure. On it, the woven threads reveal the words "Holy Whispers."

Kathy Manis Findley was ordained in 1992, becoming one of two ordained women in Arkansas and the first woman to serve as pastor of an Arkansas Baptist church. She is a graduate of the University

---

14. Quoted in Courtney Pace, *Freedom Faith: The Womanist Vision of Prathia Hall* (Athens: University of Georgia Press, 2019), 198, 209.

15. Schutte, "Here I Am, Lord."

of Alabama and Southern Baptist Theological Seminary and did post-graduate study on violence/victim studies at Washburn University. She received certification in child forensic interviewing from the National Child Protection Training Center and advanced practice certification in victimology and victim services from the National Victim Assistance Academy, Washburn University. She served for six years as a trainer for the National College of District Attorney's Annual Training Conference.

Kathy served as a Southern Baptist missionary to Uganda, East Africa; a hospital chaplain at Baptist Medical Center in Little Rock, Arkansas; pastor of Providence Baptist Church of Little Rock for nine years; pastor of Mt. Ida Presbyterian Church; and minister of worship at Little Rock's New Millennium Church. She was founder/executive director of Safe Places, an organization serving victims of violence and abuse, and was the co-founder/executive director of the Pulaski County Children's Justice and Protection Center. Kathy was appointed by Arkansas governor Mike Beebe to serve on the Arkansas State Council for Interstate Juvenile Supervision. She served as the first president of the Crime Victims Assistance Association of Arkansas and served two terms as president of the Arkansas Coalition against Sexual Assault.

Kathy received the FBI Director's 2011 Community Leadership Award, which was presented in Washington, DC, by then FBI director Robert Mueller. Other awards she received include the Women's Peace Foundation 2006 Woman of Peace Award, the 2007 Victim Advocacy Award from the American Society of Victimology, the Black Community Developer's 2006 Martin Luther King Jr. Community Service Award, and the Arkansas Attorney General's 2002 Award for Excellence in Serving Victims of Crime.

Kathy is active in the Alliance of Baptists, where she formerly served on the board. She served two terms as president of Baptist Women in Ministry. She has written three books and the curriculum "Transforming Injustice!" Currently, she serves the American Kidney Fund as a certified kidney health coach, ambassador, and legislative advocate; and the American Association of Kidney Patients as a certified patient mentor.

Kathy is an avid artist, iconographer, writer, and blogger. She is married to her life partner of fifty-two years, Fred Findley, and is the mother of one son and the grandmother of five.

The Eighth Story

A Divine Ajíaco: My Calling to Ministry

Rev. Dr. Cristina García-Alfonso

My call to ministry, hearing God's whisper in becoming a woman in ministry, is best described as an *ajíaco* (stew)—a rich mix of corporal, emotional, intellectual, ancestral, and earthly experiences that offer a unique flavor to all that constitutes who I am. The ingredients of this *ajíaco* are many, including Catholic, Afro-Cuban, and Baptist. These faith expressions reveal a distinctive image of God as Companion and Liberator.

Liberation is the theme and the story of my life. Throughout the years, first personally and then academically, I have sought to liberate myself from all that has been oppressive. Personally, I continue to grow by relying on community, people, and my personal work that invites me to pay attention to the ways I need to be more integrated as a human being. My academic training as a Hebrew Bible scholar has been a soothing place for renewal and liberation as I process, from my head and through the biblical texts, the oppressions (mainly ecclesial) I endured in the past. From the biblical characters' strengths, I draw the courage to free myself, my heart. My feminist reading and interpretation of the biblical text founded on the Baptist principle of "the freedom of the individual, led by God's Spirit within the family of faith, to read and interpret the Scriptures, relying on the historical understanding by the church and on the best methods of modern biblical study," continues to shape this journey of liberation.[1]

Growing up in Communist Cuba, I was raised in a home that did not openly embrace any faith tradition. Prior to the Cuban Revolution in 1959, both sides of my family were Christians (Catholic tradition) but did not practice their faith. When Castro took over, many people, including most of my family, embraced the Revolution and the disguise of equality as a new religion or form of spirituality. Those who continued to practice their Christian faith, or any other religion, suffered discrimination and oppression by the government. Against this backdrop, my experience of God emerged from the Catholic pictures present in the house where I was raised, Jesus' Sacred Heart and a small picture of twelve guys (Michelangelo's *Last Supper*) around a table eating supper. When I was five years old, these two images and the memory of my paternal grandfather making a funny sign in front of his face (sign of the cross) before we all had dinner together convinced me of a sacredness of the ritual in connection to Jesus and the apostles. These pictures representing my Catholic and Spanish heritage depicted a God who showed love, tenderness, and vulnerability. Jesus' heart remained open to others and therefore to me. This is a Jesus who celebrated being in community with others, leaning toward the disciples and allowing them to lean on him.

Although nobody in my family spoke to me about this God/Jesus that was daily present in my home, I knew and felt God by the ways in which I felt loved inside the walls of my home. Through the love of my family, I learned about acceptance for who I am, kindness, the safety of all kinds of people, and respect for my autonomy as a unique person. Outside these walls there was a different world, society, and eventually a church where I experienced fear and oppression, the opposite of what I felt in the safety of my home. The unspoken God that I came to know through those images was incarnated in the love and care that I experienced in my family, friends, and community. Thus, it imprinted on my heart a belief in humanity and the invitation to remain open to others in their goodness.

---

1. The Alliance Founding Covenant and Mission from 1987, Statement number 1, allianceofbaptists.org/founding-covenant-and-mission/.

My early childhood memories of seeing the Catholic pictures, climbing guava and mango trees in my backyard, dancing to Cuban music, being immersed in the clear blue waters of the Caribbean Sea, and hearing about God for the first time in the orange orchid field when a classmate enriched my spiritual and religious heritage and awoke me to the Divine. In my awakening, God has been and is *felt* though my body. In addition, my DNA carries African blood and thus the history of a people who were forced to come to Cuba as slaves. They came with their African history, their gods (*orishas*), and their religion.

These were the people of the Earth. They knew and felt God, as I do, through their bodies and through the music, water, passion, dance, and drums. For instance, at a point in my Christian journey when I felt powerless awaiting the decisions of both the United States and the Cuban governments to allow me to leave Cuba for the States, a friend from church led me to meet with a santero, a priest in the Afro-Cuban religion. In that encounter, I learned that I am a daughter of two orishas: Changó and Ochún. I carry not only genetic and religious Spanish heritage but also African blood. Such blood connects me to a people with a religion that influences how I see and feel God today. Changó—as a warrior, the master of dance and passion—nurtures my love and passion for dancing and feeling the beats of Cuban rhythms. My love for swimming, being immersed in the waters, appreciation for beauty and expressed femininity connect me with my other orisha, Ochún. Through these African connections, I have come to embrace expressions of the Divine that I deeply feel in my body, making me more awake and alive.

While I unconsciously held the richness of my Afro-Cuban heritage within me, I also integrated my Baptist heritage that started in nature as well. One of my Baptist high school classmates in boarding school secretly told me stories about God in the orange orchid field and introduced me to the Bible. All of a sudden, the unspoken God of my childhood and the pictures depicted in my household kitchen made sense as a part of my encounter with the earth, playing, dancing, and swimming. This was the beginning of a spiritual and transformative journey where I chose to dedicate my life to God. I grew curious about God and opened my heart to be touched by the Divine who made me feel more alive than ever.

Finding my church community at First Baptist Church of Matanzas allowed me to take my first steps into my Christian faith and journey. Through prayer, life experiences, worship services, Sunday schools, and other spaces where I felt increasingly at home, I sensed that a significant internal shift was happening in terms of the direction of my life and place in the world. At the age of nineteen and after much "wrestling with God," and finally feeling affirmed and confirmed of my call to ministry, I switched my career path from Spanish Literature to Theology. Attending the Protestant Theological Seminary in my hometown was in itself a transformative experience. As a young Christian woman in my faith, I came into my theological studies with openness, curiosity, zest for knowledge, and excitement about connecting with students and teachers from various Christian denominations. Throughout my theological training in seminary and my embrace of the Baptist tradition, important values were affirmed. From my various theological, family, and spiritual experiences, I learned the importance of inclusion, diversity, equality, respect, and integrity.

As I journeyed through my seminary years in Cuba, it became clear to me that I was called to serve God even when the only venue available and supported by my denomination was to be a pastor at a local church. However, the more I engaged the biblical texts, particularly the Old Testament, the more curious I became about deepening my knowledge of it. I became fascinated by the stories in the Hebrew Bible, stories of resistance, resilience, courage, and utter trust in God. These stories, for the most part, were those of women in biblical times who learned how to survive within oppressive systems, to find their voices and thrive. These stories of the Hebrew Bible also became parallel to my own story. Like these women of the text, I found myself figuring out ways to resist, reclaim, and find courage to follow my inner voice. The voice was calling me to serve God, guiding me into teaching (academia) more than preaching (parish ministry).

Along with claiming my voice came the pain of isolation and exclusion. There were times when I felt lonely and sought community and guidance with my mother's Catholic priest, spiritual director, and friend. He was a safe person for me as I wrestled with my struggles in ministry. He allowed me to explore my pain and my vocational calling as a theologian and biblical scholar. I also relied on God journeying with me. I searched for hope and community with the biblical text, specifically with my feminist writing and interpretation of Tamar in Genesis 39—a woman who also finds a way out of her struggles. Tamar cried out for me when I did not know to cry for myself.

I passionately wrote about those stories in the Hebrew Bible. My writing became a channel for my wounded heart to heal. From this experience of suffering, I started experiencing a God that was very real and felt incarnated in my body. In my experience of suffering and oppression in Cuba, it was my family and a few friends within my faith community that, along with God, sustained me on my journey.

In my calling and ministry, I have come to believe and experience a God who has dreams for our lives, as God sees the potential God in us. However, we also work with God in creating our present and future. We are co-creators with God, who created us to be in relationship with the Divine, with ourselves, and with others. The ways we relate to other human beings reflect the ways we relate to ourselves and God. Co-creating with God means that the journey can always take me to surprising places. When I served as the minister at a local church, it became clear to me that within the many ministries of the church, teaching Sunday school (teaching) and pastoral visits with my parishioners (pastoral care) were the places where I felt most called and alive.

My short-term work in this church and later in my home church continued deepening this calling to teach and pursue further theological studies. However, such calling to teaching was met with great resistance and opposition from my denomination. Although I appreciated my church's support to ordain me as a woman in a progressive Baptist denomination, it did not ensure that I would be free from other types of discrimination and sexism. For three years between my seminary graduation and immigration to the United States, I navigated difficult situations, choosing to claim my power, honoring my calling to ministry, and facing the consequences.

Embracing my love for the Hebrew Bible to its fullness has been a great joy that materialized as I immigrated to the US and entered the academic world. Wrestling with biblical texts and exploring them from my perspective as a woman, immigrant, and Cuban was a significant endeavor as part of my journey as a biblical scholar. The possibility of teaching about the biblical texts and its impact on people's lives when read from various social locations and cultural backgrounds paired with feminist, cultural, and ideological themes seemed like the best context to reveal my vocation and service to God. I dreamed about co-creating with seminary or college students through interpretations of biblical texts that were life-giving and challenging to each person in their context of ministry. I hoped for a relational kind of teaching with my students where transformation *with* and *from* the biblical text was possible. However, the more I entered the depth and difficulties of a field that is predominantly white and male, the more disillusioned I became with the potential of claiming academia as a home where my calling was to be fulfilled. Although the engagement with the Hebrew Bible remained relevant, once again there was a soft ongoing voice within me that felt that something was missing. Once more, my journey kept taking me to surprising places and sometimes scary places. My core belief that I continued to actively co-create with God allowed me to trust the process and pursue my inner voice, wherever it was taking me.

Exhausted after eight nonstop years of graduate studies in the United States, with a great deal of personal, financial, and emotional investment, I found myself wrestling with my vocational journey upon my doctorate program graduation in 2008. Amid the collapse of the financial market, the academy was not an exception. In prayer and community with God and others, I continued doing my part as I interviewed for countless Old Testament/Hebrew Bible positions. As I look back at that time, it is clear to see how all those doors to academia were closing, one after another. This was a time for discernment, often a confusing process between me and God. It is here in this discerning process that I made sense of my vocation and where to practice my calling to serve God. In a way, my professional path was created anew, leading me to one field that I had not yet explored yet: pastoral care and chaplaincy.

From my graduate work in the United States, I came to understand chaplaincy as one of the many ministries possible for those who wanted to serve God. This was new to me as it did not exist in Cuba. While in the academic track and concentrating my studies in Hebrew Bible with the purpose of teaching, I was not required to take any pastoral care classes in seminary, let alone do a unit of clinical pastoral education (CPE). My exposure to chaplaincy was through close friends who were in this field and shared their experiences with me. From them I learned the differences between chaplaincy ministry and parish ministry. This sparked an interest in me during my dissertation writing process, as I sought to take a unit of CPE that did not materialize. Still, the seed was already planted and it was just a matter of time for it to take root.

I entered the field of chaplaincy, pursuing CPE training while at the same time continuing to keep one foot in the academy, hoping and praying that I could find a place where my training as a scholar was welcomed. However, the more I continued chasing my dream in the academy, the more passionate I became about chaplaincy as a ministry that invites both my heart and mind into its work. Being with patients and families and discovering their stories as "living documents" invited me to expand my framework of ministry in walking alongside people. Through my CPE training and later years of work in hospice care, I gained theoretical, theological, and other skills as a spiritual care provider. I grew more confident in my work as someone who walks with people on their journeys of suffering and hope. All the while, I was still dealing with feelings of grief, sadness, and the shame of not being able to secure a teaching position. I couldn't imagine letting go of the community that nurtured me for that journey. Once again, in my work of co-creating with God and tuning into the particulars of my vocation, I was led into teaching. However, this teaching was completely different than what I had prepared for all those years before. It invited all of me, heart and mind, to serve God.

My supervisory training to become a CPE Educator was a space where all of me, the pastor and teacher, could reside. It became the space where I could live into the vocation I felt called to when I pastored my church back in Cuba years before. Parker Palmer describes the vocational journey best when he says:

> Before you tell your life what you intend to do with it, listen for what it intends to do with you. Before you tell your life what truths and values you have decided to live up to, let your life tell you what truths you embody, what values you represent.[2]

These words ring true as I reflect on my journey with God. From those early memories of God at the dining table, at the orange orchid field, and in my seminary years both in Cuba and in the United States, it seems that God has whispered many words at different times. There were words for each season, the ones I needed to hear at different points. Along the way, I listened to what my life intended to do with me. It was a journey of twists and turns filled with wisdom and all that life brings. In all of it, God was present, whispering my name over and over, calling me into being. Such being, mainly in ministry, continues to evolve.

My vocational journey today feels more congruent with Palmer's words of letting my life tell me what truths I embody and what values I represent. My work as a CPE educator and saying yes to God's guidance to this place of ministry is a reflection of letting go of other worlds (academia) that I sought to inhabit. God, the Companion and Liberator, invited me into deep trust in the journey. Although it has been challenging at times, I have come to understand that my consent for God's guidance to enter my journey has meant that I am able to embody the life I am supposed to live and the values I am invited to represent, not the other way around.

These discoveries are life-giving as I seek to educate students in the art of CPE, in being able to accompany patients at the bedside who have their own unique stories of God and with God, and who

---

2. Parker J. Palmer, essay in *Let Your Life Speak: Listening for the Voice of Vocation* (San Francisco: Jossey-Bass, 2000), 3.

seek companionship and liberation. I have learned that the more I accept and integrate the rich and various flavors of my spiritual persona and theological *ajíaco*, the more I am able to remain open and embrace the richness of my students' flavors—all of who they are. Honoring the uniqueness of my journey with God allows me to honor the uniqueness of my students' journeys and join them as they expand, challenge, celebrate, and embrace their theological paths.

Cristina García-Alfonso is a native of Matanzas, Cuba, and an ordained minister with the Fraternity of Baptists Churches of Cuba (FIBAC), a partner denomination with the Alliance of Baptists in the USA with whom she is also endorsed as a chaplain. She has been in the United States for twenty years, where she has attended various theological seminaries. She was awarded the doctor of philosophy in biblical interpretation (Hebrew Bible/Old Testament) from Brite Divinity School in 2008. In the same year, she began a career in chaplaincy and clinical pastoral education. Cristina is passionate about integrative learning that considers the fullness of humanity (heart and mind). She is an ACPE Certified Educator with the Association of Clinical Pastoral Education (ACPE) and works as CPE specialist at UNC REX Healthcare in Raleigh, North Carolina.

Cristina has been a contributor to books and journals in the field of the Hebrew Bible. She is the author of *Resolviendo: Narratives of Survival in the Hebrew Bible and in Cuba Today* (2010). Her first publication in pastoral care is titled "Holding Containers, Conscientious Education, and a Divine *Ajíaco*: My Theory of Supervision," in the *Journal of Reflective Practice: Formation and Supervision in Ministry* 38 (2018). This publication brought recognition for her in the 2018 Len Cedarleaf Award for Outstanding Theory Papers of the Year with ACPE.

The Ninth Story

Coming and Going and in the Meantime

Rev. Carolyn Hale Cubbedge

I was seven when I first heard God whisper my name. I said to myself, "I would be a preacher when I grow up, if I were a boy." I did not tell anyone that the thought had crossed my mind. I had never seen a woman preacher and must have assumed that only boys could fill that role. I only saw my father, who was a Baptist preacher.

I started going to church when I was eight days old. I was active in Sunbeams[1] and Girls Auxiliary (later Girls in Action, GA).[2] I loved hearing stories from missionaries during the Weeks of Prayer for Home and Foreign Missions. Nothing was more exciting than getting to meet real, live missionaries. The thoughts of being a preacher gave way to thoughts of being a missionary to "deepest, darkest Africa." And yet there was little that kept me moving in that direction. It was not until college that my vocational calling began to find clarity.

---

1. Southern Baptist Convention, "Sunbeams," December 25, 2021. This program of the SBC Woman's Missionary Union (WMU) was designed to teach preschoolers about missions.

2. Southern Baptist Convention, Girls in Action (GA). This program of the SBC Woman's Missionary Union (WMU) was designed to teach girls about missionaries and doing missions both locally and globally. See "Girls in Action (GA)," *WMU*, wmu.com/missions-discipleship/children/.

I attended Georgetown College in Kentucky. Its strong Christian liberal arts emphasis influenced me in many ways. I became involved in a local church. I had gone only to Baptist churches, but one Sunday I wanted to attend the Presbyterian church just to see what it was like. To make sure that my church attendance would count, I went to the early service at the Baptist church and the Presbyterian one at eleven. Much to my surprise, it was just like going to real church! It was an eye-opener for me.

Our professors encouraged us to strengthen and grow our faith, which was sometimes painful, as we were introduced to historical critical thinking. However, those professors did not leave us to struggle alone. The Baptist Student Union (SBC college ministry), youth revival teams, and choir tours provided leadership opportunities. On one choir tour, I had a speaking part that said I would "preach the Word." In deference to the times and gender, we changed the wording to "teach the Word." During a couple of summers, I served as the youth director at my home church. We never used the term youth "minister."

Vocational clarity turned from missions to education. Following college, I taught English at my home high school. One of the classes I offered was an elective called "The Bible as Literature." I loved that class. Student questions challenged my thinking and shaped my teaching.

I will long remember a Mother's Day sermon that purported that the role of women was to marry and have children, stay in the home where they would influence and form children, and not take a job from a man. Throughout that sermon, the preacher literally kept looking at me as I sat in the front near the organ. In a small congregation, it was obvious that I was the old-maid schoolteacher. And then came the guilt trip. I wasn't doing God's will for my life as a single woman. I was taking a job away from a man by teaching school, and I was not helping to influence and form children. At that point, I began the search for a new church home that did not define me by my marriage status.

After seven years of teaching, I was offered a position in student activities at Georgetown College. At the end of my tenure there in

1991, I was serving as Dean of Student Life. I worked with students in all manner of extracurricular activities. On occasion, I taught in the education and psychology departments. I loved serving in Christian higher education and thought I had found my niche—until I began to work with women students who were seeking to flesh out their vocational calls to ministry.

I joined Faith Baptist Church in Georgetown. Faith BC was born out of racial conflict in the 1960s. It stood for full inclusion of all people regardless of race, economic background, or educational background. It affirmed the priesthood of all believers and supported all people in following their call from God. In 1974, Faith Baptist Church became the first in the Kentucky Baptist Convention to ordain women deacons. They ordained me in 1979. Twice I served as deacon chair, and in that role I learned about local and state Baptists. I attended annual meetings and saw firsthand how the denomination of my birth lived out being Baptist. This gave me an opportunity to introduce college women to Baptist life beyond their local churches. We attended the meetings and spent time together as they worked to discern God's call. During this time, it became clear to me that God was still at work in my own life.

Two pastors at Faith were highly influential. Bill Treadwell introduced our church to the liturgical calendar, which enriched my worship experience. He included me in Advent worship leadership. I loved the planning and the involvement of children and adults as we prepared for Christmas. I loved the images and symbols, and I loved teaching about them.

The second influential pastor was Steve Hadden. I had the opportunity to teach him about Advent. Steve was generous in his inclusion of laity in worship leadership. His inclusion of me was transformative. Steve had an accident with a riding lawn mower, and due to a severe injury to his foot, he was out of the pulpit for several weeks. I was vice-chair of the deacons, and the chair was out of town on an extended vacation. Because our deacon body was responsible for worship, it fell to me to plan worship during Steve's absence.

There were several preachers in our church. All were willing to preach. As Steve convalesced, I jokingly gave him a deadline for returning to the pulpit. I warned him that if he did not return by the deadline, I was going to preach in his place. He did not meet the deadline. So I preached.

God also used others to give me clarity. One was a young pastor who was attending our church with his children. His wife had been deeply hurt by their former church and gave up on the church. He sought me for counseling. A young girl who had been in my deacon family ministry group called to tell me that she would be making her profession of faith the next morning, and she was sure that I would want to know. I surely did. The other was a builder who died of lung cancer probably brought on by asbestos exposure. In his funeral plans, he requested that I help officiate at his funeral. Steve Hadden said that all of these congregants were seeing in me a call to pastoral ministry even before I was willing to articulate it for myself.

In 1990, I surrendered to the call that God had whispered to me when I was seven. I made that decision public at Faith Baptist Church, and I began my seminary studies at the age of forty-one.

I attended Lexington Theological Seminary in Lexington, Kentucky (LTS). LTS is a Christian Church (Disciples of Christ) seminary. Its proximity allowed me to attend early classes and be at work when I was needed. Even though it was near, I knew that Southern Baptist Theological Seminary was not a place where I could be affirmed as a woman called to pastoral ministry. I had met Dr. Sharyn Dowd, a good Baptist who taught New Testament at LTS. I knew I would learn from her and her colleagues. I was welcomed as a Baptist in this Disciples community, and I was encouraged to articulate why I was a Baptist and then to be the best Baptist I could be.

Ecumenical influences were numerous at LTS. I sat in class with Jewish, Catholic, Methodist, Presbyterian, Lutheran, Disciple, Baptist, Church of God, and Episcopalian congregants, among others. We learned from each other. A fellow student told me that it was not fair that Baptists knew so much Scripture. However, knowing a lot of Scripture did not serve me well in Greek class with Dr. Dowd. Rather than translate a verse, once I got the first two or three words, I would just spit out the rest in King James language! Fortunately for me, I was auditing the class.

While in seminary and working fulltime at Georgetown College, I was called to Faith Baptist Church as associate pastor with responsibilities for youth. Faith had about one hundred youth who needed full-time attention. Joining in that effort were two young college couples who provided the hands-on ministry to the youth.

On the first Sunday of Advent in 1991, I was ordained to the Gospel Ministry. My ordination council included a veritable who's who of Baptist ministers in central Kentucky, including former pastors and college professors. Dr. Sharyn Dowd was there, and gratefully she did not ask me to translate any Greek! Along with these, Dr. Molly Marshall joined in the ordination service. She brought with her several young women who were then students at Southern Seminary where she was still teaching. She wanted them to see the fulfillment of a dream. And in the congregation were several seminary classmates, including one Roman Catholic friend.

My ordination experience was the most moving and empowering event in my life. The ministers and lay members of my church affirmed my call and the potential they saw for my life in ministry. I have often wondered why any religious group would deny such a gift to anyone seeking to follow God's call.

LTS provided many opportunities that God used to hone me. We were encouraged to seek out a spiritual director. Dr. Richard Landon served in that capacity for me. There was no end to the guidance he gave in helping me discern what God was doing in my life. He gave me life support when my position at Faith Baptist ended after fifteen months due to financial restraints and a mismatch of gifts and needs. The church that had affirmed my call was asking me to step aside. I understood why, but that did not make it easy. We all grieved deeply. Because I needed income, I took a job through a staffing agency, and I was grateful for God's provision. My despair overcame me one day at Walmart. As I handed the cashier my check, she asked me where I worked. I confessed that I did not *do* anything, and I cried. It took a long time for my *being* to overcome my penchant for *doing*.

I found much support from professors and fellow students. I took a part-time position in Christian education at Christ Church Cathedral (Episcopal) in Lexington, an enriching ecumenical experience for me. I had preaching opportunities in rural Disciple churches. After seminary I became director of continuing education at LTS, where I again served in Christian higher education.

While the fundamentalist takeover of the Southern Baptist Church was disturbing and painful, in actuality it provided formative opportunities. Before the Cooperative Baptist Fellowship (CBF), Kentucky Baptists formed the Kentucky Baptist Fellowship (KBF). I served as its secretary and communications coordinator, with a state office from my home. In this, I had the opportunity to influence and shape the work of moderate Baptists in Kentucky and even in the CBF. I served on the first CBF Coordinating Council in 1991, chairing the Equipping the Laity Ministry Group and then the Theological Education Ministry Group. At the time, I was the only council member who was a current seminary student.

The relationships that formed during those days were life altering and humbling. At the first Coordinating Council meeting, the man beside me stretched out his hand and said, "My name is Duke." While I had heard of him, I had never met Dr. Duke McCall in person. Looking back, it is easy to see how God was putting me in places with people who would play a major role in God's fulfilling my pastoral call, but the fulfillment was slow in coming by my way of measuring time.

My pastoral search began immediately after seminary. Early on, I turned down an offer to be recommended to the United Methodists. I wanted to be a Baptist pastor who could be a role model for Baptist women. I had no such role model. It was only with my sisters in Kentucky Baptist Women in Ministry, Baptist Women in Ministry, and Baptist Women in Ministry of Georgia that I found those women who were answering the call of God's whisper. And it was in these groups that I was able to speak out for all women who were hearing God's call. I was honored to chair all of these groups at various times.

It would take six years before I was called to my first pastorate. In the meantime, God allowed me to work in the disability community. I served as chaplain and houseparent at Quest Farm, a residential farm setting for adults. I later served as director of Bob Brown House for the Handicapped. Both settings helped me become more inclusive in local church settings.

I lost track of the resumes I sent, but I did keep a folder of the rejection letters, all of which said the same thing: "We do not believe that God is leading us to you, but we pray that you will find God's place for you soon." I was not surprised by many of the rejections when I heard the names of the people who were called by these churches. They were all male, and many of them were former professors who were leaving the SBC seminaries. I was in good company among the resumes, but I did not readily climb to the top of the pile.

In 1997, I had my first interview in North Carolina. The search committee was open to a woman. I met every characteristic and skill the church body had defined—except for gender. I was invited to visit in view of a call. The visit went well, but the vote did not. The interim music director, not a member of the church, told the congregation that the interim pastor wanted the job but that the committee was "hell-bent" on hiring a woman. The interim pastor was well loved, and some voted against me in hopes of getting him. Actually, he did not want the job. While I entered the process with high hopes, I felt a peace that I could not understand as I returned home. God had another plan for me. That plan came to fruition in 1999.

The call came from Memorial Baptist Church in Savannah, Georgia. Friends from across the CBF aided in my search. Frank Broome of CBF of Georgia and Beverly Greer of South Carolina CBF sent my resume. Cecil Sherman was one of my references. Broome, being the honest man he is, told the congregation that they would need to consider a woman if they wanted to get a full-time minister for the salary they were able to pay. This was the church's second search in fifteen months. My predecessor unexpectedly took a position as an associational missionary. I later learned that my name had been in the running fifteen months before, but the search committee had predetermined that the church was not ready for a woman. They did not even look at the four resumes from women. Instead, they sent the letter that said, "We do not believe that God is leading us to you . . . ." I filed that letter with so many others without knowing about the church. I had not sent my resume there. Someone else had. After I had been on the job for a year, I went through my file of rejection letters. Only then did it register that my resume had been sent to Memorial for their previous search. One of the men on that committee was James Cubbedge—who would later become my husband!

My invitation was to serve as pulpit supply. The chair wanted the congregation to hear a female voice before being asked to vote on one. The weekend with those good people was all I ever dreamed it could be. I met with the committee, was hosted at a church-wide open house, visited all adult Sunday school classes, and preached for worship on Sunday. Following lunch, I met with the entire congregation for a question-and-answer session. I asked the first question: "How can I justify being called to pastoral ministry?" That evening I met with the youth group whose burning question was if I had ever eaten grits! I had. The only theological question all weekend was the one I asked about women in ministry.

I met with the search committee one more time and was thanked for my time. As I was preparing for bed, my hostess asked if I could come back to meet with the committee. They had voted to move my name forward to the deacons, whose job was to recommend to the congregation. After I returned home, I learned that the deacons had unanimously recommended me. The congregation voted the following Sunday, and I was called. It was not a unanimous vote, but for any woman to receive 76 percent of the vote was significant. I joined Wendy Joyner Peacock as the second Baptist woman pastor in Georgia.

My call did not go unnoticed. The local Baptist Association's membership committee requested a meeting with the deacons to ask them to withdraw the call. I was on the job when the meeting took place. When we met, we assured them that Memorial was exercising its autonomy as a local church and believed that God had led us together. We expressed our desire to share ministry and did not wish to leave the association. They were not satisfied with our responses and began the proceedings to have our membership withdrawn for reasons "untoward" the association. That was the language of the association's bylaws, which never mentioned women pastors.

In line with the national votes during the SBC controversy, we were removed from the association by a 60-40 percent vote. Only seven of around eighty pastors spoke to me personally. One of those voted for our removal, but he wanted me to know that it was not personal. He just did not believe it was biblical for women to be pastors. I appreciated his talking to me and not about me.

Shortly thereafter, the SBC altered the Baptist Faith and Message to prohibit women pastors. The Georgia Baptist Convention affirmed the new version, and Memorial chose to withdraw from the state convention and the SBC, neither of which any longer represented who we were as an autonomous church.

Our withdrawals garnered attention. The local news outlets wanted to defend the church that had been treated badly because it had called a woman, but they had little understanding of how Baptist polity works. They assumed that because we had lost our membership, we would also lose our building and financial support. Only one reporter got it right, and he grew up as a Baptist and was a Carson Newman graduate.

We attracted national attention when President Jimmy Carter announced that he was no longer a Southern Baptist because of the SBC stance on women pastors. *People* magazine sent a reporter and photographer to get the story. Their visit was disruptive to say the least. They interviewed congregants and me. The photographer took no less than two hundred photographs during the service. We were to be a part of a larger article, with Jimmy Carter being the other part. Because President Carter had already held a news conference about the issue, he declined the interview. The story and the pictures were sent to the editor, but the story never ran.

On Epiphany Sunday 2001, Memorial entered a new era. We were no longer an SBC congregation, but we were still Baptist. We were born in the SBC, trained in its programs, and inspired by and involved in its mission endeavors. For all of that we gave thanks. We gave thanks for those tenets of our past that had nourished us, and we looked to the future God had for us as we moved ahead as a full partner with the Cooperative Baptist Fellowship. Dr. Daniel Vestal, CBF executive coordinator, was our preacher for the day.

I served at Memorial for five years and four months. Much good happened for me there, not the least of which was marriage to one of my deacons—the one who had served on the pastor's search committee that had not considered a woman! He then became a major player in decisions I was called to make in my ministerial calling. We decided to stay in Savannah and began to attend First Baptist Church, the only other CBF church in the area.

First Baptist Church soon called me to serve in an interim position that led to a permanent part-time position as the Christian educator with responsibilities for missions and senior adults. My other part-time work was with Morningstar Children and Family Services, which served adolescents who had dual diagnoses of mental and behavioral disorders. I worked with Morningstar on and off for about fifteen years.

My jobs with First Baptist and Morningstar suffered the same demise as had my jobs with Faith Baptist, the Kentucky Baptist Fellowship, and Lexington Theological Seminary. All ended in budget cutbacks! National economic crises are never good for nonprofit organizations whose lives are dependent on donations. Each of these situations created a great deal of disappointment and stress for me; but I claim that through all of them, God was, and continues to be, faithful. I never missed a meal or had to spend a night on the street.

As I approached my sixty-fifth birthday, I found myself in need of another job. It came about in a wonderful ecumenical setting at Wesley Monumental United Methodist Church in Savannah. I had met Ben Martin, the church's pastor, on a 2002 study trip to Greece. He served in the greater Savannah area at the time, and we became friends. I reached out to him for information and recommendations only to learn that his congregation was looking for a part-time minister to senior adults with pastoral care responsibilities. The church called three ministers at the same time. We were all part-time, and none of us were Methodist. Two were Presbyterians, and I was Baptist. We fit right in. The church has a large membership, and its members come from many denominations.

The next five years were pure bliss for me. I was never asked to become a Methodist. I was introduced as their Cooperative Baptist.

I actively gave pastoral care to CBF Field Personnel and participated in several mission trips for CBF. Every time I served, I was commissioned by and prayed for by these supportive Methodists.

My retirement came in 2019, eight days before my seventieth birthday. Unlike all those other jobs, my retirement was timely and right. My husband and I wanted to spend more time together, and it was time for me to spend time with my mother, who is in her mid-nineties.

I preached on my retirement Sunday, June 30, 2019. My sermon was titled "Coming, and Going and in the Meantime." John 13:3 says, "Jesus, knowing that the Father had given all things into his hands, and that he had come from God and was going to God, got up from the table, took off his outer robe, and tied a towel around himself. Then he poured water into a basin and began to wash his disciples' feet." No harder example of meantime living has ever been known than those days lived by Jesus.

I have done a lot of coming and going, but it has been in the meantime living that I have known that my whisper from God was real. God's call is to serve. And we do, knowing that the God who led us to each time and place is the God who leads us still.

Carolyn Hale Cubbedge is a retired minister of the Christian gospel whose ministry has been lived out in the church, in Christian higher education, in public education, and in the presence of adults and children with developmental disabilities. At her core, Carolyn identifies as a Baptist who has had the opportunity to share ministry in several ecumenical settings. She holds an MDiv from Lexington Theological Seminary (Disciples of Christ) in Lexington, Kentucky, and an MEd in secondary education and a BA (*cum laude*) from Georgetown College, Georgetown, Kentucky. At Lexington Seminary, she was the recipient of the Richard Pope Award in Church History for a paper titled "An Open Door: New Hope for Southern Baptist Women in Ministry." Carolyn was an original member of the

CBF Coordinating Council and was an outspoken advocate for the role of women clergy in the formative years of CBF.

Following a career of teaching English, drama, and speech in Ohio, she returned to her alma mater to serve as the dean of student life at Georgetown College. While there, she began her seminary training at Lexington Seminary, where she later served as director of continuing education. She was ordained by Faith Baptist Church (Georgetown) in 1991. She had previously been ordained as a deacon in 1979 by Faith Baptist, the first Baptist church in the state of Kentucky to ordain women as deacons in 1974. She was the second woman to be ordained to the ministry by Faith Baptist Church.

Professionally, Carolyn served as associate pastor of Faith Baptist Church in Georgetown; assistant director of Christian education at Christ Church Cathedral (Episcopal) in Lexington; senior pastor of Memorial Baptist Church in Savannah, Georgia; assistant minister for senior adults and missions of First Baptist Church in Savannah; and minister for congregational care at Wesley Monumental United Methodist Church in Savannah. Running concurrently throughout her church ministry has been a deep involvement with adults and children with developmental disabilities. She served Quest Farm and Bob Brown Housing for the Handicapped—both residential facilities in Kentucky; and Morningstar Children and Family Services in Georgia, a residential facility for neglected and abused children who were dually diagnosed with mental and developmental disabilities. Work in these facilities led her to become an advocate for inclusion of the disabled in local church life.

Carolyn was an active participant in Baptist life following the formation of the national Cooperative Baptist Fellowship and Cooperative Baptist Fellowship of Kentucky. As part of her service on the original CBF Coordinating Council, she chaired the Equipping the Laity Ministry Group and the Theological Education Ministry Group. A strong supporter of global missions, she served on the member care team that provided pastoral care to CBF field personnel. CBF and church mission trips took her to Singapore; Macau, China; Phnom Penh, Cambodia; San Juan, Puerto Rico; twice to Cuba; and to the Gulf Coast following Hurricane Katrina. She served as the communications coordinator for CBF Kentucky, operating the first state office from her home. Her involvement with Baptist Women in Ministry included leadership in the national organization as well as state groups in Kentucky and Georgia. In 2011 she was named Distinguished Church Woman of the Year by Baptist Women in Ministry of Georgia.

Carolyn and her husband, James, have two adult children and five grandchildren. She enjoys sewing and computerized machine embroidery. She owns and operates her own needlework business called The Cubbedge Patch. She especially likes liturgical embroidery.

The Tenth Story

Reflecting on Winds of Change

Rev. Dr. Christine Y. Wiley

As long as I can remember I had a heart for God. I remember praying for God to help me find the marbles I lost. I remember telling my friends when I was about four years old that if you just ask, God will help you. My stepfather was in the Air Force, and I remember going to Sunday school, then to the Protestant Chapel for worship where my mother sang in the choir. I was in the cherub choir and was always very concerned about God seeing me, so I didn't want to get caught doing anything bad. It was years later that my childhood guilt was transformed to a sense of authentic love from God.

At first, I did not know what to do with Jesus because if I had God, why did I need Jesus? When my first marriage crumbled due to my husband's infidelity, I needed someone to identify with, someone near who could comfort and care for me. I remember spending a night on the floor, crying and praying that I would do anything if God would just tell me what to do because I felt so broken. The next morning, I awoke in the same position on my floor with my hands clasped tight, but something felt different. I got my little girl, who was about 18 months old, ready for the babysitter. After I dropped her off and was driving to work, I had the sensation that Jesus was sitting next to me and in me at the same time. I felt both his presence and his love. The colors were brighter, the sky was bluer, and I felt a joy that was almost incomprehensible. I felt that Jesus was my friend who knew what I had been going through. My life changed at that point, and I determined I would continue to develop this relationship with Jesus and devote my life to doing his will.

It was while serving in the church and working with mentally ill patients in a psychiatric hospital that I partnered with the chaplains of the hospital to help patients get reintroduced to the churches they once attended. The chaplains introduced them to the pastors and got them familiar with the churches and congregations as they were discharged from the hospital. It dawned on me that I felt a genuine pull to talk to people and patients about spiritual things. I did not know exactly what God wanted me to do, but I felt if I went to seminary, it would become clear. As I matriculated, I had a deep sense of call to preach and teach.

I was licensed to preach in 1983 and ordained in 1986 but soon found out that the Baptist church did not affirm women as preachers. Several persons left our church after I was allowed to preach my initial sermon. I must admit that the first woman preacher I ever heard preach was myself. Following my ordination, my church was dis-fellowshipped from the Washington DC Baptist Ministers Conference. The *Washington Post* published a picture of me with an article titled "Woman Ordained Baptist Pastor in DC." The second page of the article was headlined "Baptist Ministers Defy Rules to Welcome Female Colleague." The article mentioned that the DC Baptist Convention (DCBC) was considering me for a position in youth ministry. More backlash followed.

The convention, which was aligned with both the Southern Baptist Convention and the American Baptist Churches, USA, called their seventy-three churches to a meeting to vote on whether I should get this position. There was much debate in that meeting; some argued a woman could not teach a man and that God did not call women to preach. Finally, one of the pastors got up and said, "Aren't we aligned not just with the Southern Baptists, but also with American Baptists, who have been ordaining women for many years?" The Rev. James Langley, head of the DC Baptist Convention at the time, acknowledged that Langley was correct. Finally, the conference voted. With forty-five churches represented, four churches voted against my working in youth ministry, and forty-one churches voted affirmatively—and cheered. I was the first ordained clergywoman to be employed by this Baptist convention. Winds of change.

After thirty-seven years of serving one church, my eyes have seen and my ears have heard so much as the winds of change were blowing through. I saw an increase of women in ministry in Baptist churches, chaplaincy, campus ministry, nonprofit ministry, ministry to the homeless, street ministry, and so many other forms of creative ministry.

Those winds blew in the advent of AIDS while I was working as a case manager/therapist in a community mental health center. Several clinicians' clients were in DC General Hospital just across the yard from our clinic. My former colleagues knew I was a minister and gave me a list of their clients who were sick with AIDS to visit in the hospital because they feared this new disease. This experience of visiting AIDS patients gave me a deep sense of compassion because fear kept many people away from them.

The part of me that was opened to ministry with all kinds of people despite their circumstances had been instilled early in my life. The stories of my family history had imparted lessons that loving every person as oneself is the highest pinnacle of compassion and the strongest foundation for ministry. These lessons would guide me for years to come.

I was born in London, England, in 1950 to a British-born Black woman, Beatrice Elizabeth Thompson, who was called Betty. My grandmother was Jewish and estranged from her family for marrying a Caribbean man. Because of this unique upbringing, my mother always told me never to think that I was better than anyone. Because my grandmother was ostracized from her community, I grew up learning the importance of loving people, without judgment, where they are. A white woman marrying a Black man in the 1920s was almost unheard of. Though my grandmother was excluded from her own family, other people stepped into her life as both friends and chosen family, including members of the gay community, who embraced her and her entire family.

As my mother shared these stories with me when I was young, I was unaware how significantly my past and my heritage would inform the way I would move through the world and through the years with love and acceptance. I feel as if my family's stories provided stones on the path I followed as a woman called by God.

Around the same time that I was working with AIDS patients at the community mental health center and visiting them in the hospital, our church allowed the Max Robinson Center, a medical clinic for those living with AIDS, to use space in our building when their roof fell in. The winds of change were blowing as several staff and patients of this center came to worship with us and joined our church. We embraced them as we developed deep relationships with them. A couple of years later, I led ministers and laypeople from our church to lead a weekly spirituality group for people living with AIDS in the center's new building. These winds changed our hearts and minds.

As the breezes blew over the years, it was heartwarming to see the children of our church grow up, go to school, get married, and have families of their own. But gun violence in our community grew during those years, and our city earned the infamous distinction as the "murder capital of the United States" as the homicides peaked in 1991. Most of these murders were committed in our church's part of the city, Ward 8, which had the highest density of people, the highest poverty rate, and the lowest income level.

To combat these challenges, we became very involved in the community. From our food bank, we supplied groceries to five hundred families per month. Inside the walls of our counseling center, licensed clinicians offered services to individuals, couples, and groups on a generous sliding scale. Then there was the ChristAfrican Theological Institute where we invited the community, church folk, and scholars to do theology from the ground up, as well as from the top down.

We all came together to learn from each other. We offered compassionate care in our Family Crisis center where we had family support workers and social workers. We also participated in neighborhood watch assignments and marched against putting a prison in our ward that would have been part of the prison industrial complex.

The wind blew hard against us as our church worked to become open and affirming of LGBTQ+ people. We affirmed Holy Union ceremonies in our congregation when Massachusetts was the only state that had legalized same-sex marriage. The winds were still blowing when we invited a Black Lives Matters group to hold meetings in our church. We were so amazed when six hundred people—Black, white, brown, and Asian—showed up for that first gathering.

Finally, in 2017, when we realized it was time for gentle winds of change, my husband, Rev. Dr. Dennis W. Wiley, and I answered the call to retirement. One of the first things we were asked to do upon our retirement was to preach and lecture on antiracism in a large white Episcopal church in Washington, DC.

The winds keep blowing, and my husband, who is a liberation theologian, continues to write. As for me, in addition to my teaching and clinical work, I find myself with a group of Baptists who have taken a bold move: The Alliance of Baptists not only have strongly and unhesitatingly affirmed their call to be an antiracist organization but also, with great courage and vulnerability, put into action unambiguous antiracist policies and ways of being.

I have been following these winds of change, this breath, this air in motion, this Spirit of the living God for quite a while now. This *ruah*—this *pneuma*—is blowing now through the Alliance of Baptists. We know these winds, this spirit that is active when we see the effects of God's work. This wind of change "blows where it chooses, and you hear the sound of it, but you do not know where it comes from or where it goes" (John 3:8 NRSV). Like the wind, the Spirit of God fills me as I serve with the people of the Alliance of Baptists to bring forth holy change as we become an antiracist organization knowing that the breath of the Almighty gives us life.

John's Gospel continues, "So it is with everyone who is born of the Spirit." Throughout my life and ministry, I have felt the winds of change blow against me, blow inside me, blow through my life, and energize my spirit. I have clearly heard the sound of it on my journey and in whatever place I was called. Certainly, my journey has been blown about by winds of change. Many times, and in so many ways, the rush of Spirit stirred me and disturbed me and compelled me to change and grow. In other seasons of my life, *ruah* blew gently, something like a God whisper, that stirred my heart and mind and brought holy transformation.

In faith, I have been following these Spirit winds of change, these transformative winds. Through many seasons of ministry, the Spirit of the living God has been my Comforter, my encourager and the inspiration of my soul. The renewing, refreshing Spirit wind, whenever it has blown across my life—with strong gusts or with a gentle breeze—has moved me to another place where God's heart becomes my impulse. And most assuredly, every time God has whispered my name, I have prayed, "Take my hands and let them move at the impulse of thy love."[1]

Christine Y. Wiley is pastor emerita of Covenant Baptist United Church of Christ in Washington, DC. She has been a significant leader for justice in the Washington, DC, community and the country. She has served on the strategy leadership team of the Washington Interfaith Network and was a founding leader of DC Clergy United for Marriage Equality. She has served as coordinator of field education and as instructor in pastoral care and counseling at the Wesley Theological Seminary. She also served as the director of the Field Education Department at the Howard University School of Divinity. She is recognized as an astute practitioner and consults with church, community, and government organizations. As a graduate of Garrett Evangelical Theological Seminary, she received the doctor of ministry degree in pastoral psychotherapy. She has authored many articles regarding counseling and therapy, including a chapter titled "Psychotherapy with Members of African American Churches and

---

1. Frances Ridley Havergal, "Take My Life and Let It Be Consecrated," hymn, 1874, public domain.

Spiritual Traditions" in the *Handbook of Psychotherapy and Religious Traditions*.

Dr. Wiley serves as an adjunct professor at Howard University School of Social Work and is the director of Pastoral Clinical Services, a counseling and consultation center. She provides consultation with churches, the academy, and government entities. She has three wonderful adult children and six adorable grandchildren.

The Eleventh Story

Dancing on Earth as It Is in Heaven: My Rhythm of Divine Calling

Rev. Jenna Sullivan

I caught my breath at church. Sometimes we spend years holding our breath without knowing it. This requires an armor of adaptation. I could be the star student of Mrs. Samler's second grade class. I could be the twirling ballerina. I could be happy. I could be sweetly obedient. I could hold my tears. My breath could wait. But resurrection never waits. It was in the warm sunshine of Second Baptist Church of downtown Little Rock, Arkansas, that God decided my time to breathe had come. I was a middle schooler, and my mom and her partner were looking for new places to attend church. We found this community of faith that was known to be more progressive. I had already been baptized as a young girl at a large Southern Baptist church that was home for much of my extended family.

God knew that I needed a community that would affirm all of me. I am so grateful that we moved to Second Baptist. I began to build beautiful relationships with folks of all generations. I was known by name. I was safe. For once, I felt like I could bring my fullest self to the body of Christ and be held. Nothing about Jenna needed to change. I was beginning to breathe. I laughed until I cried with my friends in the rented youth group van as we traveled on summer trips. I began teaching Sunday school to my peers—but not to earn my worth or impress anybody. I was just so excited about my faith and eager to deepen it. I was beginning to experience abundant life in faithful community and I could not get enough of it.

Every year, there was a Senior Sunday at church. This was a day when high school seniors had the opportunity to preach or lead in worship. I had never seen a teenager preach at Second, but I knew it was an option if you were sensing a call to ministry. Was I? I certainly knew that church was my favorite place in the whole world. I knew that I loved God and felt awakened to a sense of purpose. I was riding on a school bus for a youth group function when the youth minister at the time leaned over to me and asked me, "Jenna, would you want to preach on Senior Sunday this year?" I was shocked but thrilled. "Sure!" I said. I assumed that I would simply offer a testimony or small reflection that day. But the youth minister and pastor explained that I could offer the full-length sermon.

They believed in me. I told my parents excitedly. My dad celebrated with me and was eager to help me brainstorm. A passionate minister and chaplain himself, he and I had always talked frankly about theological questions and stories of Scripture. My mom seemed excited too. And so I began the preparation. Which text would I choose? It was all up to me. I was given such holy freedom and affirmation in this process as a seventeen-year-old young woman. What a gift. I decided to preach about the story of Jacob wrestling with the divine being in the night. Something about this Hebrew Scripture text captivated me. It spoke to the struggle of wrestling.

I spent hours reading and absorbing the Scripture. I had never felt these kinds of feelings. I felt deeply connected to God. I loved exploring the text and dreaming alongside it. How would God help me tell this story anew? My breath was full, and my heart was alive with a curious imagination. God was so near. God was surely whispering my name. We had such a sweet conversation. I was known by God. And even more importantly, I was beginning to know Her.

Finally, the day came. It so happened that the Sunday I preached was the day after my senior prom. While my peers recovered in a sleepy haze, I woke up early with a peaceful grin. It felt like all of me was smiling as I imagined taking to the pulpit that day.

I arrived early and the technical crew gave me a microphone to wear. It had the name "BETSY" inscribed on a label. I was wearing Betsy's microphone. As my first youth minister, Betsy had been my closest mentor who truly got to know me and celebrated my giftedness. In many ways, she allowed me to see that women were just as equipped as men to serve God. So I carried her with me to the pulpit. Her voice and leadership had led the way. I felt so proud and excited. My girlish grin turned to a sober mindfulness as the service began. I remember my hands shaking as my time to preach came. I was so nervous and yet so excited. I walked up to the pulpit. I was home.

What happened next is hard to explain at times. It was as if I was a fish landing in water. I was home. My body instinctively knew what to do with a pulpit. Even though we had never danced together before, somehow I already knew the steps. The steps to the dance were inscribed in my heart. I just showed up. I felt such deep joy as I began to preach. I even walked away from my manuscript and used my own memory and natural expressions to introduce the sermon. How did I already know the steps? This dance was one that didn't ask me to change who I was. There was no adaptation needed to survive. It was simply a dance between God, me, and the congregation. I was mesmerized. And I was certainly hooked. There was no going back.

You could almost hear the shock in the room as I preached. They were watching this dance unfold too. They were watching me discover my calling. Later, when I was ordained at Second Baptist, one of the committee members told the group, "Something shifted for the congregation that day. We still remember it." It was such a holy seventeen minutes for that seventeen-year-old girl. It held such promise for all that could be. Matt Cook, the pastor at the time who had graciously trusted me with the pulpit, told me after the service that I should consider entering the ministry. I didn't know what my path looked like. But I knew that nothing would quite be the same after I opened my mouth and communed with the world and God in that way.

I went on to Rhodes College that fall and ended up majoring in Religious Studies. Still unsure of my vocational path, I knew that learning about God in community was the right next step. I had a few more preaching opportunities here and there. I still heard the whisper of God through my challenging classes, the support of professors, and opportunities to serve the wider community of Memphis. After four transformative years, I had learned to love God with my mind as well as my heart. I discerned a call to go to seminary. I decided to attend Wake Forest University School of Divinity. I would keep dancing with God.

My time at Wake was rich in many ways. I developed beautiful friendships. I felt the freedom to ask big questions and wrestle with my own theology. My faith grew deeper roots. I was challenged to see my own privilege as a white woman. I heard from my peers and listened to their experiences as Black ministers in white institutions. The dance with God was getting more complicated. After three years at Wake, I was excited to serve a congregation. I was so eager to put all of this knowledge and passion into practice. Looking back, I think it is interesting how quickly I went from degree to degree. I think it speaks to a sort of frenzy of productivity and achievement. For better or for worse, I felt a lot of pressure on myself to succeed.

I accepted a position as associate pastor at Magnolia Road Baptist Church in Jonesboro, Arkansas. This was a small church associated with the Cooperative Baptist Fellowship. I was excited to go much closer to home. I thought this would be a place I would lay down roots. My two years there were formational. It was like ministry boot camp. I struggled with so many parts of ministry. I realized how relational the work was and how much of my own spirit needed support and maturity. God held me close during those years. I learned so much about pastoral care, the challenges of small church systems, and how to stay resilient.

It was not an easy two years. The church was full of good people but had some real challenges in terms of identity and a vision of the future. I was also on a journey toward accepting myself with love. I was insecure, and much of my own woundedness showed up in my ministry. I desperately wanted the approval of every single person I ministered to. It turns out that people are complicated and not always as deeply affirming as we hope for them to be. And the even better news is that we ultimately do not need their affirmation. That would take me a long time to learn. It would take learning to practice yoga, being vulnerable in therapy, and deepening my healing journey with God. Despite the many challenges, Magnolia Road is where I learned to be a pastor. I learned what it felt like to show up at Bob's hospital bedside, see his humanity, and laugh at the stories I had already heard. I sat next to him in his camouflage-patterned recliner, helped him grieve the loss of his wife, and reminded him to take his medicine.

I facilitated an amazing ministry called FANN—Friends and Neighbors Network. This was a group of low-income families that met at the church every other week to gather and distribute groceries together. I loved being part of their community and showing up as their pastor. I held space for women who had experienced church trauma, showed up at the first Pride rally as a public preacher, and developed meaningful relationships with folks who had never found belonging inside the walls of a southern church. I discovered the unspeakable joy of being a pastor and got a lot of practice at dealing with the inevitable angst of it.

I also continued to love church, even when it was messy and hard. I loved casseroles and Christmas carols. I loved seeing laypeople excited about the gospel. I loved teaching Scripture in creative ways and watching people expand their imagination. I loved doing life alongside imperfect, hilarious, loving people. I loved being a pastor. I knew I had become a pastor when I did my first funeral homily. It was a tragic death by mobile home fire. I was called on to do the funeral, and I prepared my best to help remember someone I had no prior relationship with. After I gave the sermon, a man from the family walked up and said, "Thank you, pastor." He removed his hand from his dressiest pair of blue jeans and shook my hand. In that moment, all Southern Baptist notions of what women could be vanished. He saw me as his pastor. And in that moment, I did too.

I decided that I would keep doing this ministry thing. But I knew I needed to leave Magnolia Road. It was time to move to a place where I could be surer about my long-term role. I wanted to plan for my future, and it was hard to do that at this church. I knew I deserved to know what my future held and I wasn't sure we were all on the same page about what that future was. It was hard to leave. Sometimes, I felt like I was betraying people or leaving them behind—especially when they didn't quite understand. Overall, folks were supportive and gave me their blessing to leave.

I applied for a pastoral residency at Wilshire Baptist Church in Dallas, Texas. I had known one of the current pastoral residents from my time at Wake Divinity. This would be a place for me to process my first few years of ministry and continue to develop my pastoral skills. I have been at Wilshire now for over a year. In many ways, it is so different than where I came from. It is much more formal in nature, and I have a lot less responsibility than I had before. This has real gifts and real challenges. My time here has also been marked by surviving a global pandemic. One of the biggest blessings during it has been my friendship with fellow resident Ashley Robinson. Ashley is wildly accepting and loving of all people in their messy humanness. Her hospitality towards the queer community as a committed ally struck me from the day I first met her.

In my time in Dallas, I began doing some somatic experiencing therapy with a trusted counselor. As I felt safe to process some childhood pain long held in my body, I also became more trusting of a new supportive faith community. In all this processing, I came to terms with my experience of being queer. I had known for years that I had an attraction to women, but this knowledge was concealed and buried in pure terror. I was terrified of what it would mean for my life and reputation. I was sure I could make it work with a man if he was the right one. But resurrection . . . really catching my breath . . . was beginning to make it clear that I would choose holy freedom. And I knew that if I was true to myself and lived the most expansive life I could, there was a good chance I would eventually fall in love with a woman.

I gave myself the most beautiful gift this year. I came out publicly. It was terrifying, painful, and extremely vulnerable. The best way I can explain it is that we know things about ourselves when we feel safe enough to know them. For years, I had been holding my breath around my authentic sexuality. I was so concerned with being safe and predictable and respected. My sexuality was too complicated and unpredictable. And while I have learned to be an expert at adapting for others, this is one thing I have not been able to adapt for myself. My epiphany cracked me open, and I became in touch with something more important than the approval of anyone else. I found myself.

She is free, fluid, and unpredictable. That still annoys me. But I am learning with the support of others to allow her to breathe. When I came out, I took a deeper breath than I had ever taken. As supportive messages poured in, I realized that pastor Jenna and queer Jenna did not have to be mutually exclusive. They could dance together in the unfolding story of me.

In my ministry here, I have begun to grow in important pastoral ways. I have mentored young queer teenagers in our youth group. They look at me differently. They find shelter in my story. My preaching voice is louder and stronger. My lived reality and joyful acceptance of myself has challenged Wilshire to embody its values in practical ways. It has been hard. But God has moved in and through my story to help others feel much less alone.

To the sisters who are reading these stories, I have a special word for you.

Dear sister, you are allowed to be complicated. You have permission to evolve, expand, and deepen your understanding of yourself . . . and that includes your sacred sexuality. You do not need the approval of anyone except God and your own sweet heart. Learn to love yourself. Give yourself grace. Stay close to those who give you unconditional support. As you enter ministry, know you are entering a hard and holy dance. God will sustain you when you know the choreography by heart and when you stumble awkwardly through the moves. You are bringing gospel hope to a world that needs it and will often protest when you offer the thing it needs most.

Stay true to yourself and know that you are enough. Breathe deep and remember that God gives you breath. You are never alone in this work. I cannot emphasize enough how important it is to take care of your soul amid your journey. Remember that you are not responsible for fixing the pain and misery of others. You are simply tasked with noticing the holy and naming it. Keep bringing your full self to your ministry. Do not compartmentalize or fragment your soul. You are whole. You are enough. I can't wait to see where you and God dance to.

I stand amazed at my story. I see one important thread that has held it all together: a beautiful and majestic Creator. God knows me, loves me, and continues to call me forth into a beautiful future of ministry. I am not sure what is next, but I'm excited to keep dancing. I am so grateful that God whispered my name. I will continue to do my best to accept the unpredictable and, at times, inconveniently beautiful truths of myself and of others. I will always accept the invitation to dance with God. Somehow, I always remember the steps.

Jenna Sullivan is a disciple of Jesus, feminist + queer preacher, certified yoga instructor, and community pastor. She plans to joyfully spend her life embodying the ancient gospel of Christ-like love, compassion, and justice. Whether dancing with abandon on Instagram, bearing witness to unspeakable church wounds, or getting into holy mischief with friends, Jenna stays both reverent and relevant. She is an emerging church mother—living fearlessly into her womanhood, queerness, and boundless love for all of God's creation.

The Twelfth Story

Empowered by My Promised Inheritance

Rev. Sheila D. Sholes-Ross

I cannot. I will not. I have never heard of such. I will not accept having a woman "in charge" of my spiritual development. These are just some of the many comments I heard from family members and friends when I informed them that I was being called into ministry. At the age of forty-five, I heard God whisper my name in order to receive my rightful inheritance and placement as a woman of God called into ministry. But this call, which I either did not recognize or ignored, had echoes back to when I was as a seventeen-year-old African American girl in New Orleans, Louisiana. I had never seen a woman pastor, let alone a woman of color, in the male-dominated Baptist church pulpit. The age reference remains clear in my memory bank since I was being pressured to select a major, an ambition, for my 1974 senior yearbook picture since I would soon be heading off to college after graduation. In my home, it was often spoken that I had to go to college and have a profession that would enable me to take care of myself so that I would not have to rely on a man through marriage.

During those times, girls going off to college were expected to become nurses and teachers; at least, my family expected me to select one of these choices. However, I could not write in the yearbook space, calling for a proposed major and ambition, one of these wonderful professions. So I left it blank until the school principal called me in his office to see why I had committed this grossly inferior act. I could not tell him that I left it blank because I knew God was calling me to "something" but I could not, for the life of me, comprehend what that "something" was.

The principal was livid. He would not accept this from a person who was graduating in the top ten of her class of over four hundred graduating students. So I placed on the major and ambition line "legal secretary," another wonderful profession, but I knew I was not called to become a legal secretary. I just wanted the male principal to stop with the pressure. Upon entering the university of my choice, I declared a double major of music therapy and voice. I did not believe I was called to be a singer and therapist either, but pressure from family members propelled this declaration because of my giftedness and talent in music.

Upon university graduation, I did not seek a career in music because I did not have a passion to do this aspect of work. It was becoming more and more evident to me that God was calling me to something, but it was not clear as to "what" the something was. I just knew that whatever it was, it had to be either special or difficult because God did not want to present me with the information in a clear manner that I could understand. Maybe it was because I would not have fully comprehended or accepted God's call. Like many, I would have said, "Why me? God, you know there are no women preachers around here."

Growing up, I always thought, "Why did men ever want to become ministers . . . preachers?" I must ashamedly admit that I believed it to be a lowly vocation and one only for men. Maybe that is why God did not respond when I asked, "What are you calling me to become?"

As a nineteen-year-old college sophomore, I was chosen as the youth speaker for the annual evening Women's Day Celebration in my New Orleans home church, which was 100 percent African American. I was so proud, delighted, and terrified to accept the invitation. When the time came for me to offer the message, instead of going down to the floor podium where women speakers usually spoke, I entered the pulpit. Dead silence. Usually, when a young person got up to speak, especially a female speaker who might be a little timid, the church would break out with hand-clapping and many amens, along with "Take your time, baby. God will help you!"

Entering the pulpit was not a conscious decision. I was by no means trying to rock the boat. I asked myself afterwards, "Why did you do this?" Surprisingly, I had felt completely comfortable. Following the message, everyone told me how great it was and lavished me with praise—even the senior pastor who was sitting near the pulpit during worship. I remember seeing the look of shock on his face when I entered the pulpit, which possibly explains why I was never again asked to serve as a Women's Day youth speaker.

After college I had a number of professional positions, none of which coincided with my music degrees. In order to fulfill the needed expertise for these positions, I found myself back in the classroom acquiring several more degrees. With each new position, I was challenged with the question, "God, is this what you want me to do?" And I added, "If not, guide me to what you *are* calling me to do. What am I missing?"

Years passed. I got married and still was challenged with this proverbial question to God. I struggled to the point that I informed my husband that I believed God was calling *him* to ministry, and I had no desire to be married to a clergy person. I loved dancing, great wine, and bourbon. In the African American Baptist church tradition, good church people claimed that they did not dance or drink, but many did, even the ministers. This hypocrisy among many who had accepted the call from God may have been one of the reasons I had a problem with the vocation. After looking at me for what seemed like a long time, my husband responded, "God is not calling me into ministry. I do not believe God needs a third party to advise me of a ministry call." He smiled and advised me to continue asking God what the Holy One wanted of me. Smart husband. "Okay, God, you now have more of my attention. It is not my husband you are calling. What do you want of me?"

After working in several wonderful positions in my hometown of New Orleans, I was recruited to the University of North Carolina at

Chapel Hill. So off we went to North Carolina. I successfully spent a few years as a school-based health developer of statewide programs, all the while becoming more and more restless. I became increasingly weary of presenting the same unanswered question to God, until finally I understood the Holy One's whisper: "You feed my sheep." Still, I ignored the whisper.

During my tenure in North Carolina, I did see women in ministry. I did see women of color in ministry, but for whatever reason, I continued to avoid accepting God's call upon my life. That is, until a strange occurrence took place. This is a personal and funny story that you may not want to visualize, but it does speak to my ultimate acknowledgment and acceptance of God's whisper.

While I showered one night in 2004, a light bulb tightly secured in its fixture setting suddenly fell, barely missing my head. It should have broken once it hit the shower floor, but it did not. It remained intact, and I escaped injury. I was terribly shaken because, as far as I could tell, nothing could explain its sudden release and miraculous indestructibility. My husband was out of town on business, but upon his return he found me curled up in a fetal position in bed. I told him, "God is not calling you; God is calling me." My husband responded, "I told you God did not need you to tell me about any ministry call upon my life." I was then ready to walk into my "promised inheritance" call from God.

I am such a blessed woman because my husband and his immediate family members have been supportive throughout my ministry journey call and in my present position as Senior Pastor at First Baptist Church of Pittsfield, Massachusetts. I cannot say the same with my immediate family members and friends. There are former male friends currently serving as pastors in renowned churches, and they do not recognize me as a pastor. These are men I grew up with in the church where I was bold enough to enter the pulpit at the age of nineteen to offer my Women's Day message.

As I began to walk towards full acceptance of this call upon me, I entered seminary in the fall of 2005. This was when I was introduced to the Hebrew Old Testament texts of Numbers 27:1-11 and Joshua 17:3-4 (NRSV) via my female Zimbabwean Old Testament professor. I immediately fell in love with these texts, as they spoke well to my journey as a woman in ministry—a woman facing obstacles but determined to actively participate in her inheritance call.

The biblical story documents that Zelophehad was from the tribe of Manasseh. He had five daughters but no sons and therefore no male heirs to receive property inheritance upon his death. Zelophehad died. The text tells little of Zelophehad himself but speaks about his incredible five daughters named Mahlah, Noah, Hoglah, Milcah, and Tirzah. They stood up for themselves to guarantee their share of a property inheritance. Numbers 27:2-7 (NRSV) states:

> They stood before Moses, Eleazar the priest, the leaders, and all the congregation, at the entrance of the tent meeting, and they said, "Our father died in the wilderness; he was not among the company of those who gathered themselves against the LORD in the company of Korah, but died for his own sins; and he had no sons. Why should the name of our father be taken away from his clan because he had no son? Give us possession among our father's brothers." Moses brought their case before the LORD. And the LORD spoke to Moses, saying: "The daughters of Zelophehad are right in what they are saying; you shall indeed let them possess an inheritance among their father's brothers and pass the inheritance of their father on to them."

God had spoken to Moses, and I choose to view God's response as the Holy One defending the rights of women. What is so intriguing regarding this story is that even in antiquity's patriarchal setting, Moses listened and obeyed God's command. Moses may not have fully understood or agreed with God, but he obeyed God. This text should be a starting point with many fundamentalist and evangelical male clergy. However, there are also twenty-first-century women who persist in maintaining the traditional mindset that only males can be pastors. They would benefit from the biblical understanding that Moses, a man, obeyed God regarding the rights of Zelophehad's daughters. Many may still not accept, and various interpretations of the text will differ, but I choose the interpretation of the text focusing on women's rights.

I often reflect on what God might have done if Zelophehad had sons. Would God still have granted the daughters this inheritance if they had asked, due to patriarchal traditions? This could be another chapter in and of itself. Because of its significance, the story is reiterated in Joshua 17:3-4 (NRSV). God had already made a provision for the women to receive their allotted claim. The Holy One gave Moses the commandment to honor the women's request; yet they had to be willing to come forward and speak God's truth on their own behalf with confidence.

Women telling humanity about hearing "whispers" from God calling them into ministry is not easy. But when women are called, God has already made the provision for them to walk toward that ministry. Why? Because God is a God of justice. Many people will never accept the biblical support of women in ministry as clergy. They will overlook the Scripture stating, "I will pour out my spirit on all flesh; your sons and daughters shall prophesy" (Joel 2:28, NRSV). How can women prophesy if they do not speak up with confidence and live into what God has called them to do?

As a woman called into ministry, I can attest to the difficulty of this task. Many events in life that entail speaking up for justice and fairness come with a price. Still, in the twenty-first century, when a woman accepts the call to ministry, she sometimes faces alienation along with an uphill battle to be recognized as equal to her male counterparts. However, the first step is to speak up and acknowledge the call.

I spoke of my inheritance acceptance first to my husband, who wholeheartedly supported my call. Soon after, on a stormy night, I spoke of it to two close friends. I telephoned them and said I had something to share with them of an "urgent" nature, but I could not provide any more information until they arrived. They must have been terrified because they arrived at my home within ten minutes, a trip that normally took fifteen to twenty minutes.

My husband, fully aware of the pending conversation, wondered, as I did, how our friends would respond to my proclamation. I started with "Friends, God has called me to ministry, and I have accepted God's call." The response: "Okay." Then one friend proceeded to change topics, as if I had not made such a life-changing announcement. I found myself in a state of disbelief for what felt like an eternity until his wife said, "Do you hear what this woman is saying?" Gratefully, her response assured me that what I had just shared was not some trivial news to be "blown off." As our conversation ended, my dear friend offered a prayer of blessing and protection for the journey.

My immediate family—my sister, brother, aunt, and godmother—did brush off my announcement. They were unapologetically unsupportive. It was my sister who finally conceded that she believed I was called by God upon hearing the delivery of my initial sermon. My brother, however, never offered support or encouragement in respect to my call. My mother and father were long deceased by this time. I have often wondered how they would have responded to their youngest daughter being called to ministry.

My sister attended my seminary graduation, coming up from New Orleans to North Carolina, and cheered so loudly that it brought me to embarrassment and tears. Although the seminary president asked attendees not to be demonstrative with individual graduates, this did not preclude my sister from wildly cheering. Thankfully, many of my family members and friends, initially skeptical of my call, eventually came around to embracing its authenticity. But there were still many others, including colleagues, who did not share this view. To illustrate my point, allow me to share an incident portraying this attitude while I was serving as an associate minister at a local megachurch in North Carolina.

It was a citywide revival, and I was late arriving to worship. I took a seat in the sanctuary, not attempting to enter the pulpit where other, mostly male ministers were already seated. The senior pastor at the time called ministers in the sanctuary not presently seated near the pulpit to come forward. Even in the crowded sanctuary, he recognized my immobility and again reiterated, "*All* ministers." This pastor was one of my mentors and supportive of women in ministry. As I rose to take a seat at the pulpit, a well-known pastor placed his handkerchief in the chair next to his in order to indicate to me that I was not welcome to sit next to him. I stared at him in shock but, not wanting to cause a scene at the time, I proceeded to take another place to sit near the pulpit. Oh, how I wished the Numbers 27 text had come to my mind. If I had remembered this beloved text, maybe I would have remembered the importance of courage and spoken up against the minister's act of rudeness and injustice. With confidence, I would have picked up his handkerchief and stated, "I believe you misplaced this item."

Long after this event, I shared the incident with the senior pastor, but upon questioning, I refused to give him the name of the male clergy person. How I wish I had given him that name! It would have provided another opportunity to address a patriarchal mindset. My male mentor was prepared and willing to do it, but I was not.

As I have matured in ministry during my course of almost eight years as senior pastor, I acknowledge that I was taking the "easy" way out. Standing up and confronting injustice takes great courage. Yes, I had heard God's whisper and accepted the Holy One's call to ministry, but in that moment of demonstrated patriarchy, I faltered in my confidence of my promised inheritance. I relinquished an opportunity to speak up for something that was rightfully mine and ordained by God.

As I reflect on the lives of many women in ministry, across race and ethnicity, I think of the struggle endured and particularly the perseverance by women of color in ministry. I am reminded of the Rev. Dr. Prathia Hall, noted preacher, theologian, ethicist, and civil rights activist. Her life is documented skillfully, beautifully, and eloquently by scholar, the Rev. Dr. Courtney Pace in the book *Freedom Faith: The Womanist Vision of Prathia Hall*.[1]

Dr. Pace is the Prathia Hall Scholar with Equity for Women in the Church, Inc., a nonprofit ecumenical movement advocating on behalf of women in ministry. In her book, Dr. Pace states that "Rev. Dr. Hall was one of the most profound, prophetic preachers of the twentieth century. A man with her talents and successes would have been a nationally recognized civil rights leader, held a prestigious pulpit, and served as president of a major denomination. That path was not open to Hall, despite the influence she held."[2]

---

1. Courtney Pace, *Freedom Faith: The Womanist Vision of Prathia Hall* (Athens: University of Georgia Press, 2019).

2. Ibid., 1.

Like Prathia Hall, women in ministry today are still disenfranchised from senior ministry positions. However, Dr. Hall remained steadfast in her promised inheritance and thereby opened doors for future clergywomen. In 1977, Hall became one of the first African American Baptist women to be ordained by the American Baptist Churches, USA. I, too, was ordained by the American Baptist Churches, USA. I am proud to follow in her footsteps. I have seen videos of Dr. Hall's preaching style in the pulpit, and she was a trailblazer with a force. How many clergywomen have not had this force within them to remain steadfast in their giftedness because of patriarchal hindrance? I, for one, stand on the shoulders of Rev. Dr. Prathia Hall.

Dr. Pace also notes that it was Dr. Hall who coined the phrase "I have a dream."[3] It was in 1962, after many church burnings, that Dr. Hall was invited to a prayer vigil in Albany, Georgia. She was invited because of her civil rights involvement and eloquent orations regarding the movement. It is reported that she used that phrase there in Albany. Although it became a part of Dr. Martin Luther King's signature message, it was Dr. Hall's initial dream. I wonder, if Dr. Hall had staunchly claimed ownership of the phrase, how people would have responded. Would she had been viewed as creating a "scene" like I tried to avoid at the citywide revival? Or what if Dr. King, in his message, had attributed more credit to Dr. Hall? Would he have become an acknowledged ally of women in ministry?

The path was not fully open for Hall, like it is not fully open today for many women in ministry. Traditional mindsets still refuse to budge. Patriarchy can learn a lesson from the obedience of Moses in the book of Numbers, a lesson so significant that it was repeated in the book of Joshua. It is awe-inspiring because Moses listened to and obeyed the command from God to honor the request of Zelophehad's daughters. The appeal voiced so bravely by Mahlah, Noah, Hoglah, Milcah, and Tirzah was much more than a request. It was about the significance and importance of standing up for what was rightfully theirs because it was ordained by God.

---

3. Ibid., 228–30.

We as "women of God" must stand up and speak up for what is rightfully ours—challenging mindsets, knocking down patriarchal barriers, and unlocking doors that have been locked far too long! A continuing question in ministry is this: How do women of God and men of God change the patriarchal mindsets that hinder women in ministry, a hindrance that prevents them from their inheritance?

I have some recommendations:

Women called to ministry must first be bold in announcing their call. Then they must live into their call. They must not expect or be dependent on the acceptance of others. Instead, they must advocate on behalf of their call. If a clergywoman is called to a senior pastorate position, she must not allow patriarchy to determine a lower salary from that of a male counterpart. The Rev. Christine A. Smith, in her wonderful 2013 book *Beyond the Stained Glass Ceiling: Equipping and Encouraging Female Pastors*,[4] documents that the average salary for female senior pastors as stipulated by a 2009–2011 American Baptist Church (ABC) survey was between $26,000 and $45,000. Clergywomen must do their research and demand salary equity even if it is their first pastorate.

Clergywomen must seek allies (male and female) for mentoring, educating them on topics from salaries to what to expect in senior pastorate positions. They should not select a ministry avenue that does not fulfill the area of ministry God has called them to. Some women have become chaplains, a wonderful area of ministry, because of limitations and hindrances in pulpit ministry.

Clergywomen who feel they are called to be senior pastors must also examine the work of planting churches where they can be recognized and accepted into pulpit ministry. Those of us who currently serve as senior pastors must collaborate more to develop strategies to better advocate on behalf of clergywomen and move them towards senior pastorates. When we become aware of churches seeking new pastors, let us challenge those churches, in the spirit of love, to develop search committees that refrain from knowing the gender of

---

4. Christine A. Smith, *Beyond the Stained Glass Ceiling: Equipping and Encouraging Female Pastors* (Valley Forge: Judson, 2013).

candidates. Certainly this is a small start, but committees would be forced to look at qualifications first rather than gender.

The breadth of experience that is easily gained by male clergy does not equate to hiring a potentially good pastor. Some clergywomen without senior pastorate experience must be given a chance to enter into the role. And even if change is initially minimal, maybe the church will begin to look at itself and hear God speak about the importance of fairness and justice.

Even though these recommendations are starting points, they may appear impossible to implement for various reasons. Because of the autonomy of churches and the hierarchal placement in denominations, this may be a difficult strategy to pursue. However, difficult and ongoing honest conversations must begin with all of us taking active roles in support of women in ministry—support with our voices and actions that will ultimately lead to change. This change will allow women not only to speak up with their voices about their inheritance but also to enter into ministry with immense support that will help them prophesy as God has commanded them after they hear the "whisper."

As for my own "whisper," the sound of it remains in my heart, continually nudging my spirit to persevere. The "whisper" unshackles my soul, empowering me by my promised inheritance. And from a place of holy freedom, I am liberated to stand boldly in the light of my inheritance and live into my calling.

Sheila D. Sholes-Ross currently serves as senior pastor of First Baptist Church of Pittsfield, Massachusetts, which was founded in the 1700s. Rev. Sholes-Ross is only the thirtieth pastor and is the first female and first African American selected pastor. Ordained by the American Baptist Churches, USA, she has a master of divinity degree (*magna cum laude*) from James Walker Hood Theological Seminary, (Salisbury, North Carolina), as well as master's degrees in public health (UNC-Chapel Hill) and administration and supervision (Xavier University of the South); bachelor's degrees in music (voice) and music therapy (Xavier University and Loyola University of the South, respectively). Rev. Sholes-Ross also received a certificate of nonprofit management from Duke University.

During her tenure as an executive director of a nonprofit drop-out prevention organization in Chapel Hill, North Carolina, she obtained two US Department of Education grants at $1.3 million each for programs addressing the educational needs of students in two school districts—one urban and the other rural. She is founder and co-chairperson of Equity for Women in the Church, Inc., an ecumenical national organization advocating on behalf of women in ministry. She also serves as a board member for the Conference of Baptist Ministers of Massachusetts (CBMM), board member of the Clergy Oversight Council–Ministerial Standing through the American Baptists Churches of Massachusetts (TABCOM), vice-chair of Pittsfield Area Council of Churches (PACC), board member of Berkshire Medical Center Patient and Family Advisory Council (PFAC), and member of Pittsfield Police Advisory and Review Board (PARB).

Rev. Sholes-Ross is married to Nelson Ross (over thirty years), who, after God, is her greatest supporter and friend.

The Thirteenth Story

My Child's Heart Remembers

Rev. Mica Togami

My child's heart remembers the days before the Covid-19 pandemic. As a hospital-based manager of spiritual care, the beginning of the Covid-19 pandemic felt surreal. The news of the contagious virus began to flood the media at a time when my brothers were traveling in Japan visiting relatives, and my concern for them was intense. Professionally, the entirety of our hospital staff prepared to provide medical care to the patients, with little knowledge and understanding of the impact of Covid-19. Fears of the deadly virus and how to maintain the safety of our chaplaincy staff and our medical staff was a core concern. Providing leadership to the spiritual care department was daunting as I worried not only about our staff but their loved ones as well.

Personally, I sat with my concern for my own family: my partner being immunocompromised after lengthy treatment for leukemia. I could not help asking myself, "What if I bring this virus to her? What am I doing? Am I called to be here, in this place?" A deep small voice within said, "You have been preparing for this moment all your life."

My work is that of a chaplain and as an ACPE educator (Association for Clinical Pastoral Education), equipping people to become chaplains. My daily work continues to broaden my understanding of ministry. More than three decades of encounters with diverse patients, staff, and chaplain students have inspired and challenged my personal development and continue to transform my understanding of faith and trust in God/Spirit. Each individual person that I have had the honor to listen to and be with as they share their story has enriched my life. My consistent response is gratitude. My calling has been a process of learning to be authentic and to share the essence of who I am in relationship with others, in hopes for wholeness amid the challenges and suffering that we all face in this world.

My formative years as a Japanese-Brazilian "missionary kid" have informed my pastoral ministry. As a daughter of Japanese missionary parents who served a remote rural town in the southern part of Brazil, attending church was a given—along with accompanying expectations of wearing frilly dresses and shiny shoes and the mandate of a cheerful disposition. For the most part, I enjoyed getting together with friends every Sunday, playing in the church courtyard, singing, and hearing Bible stories, especially from "kamishibai," which is known as "paper play"—a storytelling tool (in our case a stock paper with images of the stories depicting a biblical character or an event). Most of my Sunday school friends were like me, *nikkei jin* (Japanese descendants living in Brazil). We spoke to each other in Portuguese while our parents spoke to other parents in a fluid interplay of both Japanese and Portuguese. The language transitions between Portuguese and Japanese were smooth, harmonious, and natural. As children, we learned to understand both languages without any formal instruction.

The Sunday school teachers translated the "kamishibai" stories in the Portuguese language, teaching a specific Bible-based lesson. One of the stories I recall was about Samuel and his call to ministry. My child's heart remembers with love the part of the story when God called Samuel's name in the middle of the night. I wondered when that magical event would happen for me—and waited for it to occur. Looking back, I am aware that my calling did come not from the outside voice of God but from my inner whisper within to be true to myself, to appreciate the gift shared by others with me, and to identify and develop the gifts that I can share with the world.

Through my parents' ministry, I observed how they were welcoming of all people from all walks of life. In addition to ministering to people within the community, my parents frequently invited both friends and "strangers" to our home. My mother was an excellent cook and demonstrated her hospitality through preparing meals for potentially one extra person or for a crowd. The dining table was symbolic—expanding or contracting to accommodate those gathered. We celebrated all the holidays, including American Thanksgiving with turkey and stuffing. No matter what food was on the table, the most sought-after dish was my mother's fried rice. As a New Year's tradition, my parents invited the Japanese community to the house for "mochi tsuki"—a traditional rice-pounding activity to make mochi (rice cake) for the New Year. Each year, this celebration grew in numbers, requiring us to find larger venues than our house to accommodate the crowd.

My parents' hospitality also included having people stay at our house, not only for a night but sometimes for stretches of weeks and months. Missionary families from different denominations and countries waiting for their housing would stay with us—including local families who were in crisis due to a divorce/separation, a spouse waiting for a trial, a family traveling through as they were sightseeing. As a child, I absorbed the stories of their adventures, mishaps, joys, and pains—stories that my child's heart will long remember.

I remember my mother voicing expectations of me: the imperative to be a "good pastor's child." I was asked numerous times (more accurately "bribed") into being a "flower girl" for weddings that my father would officiate. Piano lessons were "a must," and I took lessons for seven years with, to my mother's chagrin, no real improvement in my proficiency. While encouraging me to meet family "role" expectations, my mother ironically modeled for me how to be an independent woman. Her life story was one where she felt a strong call to ministry and to be a missionary. The Japanese Baptist church authorities, however, told her that the only way she could serve abroad would be to marry a pastor, which she did.

My mother's role was to function in a subservient way to my father, traditionally supporting his work by doing the necessary administrative assistant tasks, playing the piano for the church services, teaching Sunday school, and cooking for gatherings. However, my mother had her own way of providing ministry to others. She developed a close relationship with a Presbyterian physician and his spouse who were prominent in the community. Together, the physician's spouse and my mother provided spiritual care visits to the patients at the community hospital. I remember expectantly waiting in the car with my father to pick her up after these visits. She would share stories of those whom she visited—patients who were facing different illnesses and challenges in their lives. My mother also used her previously acquired Montessori training (having trained in the United States while on the way to Brazil) and leadership skills to help start a kindergarten (which has now grown into a K–12 school). Her leadership style was relational and communal, informed by the indigenous values of the Japanese society (coming from Confucius philosophy, Daoism, Shintoism, and Buddhism) that I have carried into my own ministry.

During my teenage years in Brazil, several congregations from the Texas Baptist Convention came to bring the "gospel" to our town. One day, my father asked me to tag along and help translate for the mission team. The mission team came prepared with a cardboard record player (which rotated by using a pencil) with the message about Jesus. We went door to door in one of the more socioeconomically challenged neighborhoods. Clapping outside the house, we announced our presence and were invited into homes with red dirt floors. A Brazilian church member would lead the conversation introducing the team. I translated what the American pastor said into Portuguese and then responsively shared in English what I learned from the Brazilian family. We played the record player. After the message, there was an invitation for the family to come to church that evening.

After days of this door-to-door ministering after school, I was looking forward to being picked up to go home. The Brazilian pastor sought me out and asked if I would serve as a translator for the evening church service. He had just received a phone call that the translator was sick. I was caught off guard and felt ill-equipped to have that responsibility in front of the entire congregation. I remember thinking that women were not allowed to "preach." Even worse, I was wearing jeans and a t-shirt. My parents prohibited my wearing jeans during church services so that I could model "proper attire" for other teens. With no other recourse, I got up in front of the church and translated the entire service and the sermon led by the American pastor. As the service moved towards an ending, I realized that I was also expected to translate the dreaded "altar call." It seemed like the hymn "Just as I Am" was sung for hours in Portuguese. A fourth of the people in attendance (including the families that I had visited that day) came forward. I knew then that God was working in ways beyond my understanding.

My parents decided during the end of my ninth grade school year to retire from the mission field. They chose to go back to Japan—the place they called home. This transition was culturally difficult for me. My father served a large church in Tokyo, with an attached kindergarten. We lived on the church grounds, where there was no separation between our family life and church life. I couldn't relate to people my age due to the deep cultural divide between my Brazilian upbringing and my Japanese peers. I found a place of acceptance at the American School, where most of the children were missionary kids. Throughout high school, I engaged in sports and music and many extracurricular activities to cope with my grief over the loss of "home." As consideration of college began, I knew that my Japanese was not fluent enough for me to attend a Japanese college, so my only alternative was to go to the United States.

Both of my brothers had gone to Baylor University in Texas, and I followed their path, seeking a new place to belong. My brother Nobu, who was finishing his graduate studies, helped me settle into the dorm. As a freshman at Baylor University, I didn't have a car and, at eighteen years of age, had no driver's license. For a period of time, going to church meant riding a shuttle to any church that offered transportation. The necessity of attending a variety of churches because of transportation availability had the unexpected consequence of opening me to find meaning in places I would have otherwise disregarded. The only church I could walk to was Seventh and James Baptist Church. I was surprised to learn that the pastor of the church, Rev. Dan Bagby, was also a missionary kid from Brazil. He represented a piece of "home" for me as we connected, frequently speaking in Portuguese. Dan's care and compassion helped me to make the cultural transition.

Though not a regular Sunday school attendee, I was intrigued by the college group that focused on the importance of questioning one's beliefs and encouraged members to be involved in social action. I began tutoring Spanish speakers, helping them with reading and writing in English. The most significant part of being at the church was witnessing Beverly CroweTipton's ordination. It was the first time I became aware that a woman could be ordained and serve as a pastor. She preached and led services at the church. That led me to take a class called "Women in Baptist History" with Dr. Rosalie Beck, the first female faculty member of Religion at Baylor University. Dr. Beck's class exposed me to an awareness of the influential work of women in the church. I participated in Baptist Student Union work and was encouraged to lead Bible studies and (eventually) to serve as a summer missionary to Sydney, Australia. I felt at "home" in Australia, as the night sky was similar to Brazil (being in the southern hemisphere). My mentors Shawn Shannon and Candace Hardin were affirming and were role models of ministry for me, although they were not formally ordained. This made me aware that people's giftedness had little or nothing to do with their titles. My varying experiences and my undergraduate recreation major created an inner desire for me to explore the possibility of church recreation work. I decided to go to seminary.

My parents were thrilled when I shared with them my decision to go to seminary. At that time, my eldest brother Yoshiya was living in Louisville, Kentucky, with his partner. I made the decision to go to Southern Baptist Theological Seminary only to experience a tumultuous time in the history of the seminary. Faculty members were resigning one by one, as they could not affirm the newly amended Baptist Faith and Message. These professors who fought for social justice with integrity and fortitude left a lasting impression on me.

Rev. Cindy Weber came and taught a seminary class on Pastoral Formation, and I learned then that her church was looking for seminary students to do internships. I admired Cindy, as I learned that she had worked as the associate and interim pastor and later as the senior pastor for Jefferson Street Baptist Center of the Long Run Baptist Association. The association, not wanting a woman pastor leading Jefferson Street, evicted the congregation. I became a member of the newly formed church, Jeff Street Baptist Community at Liberty, where I learned about the work for social justice and peace with those who have been marginalized and treated as "lesser than" in American society. What I took to heart was the value of living a simple life in a diverse community. After a few years, I was ordained to the ministry by the congregation.

As a part of my master of divinity degree, I was required to take a unit of clinical pastoral education. This CPE training invited me to reflect on my past history and to identify and deeply value both the pain and joys of my own story. I was trained by various CPE supervisors: Clarence Barton, James Pollard, Wes Monfalcone, Jo Clare Wilson, Nancy Anderson, and John Moody. I experienced them as my allies while I struggled with my experiences of homophobia, sexism, cultural dissonances, and racism. Their fearless effort to wrestle with hard questions and not accept "easy" answers, and the fact that I was being "seen" by them, was affirming and confirming of me as a person growing into my truth of myself. The path to become a clinical pastoral education supervisor (now called certified educator) took seven years for me as I wrestled with writing and articulating theory that was heavily influenced by Western Christian education.

Now, as a part of the Asian American Pacific Islander (AAPI) Certified Educator group, I have found new ways to give words to my experience. Just recently, one of my AAPI colleagues shared that our immigration experience to the United States was "trauma," and the latest rise in Asian hate crimes was a "re-traumatization" for us. I resonated deeply with my colleague's comment. The cultural message I had gotten since I arrived in the United States at age eighteen was that "you are not welcome here" and "go home to your country." These were punctuated with different derogatory slurs. I was fortunate enough to have the financial means to find attorneys to help with the visa process so I could legally stay in this country and become a US citizen. Some of these traumatic experiences also played out when I provided spiritual care as a chaplain in hospital or hospice settings. For example, when I visited patients, they would frequently ask, "Where are you from?" After a short explanation, I would brace for the next question: "You are a woman chaplain?" followed by the statement, "I didn't know a woman could be a chaplain." I wondered how many white male chaplains were asked similar questions. The painfulness of these repeated encounters of "othering" are deeply woven into frequent experiences—not only for myself but also for my AAPI and BIPOC (Black, Indigenous, people of color) community members.

The voices of Black Lives Matter uncovering the underlying racism in our country have given me words to more clearly articulate the disparities I witness in healthcare and the healthcare workplace. Embedded in these institutions are various forms of racism that present as micro-aggression and micro-invalidation. I am aware of needing to examine my words and actions in relationships with my team of spiritual care providers, staff, and patients.

I am still learning how to live out my life at the intersectionality of being a woman, an Asian, a tricultural immigrant, a Baptist, and queer. These multiple communities across my life have informed and shaped me—with each of them and all of them being a blessing to who I am.

Spiritual practices of prayer, breathing, and meditation have been a vital part of my spiritual life, inviting me to awe, curiosity, and wonder. In summary, my calling to the work of ministry has not been a straight path but an invitation to trust the spirit within myself. I wonder if "calling" is better understood not so much as "following" or being "led" but as being presented with a path to author one's life by listening deeply to the yearnings and openings within one's spirit, surrounded and supported by a chosen community.

Mica Togami has served as a hospital chaplain for over twenty-five years. As a certified educator with the Association of Clinical Pastoral Education (ACPE), she has trained chaplains across a wide variety of settings in Georgia, Kentucky, Hawaii, and California. Mica graduated with a master of divinity degree from the Southern Baptist Theological Seminary and was ordained in 1996 at Jeff Street Baptist Community at Liberty in Louisville, Kentucky. She was born and raised in Brazil as a "missionary kid." Her parents were the first missionaries sent by the Japan Baptist Convention to serve the Japanese community in Brazil. Because of their service, Mica lived in both Brazil and Japan during her formative years before coming to the United States. She has been endorsed by the Alliance of Baptists since 2004. Mica currently serves on the board for the Alliance of Baptists. She identifies herself as queer, first-generation Japanese/Brazilian American immigrant, and citizen of the world.

The Fourteenth Story

Awakening to My Call

Rev. Dr. Jann Aldredge-Clanton

Both my parents were preachers, but only one was ordained. I grew up in a small town in Louisiana in the 1950s and '60s. It was a time in the South when water fountains were labeled "white" and "colored," and LGBTQIA+ people were invisible. My father almost lost his job as pastor of First Baptist Church, Minden, Louisiana, because of his stand for integration during the civil rights movement. He did lose his position on the board of Midwestern Baptist Theological Seminary because of his support for the academic freedom of a professor who wrote a book on a symbolic interpretation of Genesis. My mother always served as a minister, but she was never ordained or paid. Her dynamic speaking ability and exceptional leadership skills made her every bit as qualified to pastor a church as my father was. She was always taking care of the underdog, never realizing that she was one. Growing up, I never saw a woman in the pulpit, except a missionary to Nigeria. And what she did was called "speak," not "preach."

When I was teaching English at Dallas Baptist University, I read *All We're Meant to Be: A Biblical Approach to Women's Liberation*, by Letha Dawson Scanzoni and Nancy A. Hardesty. This book changed my life. Although I had claimed my professional vocation, I had never questioned biblical interpretations that prescribed the subordination of women at home and at church. Not until I read this book did I discover that anything could or should be any different.

Betty Friedan's *The Feminine Mystique* had come out more than ten years before, but I'd never heard of the book or raised any questions about women's traditional roles. As I read *All We're Meant to Be*, I found more than enough biblical support for gender equality. In my evangelical church tradition, the call to gender justice could reach me only through the Bible. Recently co-authoring *Building Bridges: Letha Dawson Scanzoni and Friends* with my friend Dr. Kendra Weddle, a religion professor at Texas Wesleyan University, I recalled how the copious scriptural evidence and clear theological reasoning in *All We're Meant to Be* transformed my life with new revelations of the rightness of gender equality.

Several years later, I witnessed these revelations becoming flesh. When I was thirty-one, Dr. Raynal Barber, my friend and colleague in the English department at Dallas Baptist University, and I went to a worship service at Cliff Temple Baptist Church in Dallas. Martha Gilmore was being ordained, one of the first women in the South to be ordained by a Baptist church. We heard a sermon from Ephesians 2 on breaking down walls of prejudice that divide people, applying this text to breaking down centuries-old barriers keeping women out of ministerial leadership. Then, for the first time in my life, I saw a woman kneeling before the church as a long line of people—women as well as men—passed by to lay hands of blessing upon her. Before this night I had seen only men ordaining only men. The message I internalized was that this was a male ritual from which women were forever excluded. Now something new was happening. A woman was receiving the sacred blessing. From somewhere deep within my soul, I felt the rightness of it. The service ended, and people started leaving the sanctuary to go to the reception in the church parlor. I sat transfixed, not wanting to leave this holy place. Raynal turned to me and said, "Jann, one day we'll be going to your ordination. I see the way you relate to students, as a minister as well as a teacher." I gave her a shocked look and replied, "Oh, no! I'll research, write, persuade, give chapter and verse to support the ordination of women, but I wouldn't want all the criticism and struggle Martha has gone through." I just wanted to do all I could to support women's ordination; I didn't want to be ordained. But the prophetic word could not be unspoken. Holy Wisdom continued to call my name.

Eight years later, Raynal stood at my ordination service at Seventh and James Baptist Church in Waco, Texas, to read these words of the prophet Habakkuk: "Write the vision; make it plain on tablets, so that a runner may read it. For there is still a vision for the appointed time.... If it seems to tarry, wait for it; it will surely come" (2:2-3, NRSV).

Rev. Martha Gilmore preached the ordination sermon, proclaiming that I was "the vision made flesh, the vision that God indeed calls women to ordained ministry." Martha declared that I had also become "a statement, a promise for many women and men and a hope for many women who may be frightened to hear God's call." It helped to hear her bless me as a "statement" because that word had been used negatively in reference to me and other women who had chosen nontraditional paths. People had tried to dismiss me by saying, "Oh, you're just trying to make a statement." I realized that we were at a time in history when statements about the worth of women needed to be made. And these statements need to be made today as much as ever.

One of the hymns we sang at my ordination was "In Unity We Lift Our Song," written by Ken Medema to the tune of "A Mighty Fortress." The third stanza begins, "For God our way, our bread, our rest, of all these gifts the Giver; our strength, our guide, our nurturing breast, whose hand will yet deliver." As I sang "our nurturing breast," I thrilled to the power of female divine imagery. I had picked this hymn because I was just beginning to awaken to the importance of female divine names and images in worship.

On the night of my ordination, I knelt at the front of the sanctuary as hundreds of people from many faith traditions came by with words and hands of blessing. My father had died fifteen years earlier, but that night I felt a strong sense of his presence and blessing. My mother, sister Anne, spouse David, and sons Chad and Brett were there to affirm and bless me. Baptist ordinations traditionally include only ordained Baptist pastors and deacons, usually all men, in this ritual of laying on hands. David, an ordained Baptist deacon, was in this group. But I also wanted this ritual to symbolize the inclusiveness I strongly believed in. I definitely wanted my mother, sister, and children, all ministers though not ordained, to be included. And I wanted to include members from St. John's United Methodist Church, where I was serving as associate pastor. When no Baptist church would call me after I graduated from Southwestern Baptist Theological Seminary and the seminary's placement office would not help, the gracious people of St. John's had welcomed and affirmed me as a minister with a special appointment to a Methodist church. They did this without asking me to give up my Baptist tradition. One of the members remarked, "It doesn't matter that you're a Baptist because labels don't matter anyway." So I invited people of all genders, races, ages, and faith traditions—all who wished to come forward to lay on hands of blessing. Powerful feelings washed over my spirit like waves along the seashore. Tears of joy and gratitude mixed with tears of sadness over the hundreds of years that women were denied this sacred blessing. At the same time, waves of hope washed my soul, filling me with courage to live the vision.

In the years since, I've discovered that it's easier to see the vision than to live it. Time and time again, I've faced the challenge of breaking free from cultural traditions that limit women and all people. Living into my call and becoming all I'm created to be in the divine image is a continual challenge. Religious and cultural traditions are constantly trying to stifle our gifts and our voices, to put us back into boxes from which we've broken free. External and internal forces are formidable.

The more I tried to live my call to pastoral ministry and my call to write in support of women in ministry, the more I realized that the resistance to ordination of women is just part of a larger patriarchal culture that gives greatest value to white, heterosexual, able-bodied, financially privileged males. People other than these males are considered "other" and are marginalized and oppressed. One of the arguments I heard against ordination of women was, "If we start ordaining women, the next thing you know we'll be ordaining gays!"

I must confess that at the time I tried to argue that the two issues were separate. But Sophia Wisdom kept expanding my vision so that

I could respond, "Yes, that's the point! The ordained ministry should be open to all." I was realizing that the ordination issue is just the tip of the patriarchal iceberg. At the foundation of our patriarchal culture is an image of a male God, sanctioning patterns of dominance and submission. More and more I was understanding that the strongest support imaginable for the dominance of men is the worship of an exclusively masculine Supreme Being. So my call expanded to writing, preaching, and teaching on the inclusion of female names and images of Deity.

The importance of the Female Divine had come as a personal revelation of great power and freedom as I was finishing seminary and experiencing exclusion from ministry opportunities because of my gender. Driving home one evening, I prayed "Our Mother" for the first time. I trembled. Would I be struck by lightning? Instead, a deep sense of affirmation began to flow through me. Praying to the Divine Mother helped me feel that She was on my side and just as incensed over discrimination against women as I was. Then I began to sing one of my favorite hymns. But instead of "He leadeth me," I sang, "She leadeth me," beginning softly and timidly but then gaining strength: "She leadeth me! O blessed thought! O words with heavenly comfort fraught! What'er I do, where'er I be, still 'tis God's hand that leadeth me. She leadeth me, She leadeth me, by Her own hand She leadeth me: Her faithful follower I would be for by Her hand She leadeth me." Later I would write new words to this hymn tune: "She walks beside us all the way; She walks beside us every day. Her faithful partners we will be, for by Her grace She sets us free."

When my first book, *In Whose Image? God and Gender*, came out, I was a chaplain at Hillcrest Baptist Medical Center in Waco, Texas. *Waco Tribune-Herald* reporter Doug Wong interviewed me about the book. In my unquenchable idealism, I believed people would be convinced of the truth of my words in the book and turn from their patriarchal ways. The picture in the newspaper accompanying Doug's article shows me holding up the book close to my beaming face, as if to say, "Love me and my book! We'll change your life for the better." Many people probably thought I looked too congenial to be espousing any radical ideas. Others who read the book understood the revolutionary implications of including female names and images of the Divine. Several people called the director of the Hillcrest Pastoral Care Department with complaints about me. What worried me more than any complaint about my theology was an inaccurate quote in the newspaper, attributing a masculine reference to Deity to me. I had stopped referring to the Divine as "He" five or six years before, and I certainly wouldn't have used this masculine reference when talking about my book that advocated gender-inclusive language. How could Doug Wong have missed my point? My grandiose, naive notions about my book's changing the world began to meet the reality of millennia of worship of a male God. Doug thought he heard me call God "He" because that's all he'd ever heard.

It discouraged me to hear friends, family, and Bible study groups of many denominations who had studied the book—even those who said they loved it—continue to call God "He." A Sunday school class that enthusiastically responded to my teaching the book and who prided themselves on their open-mindedness and liberal ideas became the staunchest opponents of inclusive language in their worship services. In another class where I'd taught the book for six weeks, a man asked, "You don't mean we need to change our worship language, do you?" They wanted to learn about inclusive theology at 10 a.m. but not practice it at the high holy hour of 11 a.m. on Sunday morning. My mother, who in her own way was supportive of my writing, told me that when she prayed "Our Mother," she didn't feel she was giving God as much respect. Her comment made me sad because it also said something about the value she gave herself.

Soon I discovered that theological reasoning could go only so far, that the resistance to change came from deeply ingrained emotions. I realized the need to go beyond biblical and theological explanation to ritual experience, to engage the imagination as well as the intellect, in order to bring change. I remembered the prominent place given to hymn singing in the Baptist church where I grew up and how much I loved singing hymns. So I began writing inclusive lyrics to familiar hymn tunes with the hope that they would be incorporated into worship services and contribute to an expansive theology and an ethic of equality and justice.

When we moved to Dallas for my new job at Baylor University Medical Center, I learned anew the power of naming. A new name went with me to my new job. I had been going by Jann Clanton and then Jann Aldredge Clanton, but "Aldredge" kept getting dropped. Wanting to reclaim my identity, I decided to hyphenate my last name. Now I was "Jann Aldredge-Clanton." I insisted that this name be inscribed on my chaplain's badge, in spite of many objections. The department secretary complained that my name was too long to fit on the badge, as well as on department schedules. Some of my colleagues objected that "Chaplain Aldredge-Clanton" was too cumbersome to be used around the hospital. Also, they worried that this hyphenated name might be construed as making a feminist statement and would get them, and me, in trouble. The zealous opposition to the hyphen in my last name, like that to calling God "She," convinced me of its importance. I recalled responses I'd gotten to requests I'd made to balance male and female references to Deity: "You're making such a big deal over a few words. The Creator of the universe can't be limited; *He's* above male or female." When I agreed and said that there should then be no more problem referring to God as "She" than as "He," I got strong negative reactions. No better proof could be found for the bias against the feminine and the need to overcome it by calling God "She." The hyphen in my last name also carried power, more than I at first realized—power to confront traditional discrimination against women. My colleagues were right. It was a feminist statement, and I was proud of it.

Years before, a woman at an English teachers' conference asked me when I introduced myself, "Is that your husband's name or your father's?" I stared at her as she laughed and said, "I didn't take my husband's name because I reject that symbolism. But then I realized I still had my dad's name. How can we ever get away from being owned by men?" One of my friends had tried to escape by changing from her husband's back to her father's name and then to her mother's maiden name. Now she has her grandfather's name. As I was getting used to my new name, Jann Aldredge-Clanton, which I had to admit was a mouthful, I recognized the irony. In trying to reassert my own identity, I now had the names of both my father and my husband. But somehow, at least in my mind, the hyphen made the name my own.

Along with other biblical female names and images of the Divine, I had been researching and writing on Wisdom (*Hokmah* in Hebrew Scriptures and *Sophia* in Christian Scriptures) and Her biblical and historical connections with Christ. My exploration of these connections led to the publication of *In Search of the Christ-Sophia: An Inclusive Christology for Liberating Christians*. A year later, *Praying with Christ-Sophia: Services for Healing and Renewal* came out, providing hymns and other worship resources that make the vital application to ritual experience. One of my first hymns is "Celebrate a New Day Dawning" to the tune of "Hymn to Joy":

> Celebrate a new day dawning, sunrise of a golden morn;
> Christ-Sophia dwells among us, glorious visions now are born.
> Equal partners round the table, we make dreams reality;
> calling out our gifts, we nurture hope beyond all we can see.
>
> Christ-Sophia lights the pathway to a world of harmony;
> Sister-Brother Love surrounds us, nourishing our synergy.
> Earth joins in our rich communion, grateful for our healing care;
> leaping deer and soaring eagles, all Earth's fullness now can share.
>
> Sing a song of jubilation, dance with joyous revelry;
> clapping trees and laughing rivers join our call to liberty.
> Free at last to blossom fully, flowering forth in beauty bright,
> we become a new creation, bursting open into light.[1]

Finding a church that included "Christ-Sophia" or any biblical female divine images in worship services was even more impossible than finding an integrated church in Minden, Louisiana, when I was growing up. When we were in Waco, I joined a small group to create a worship community committed to gender and racial inclusiveness. To make our mission clear, we began by calling ourselves the "Alternative Worship Community: intentionally integrated,

---

1. Words © 1996 Jann Aldredge-Clanton, tune HYMN TO JOY.

deliberately inclusive in language, and open to all people." Soon we dropped this unwieldy title and became simply the "Inclusive Worship Community."

When our family moved, we joined one of the few Baptist churches in Dallas that ordained women. David and I agreed that we couldn't, with integrity, consider a church that still refused to ordain women. But I was dismayed to find that this progressive Baptist church still had mostly men leading the services and all the language for Deity was "Father," "Master," "King," "He," "Him," "His." About a month after we joined this church, Jo Ferguson ran up to me exclaiming, "I'm so glad you're here! I hope you'll start and lead an inclusive worship group in this church." I hesitated, telling her I was reluctant because of the controversy inclusive language had stirred in Waco and because I wanted to be low profile in the Dallas church. Because of Jo's persuasive power, I finally said I would be part of the group but not the leader because I felt strongly about shared leadership.

In 1995, I helped create a worship community called New Wineskins from the metaphor in Matthew 9:17, describing our search for new language and symbols to proclaim the good news of liberation and *shalom*. From the beginning we included female names and images of the Divine. We were at first welcomed to meet in a liberal Baptist church, but opposition soon mounted against us. We were criticized for everything from singing too loudly to heresy. The voices of opposition grew louder when one woman brought in a two-foot-tall Mary statue that she had transformed into Christ-Sophia. They also objected to our singing hymns that included female divine images. I was understanding more fully than ever the power of female divine names and images in worship—power to split the church, according to some members. To quell the controversy, church leaders decided that New Wineskins could continue meeting only if we dropped the use of references to the Female Divine in litanies and hymns and removed visual symbols of Her. We could not meet these conditions, which were our reason for being, so we found another place to meet and then another and another. Some churches of other denominations welcomed us and then asked us to leave because of conflict stirred by our theology. We have had to move fourteen times. We have renewed our commitment to our mission continually, believing we are planting seeds of change everywhere we go.

In April 2001, I preached at the Alliance of Baptists Annual Convocation. My sermon, titled "A Still More Excellent Way in Worship," emphasized ways in which including female divine imagery contributes to justice and peace. That evening the congregation also sang two of the inclusive hymns I'd written to familiar hymn tunes. I was surprised and delighted by the positive responses I got to my hymns and my sermon. Hope rose in my heart that people were becoming more open to changing worship language. Would these people go back to their churches and include biblical female names and images of the Divine in their worship? Or would nothing change, just as so many times in the past when I had preached and taught inclusive theology, received enthusiastic responses, and seen little or no change?

Several months after the Alliance of Baptists Convocation, I received an email from someone I didn't know: Larry E. Schultz. He had been at the convocation, but we hadn't met. Larry wrote that he was minister of music at Pullen Memorial Baptist Church in Raleigh, North Carolina, and that he'd like permission for Pullen to use my hymns that were sung at the convocation. I gave permission, excited that this Baptist church would be singing my hymns. A little while later came another email from Larry, telling me that he was also a composer and asking if he could create new music for the two hymns sung at the convocation. Also, he asked if I had any texts without music that I might want to send him. Until then, I'd been writing words to traditional hymn tunes, with one exception. I had recently written a hymn text trying to express the theodicy questions I had asked and had heard others voice in my ministry as a chaplain. Can the Creator be both benevolent and powerful with so much suffering and evil in the world? The lyrics came to me in the form of a child's questions.

On the morning of September 11, 2001, Larry opened my email in which I'd sent the hymn text, "Are You Good and Are You Strong?"

He later told me of the cathartic experience it was for him, after the horrors of 9/11, to take these words and compose a children's anthem and a hymn tune.² Larry and I have continued to collaborate on inclusive hymnbooks and anthems. Also, because we believe in the importance of instilling in everyone from the earliest ages the belief that we are all created equally in the divine image, we collaborated on an inclusive song and activity book for preschool children and an inclusive musical for older children.³

The Alliance of Baptists led to another rewarding collaboration. In 2012, Rev. Sheila Sholes-Ross, experiencing the lack of opportunities for clergywomen, especially clergywomen of color, initiated Equity for Women in the Church as one of the communities in the Alliance. The next year she invited me to co-chair with her this community. At first, I told Sheila that I'd like to be a member of the community, not co-chair. But Sheila persuaded me of the importance of a Black woman and a white woman sharing leadership to model racial equality. I recalled that many years earlier in Waco, I had attempted to start a church with a Black man as co-pastor. As our conversations progressed, I noticed that he kept saying he would be glad for me to assist him in various ministries, and I soon realized that he could envision me as his assistant pastor but not as co-pastor.

In Equity for Women in the Church, my vision of co-pastoring with a Black minister has become a reality. Sheila and I co-pastor/co-chair this community that, in 2014, became incorporated as an ecumenical organization with the mission of facilitating equal representation of clergywomen as pastors of intercultural churches and of

---

2. "Are You Good and Are You Strong? (Questions for a Loving God)," composed by Larry E. Schultz; words by Jann Aldredge-Clanton (based on Pss 23, 25, 27, 90, 103, 130; Lam 3:17-26; Wis 9:13-18; Rom 8:14-23; Rom 8:37-39; 2 Cor 4:14-5:1; Rev 21:1-7), Alfred Church Choral Series, Jubilate Music Group, sheetmusicplus.com/title/are-you-good-and-are-you-strong. "Are You Good and Are You Strong?" seeks to express theodicy struggles as it presents honest questions asked by children to God during times of grief. The theodicy questions conclude with the hopeful prayers that God would "keep us safely from all harm, and rock us gently in Your arms."

3. *God, A Word for Girls and Boys Coloring Book*, jannaldredgeclanton.com/books/; *Imagine God! A Children's Musical Exploring and Expressing Images of God*, music by Larry E. Schultz, words by Jann Aldredge-Clanton, choristersguild.org/store/cgk24-imagine-god-preview-kit-includes-score-and-demo-cd/2414/.

dismantling patriarchal and white supremacist church practices and structures so that clergywomen can thrive in pastoral positions.

Through educational programs and publications, Equity for Women in the Church teaches gender and racial equality based on the foundational belief that all people are created equally in the divine image (Gen 1:27). Equity for Women in the Church seeks to model an egalitarian leadership structure, with diverse co-chairs and board members sharing decision-making power. Rev. Dr. Alfie Wines, one of our board members, initiated a book, *I Wish Someone Had Told Me: Equity for Women in the Church*, published in 2020. She collected and edited stories by board members and other authors of various races, genders, ages, denominations, and occupations—powerful voices calling for the transformation of church and society to create equity for clergywomen and all people.

In 2018, I started attending The Gathering, A Womanist Church, in order to explore ways Equity for Women in the Church and New Wineskins Community could collaborate with The Gathering. All three have a mission of pursuing racial and LGBTQIA+ equality and dismantling what The Gathering calls "PMS" (patriarchy, misogyny, and sexism). Sophia Wisdom had much more in store for me at The Gathering. What I had not realized was how much I needed The Gathering for my own spiritual healing, empowerment, and growth. I had long advocated for men to experience feminism and female divine names and images not only to contribute to gender equality and justice but also for their own healing from sexist, patriarchal culture and for deepening their spiritual experience. Now I knew how much *I* needed womanism and the centering of Black women's experience for my healing from my racist, white supremacist culture and for deepening my spirituality.

Soon I became a ministry partner of The Gathering. Instead of members, this church has "ministry partners," designating our participation in fulfilling the prophetic mission of the church. As ministry partners, we use our gifts, our voices, our networks, and our platforms in working together toward our liberating, transformative vision of justice and wholeness for all people. The co-pastors, Rev. Dr. Irie Lynne Session and Rev. Kamilah Hall Sharp, invited me to write litanies for worship services. Believing in the power of liturgical experience to bring change, I was delighted to have this opportunity to use my gifts. Also, it was a joy to use my research and writing gifts to co-author with the co-pastors a book: *The Gathering, A Womanist Church: Origins, Stories, Sermons, and Litanies.*

Although it may seem that the struggle is over for women called to ministry, finding churches to use all our gifts continues to be difficult. It's still important to be open to unexpected opportunities. I never expected a Methodist church to call a Baptist minister. The first sermon I preached at St. John's United Methodist Church was titled "God of the Unexpected." Women today who are exploring a call to ministry will find fulfillment in the "unexpected."

Our reality continues: clergywomen often must combine several jobs to make a full-time salary. St. John's, a declining inner-city church, could not pay me even the modest salary I had been making at Dallas Baptist University, so I also worked part-time as a pastoral counselor at Samaritan Counseling Center and as executive director of the Waco Conference of Christians and Jews (now the Greater Waco Interfaith Conference) to make a full-time salary. Women today who are sensing a call to ministry might find themselves considering combining a variety of ministry positions or becoming "tentmakers," a term Baptists have used for ministers who receive little or no pay for church work and so perform other jobs to support themselves financially.

Women called to ministry today will create their own faith communities or revive dying churches. One of the envisioned projects of Equity for Women in the Church is to provide financial support to clergywomen who create new and renewed multicultural, welcoming, and affirming churches who practice inclusivity in language, gender, and race. Shirley Chisholm coined the saying, "If they don't give you a seat at the table, bring a folding chair." Rev. Dr. Irie Lynn Session, one of the founders of The Gathering, A Womanist Church, modified the saying: "If they don't give you a seat at the table, make your own table." This is one of the messages I would offer to the women who come after me: listen to your soul, hear clearly that God has named you "beloved daughter," follow the path you choose with courage and persistence, and "make your own table" if you have to. For me, making my own table meant finding a church willing to include biblical female names and images of the Divine. When finding such a church seemed impossible, we created New Wineskins Community.

Women called to ministry may choose to accept a call to a struggling or dying church and lead the congregation in working to revive the church. For example, Rev. Stacy Boorn revitalized Ebenezer Lutheran Church in San Francisco, California, with a new mission: "to embody and voice the prophetic wisdom and word of the Divine Feminine, to uplift the values of compassion, creativity, and care for the earth and one another." The congregation put a large banner across the outside of the church with these words: "God loves all Her children." Soon the church became known as Ebenezer/herchurch Lutheran, and today it is a growing, thriving, creative, and inclusive church.

At an International Peacemakers Conference in Dallas, I gave a presentation on expanding divine images to include the Female Divine. Excitement filled the room as everyone participated in a ritual for healing, ending with singing my hymn "We Sound a Call to Freedom." A woman from South Africa gave us a beat with her hand against the back of a folding metal chair as we danced around in a circle singing the hymn's refrain: "Free at last, O Hallelujah! Free at Last, O Hallelujah! Christ-Sophia, you have freed us! Your truth has set us free."

The conference ended with the Women of the Cloth ceremony, which included blessings from women of various faith traditions, arranged in a semicircle on the platform in the sanctuary of the magnificent Cathedral Guadalupe in downtown Dallas. We stood in front of a high altar over which hung an eighteen-foot tapestry of Our Lady of Guadalupe. Our group included a Jewish rabbi, a Buddhist spiritual leader, an Islamic holy woman, a Christian Scientist practitioner, a former Catholic nun now ordained as a nondenominational minister, a still-practicing nun, a Unity pastor, an Episcopal priest, a United Methodist minister, and me.

The organizer of the Women of the Cloth ceremony had asked me to give the closing blessing. When it came time for my benediction, I stepped up to the mic and began: "Hear the voice of Sophia Wisdom Who Dwells within Us All, 'I am the breath of life. I am the healing power. I am Freedom and Wisdom and Peace. I am a Fountain of blessings flowing freely through all creation. There is life in my words and healing in my touch.'"

From some deep well, my voice rose, surprising me with its boldness. I felt free and powerful and totally unafraid as I invited the congregation to "listen to Her voice and feel Her touch." My voice continued to swell as I quoted lines from one of my hymns: "Long we've needed Her embrace, glory and power of Her grace." My arms stretched out in a circular gesture toward all the women around me on the platform as I continued, "Now we gather up Her blessings as we celebrate Her many names: *Ruah*, Creative Spirit, *Sophia*, *Hokmah*, Wisdom, Birth-Giver, Divine Midwife, Black Madonna, Mother Eagle, Mother Hen, Comforting Mother, Our Lady of Guadalupe, *Shekhinah*, Sister, Friend, Divine Healer, and so many more." I reached up toward the eighteen-foot Our Lady of Guadalupe, then out toward the Women of the Cloth and all the people in the congregation as I exclaimed, "Look, look, for She is here! Her wisdom words have long been near. Now, now, behold Her grace, divinity in Her image." Everyone rose and clapped and shouted, "Amen!"

The International Peacemakers Conference brought threads of my life together to reveal a design as clear as that on the tapestry in the Cathedral Guadalupe. My interfaith thread shone through as I stood at the altar of a Catholic cathedral, surrounded by spiritual leaders from many faith traditions. My Baptist roots came forth in my proclamation of freedom. I felt linked to those Baptist founders who preached religious liberty into our Constitution. My Baptist heritage had also given me the model of dynamic preaching. Some of my friends from other traditions seemed surprised to hear my emboldened Baptist preaching voice, and my feminism released my voice to its greatest freedom. Not until I'd experienced the Female Divine could I claim my full power as one created in the divine image. That day, awakened again to my call, I felt Her voice rise up through mine to fill that large cathedral. And I felt the ecstasy.

Jann Aldredge-Clanton is a feminist theologian and minister who serves as co-chair of Equity for Women in the Church, adjunct professor at Richland College, co-pastor of New Wineskins Community in Dallas, Texas, and ministry partner of The Gathering, A Womanist Church. She is an Alliance of Baptists ordained minister and an award-winning hymn text writer. She writes books and a blog on gender equality, inclusive theology, and inclusive worship. Among her book publications are *In Whose Image? God and Gender*; *Changing Church: Stories of Liberating Ministers*; *In Search of the Christ-Sophia: An Inclusive Christology for Liberating Christians*; *Seeking Wisdom: Inclusive Blessings and Prayers for Public Occasions*; *Inclusive Songs for Liberating Christians*; and *Inclusive Songs for Resistance & Social Action*.

The Fifteenth Story

Magic and Mystery

Rev. LeAnn Gunter Johns

Do not miss the magic and mystery of your current service in search of your calling. Your vocation is not tied to your title; your vocation is who you are when you are with us.

My friend and mentor, Rev. Dr. Dock Hollingsworth, spoke these words at my ordination in October 2003. I was still in seminary and working as a part-time minister at Peachtree Baptist Church. I remember being so overwhelmed and confused by the day, by who showed up to support me and why. People from all walks of my life came that Sunday afternoon—friends and professors from seminary who had only known me for a year, friends who had known me during my high school and college years, members of my family, friends from the community who had no connection to a church. They showed up that afternoon to be a part of this holy and beautiful service cultivated by a congregation that had only known me for a short time, yet recognized something in me that I could not quite see in myself. I had not approached this congregation to ask for their blessing of ordination. My colleagues in ministry and lay leaders in the church first approached me. They wanted to be a part of this service that was designed to acknowledge God's calling upon my life, pray with me, and grant me a title of "reverend."

That Sunday in October felt more like a dream than any part of my journey I could have written or edited myself. And yet, evidenced by the sun dreamily reflecting off the stained-glass windows on those lined up in the center aisle waiting to place their hands upon me, bless me, and pray for me, it was real. It felt like a long journey from where my story began, but it was only the first of many beautiful road marks of God's continued calling upon my life.

I grew up in Panama City, Florida. For as long as I can remember, my parents served the church in various roles. My father was a deacon, adult Sunday school teacher, and committee member. My mother loved her role as youth Sunday school teacher and avid volunteer. My sister and I grew up familiar with the halls of our churches, the classrooms being an extension of the playgrounds, with their chalkboards and books to occupy our time as we waited on our parents to finish their meetings. My parents gave my sister and me two significant gifts. One was the desire to always connect to a church family.

First Baptist Church of Panama City was the first church that felt like a place of connection for me. No one could ever claim that I was the perfect, well-behaved child in corporate worship. However, it was in the small group missions study of GAs that I felt most connected. I spent my formative years learning about women and men who had heard God's call upon their lives and were serving all around the world, sharing God's love. My GA leaders were my first ministers who shepherded me around our city to do hands-on work in the places of greatest need. As a young child, I began hearing a refrain that seeps down into my bones: "You can do anything God calls you to do."

My family changed our church membership to Hiland Park Baptist Church, where my involvement in the youth group was as significant as my involvement in children's activities had been. My early missions opportunities were embedded in me now, and I wanted to continue to find places of service. During the summers of my high school years, I joined the camp staff of Florida GA/Acteens camp as a camp counselor. At camp, I got to relive those earliest memories of my childhood mission experiences. I wanted to make it real for the girls and teens who were spending their week with us. For a week, we transported them to different cultures and traditions, sharing how God's love was transforming lives. We helped them overcome fears and experience success through challenging ropes courses, all led and supervised by our entire female staff. Whether I was teaching the story of Dr. Rebekah Naylor, who stayed in India to perform life-saving surgeries when others called her home due to safety reasons, or securing the harness for a young camper, I was beginning to believe for myself, "You can do anything God calls you to do."

The other gift my family gave my sister and me is the belief that there is always enough room. It was common for friends to join us for dinner. Sometimes it was one of the youth whom my mom taught through church. When we heard the doorbell ring, one of us went to answer it while the other grabbed an extra plate. One of my mom's "kids" was a young teenage girl named Suzanah Raffield. She was in my mom's Sunday school class and was our favorite to have hanging around the house. She took me and my sister shopping and was our favorite babysitter. As she grew older, I overheard the conversations she had with my parents—conversations around vocation and calling. My parents disagreed with her on the role of women in the church. It was no surprise to us when she decided to go to seminary. From my hiding place, I cheered her on, all the while listening closely to my parents' response. They were loving but struggled to understand why she felt God calling her to these next steps in ministry.

Suzanah was a cheerleader for me, too. When I was old enough, she was the one passing me the camp staff applications. In the summer of 1996, I shared with my coworkers and friends that, like many of the missionaries whose stories we had studied, I was experiencing God's call to service. My understanding of the call at this time was to serve in missions somewhere in our world—not surprising since all I had ever known or seen of women in ministry involved being a missionary.

I think clarifying this call to missions at the age of seventeen influenced my decision to major in Elementary Education. I had always loved working with children and assumed that an education degree would be helpful in many of the missional environments I might one day serve. I wanted to follow the path of friends and attend a Baptist college or university, but my family's finances didn't allow me to do that. I attended our local community college for a year and a half before transferring to the University of West Florida.

While in college, I had the opportunity to serve both in my home church with children and youth and at summer camps in Georgia.

Camp Pinnacle was the perfect setting for the GA[1] and Acteens[2] camp in Georgia. I fell in love with my surroundings the moment I drove onto the property. For three summers, the lake and mountains heard my cries, laughter, and prayers about my future. I witnessed girls learning new skills and hearing stories about God's love for all people. It was at Camp Pinnacle that I got to meet Sarah Jackson Shelton, my first female pastor. I lingered around the lunch table to ask her questions about her story and her work. After lights-out check each night, I found myself rocking on the back porch still asking myself, "Why can't women be pastors?"

Suzanah asked me if I had considered seminary. The thought had never crossed my mind. The only people I had known to go to seminary from my church were men. They had all gone to the closest Southern Baptist seminary in proximity—New Orleans Baptist Theological Seminary. The idea of more education seemed impossible. My family had barely made it through my four years of college without major debt. How could I think of further costs? What does it mean to get a theological education, and would I need it? How could I use it?

All of these questions circled in my mind as Suzanah had a friend, Cindy Clark, come and talk to a group of us about McAfee School of Theology. I heard about a place where gender didn't limit the types of classes a person could take. I learned that women could even take preaching classes at McAfee (not necessary for me because I had no plans to preach—*wink*). Every step towards entrance into McAfee went smoothly. Difficult conversations happened along the way. It was difficult to explain to my parents, neither of whom was able to

---

1. Southern Baptist Convention, Girls in Action (GA). This program of the SBC Woman's Missionary Union (WMU) was designed to teach girls about missionaries and doing missions both locally and globally. See "Girls in Action (GA)," *WMU*, wmu.com/missions-discipleship/children/.

2. Southern Baptist Convention, Acteens. This program of the SBC Woman's Missionary Union (WMU) was designed for older girls to have missions experiences that would lay a foundation for coming to faith in Christ as Savior and make missions an important part of their daily lives. See "Acteens," *WMU*, wmu.com/missions-discipleship/students/.

complete their four-year degree, why I would spend time and money getting a degree that would take me an additional three years. And how would I pay for it? There were conversations with my home pastor about why I was choosing a "liberal" seminary.

My first semester of seminary encompassed all things. There was joy at newly discovered classes. (I had no idea you could have an entire class in New Testament!) I was overwhelmed at learning new languages. (It's still all Greek to me!) I found friends who would become family to me. (When everything you thought you believed is stripped away, there is incredible vulnerability that creates lifelong bonds.) Many of these were expected surprises for someone entering a new phase of their educational journey in a new city. Unexpected struggles came at the same time. I believed God had been with me every step of the way on my journey into seminary. Yet, with many more options for ministry opened to me, I struggled with what my future would hold. Perhaps the hardest part of that time of my life was dealing with a broken heart. My friend and college sweetheart had decided that it was "God's will" to date someone else. As I struggled with the loss of this important relationship, the question circled my mind, "If I am pursuing God's will for my life in ministry, how is it possible that God's will for someone else is causing so much pain for me?"

Things in my head and heart got so complicated that I seriously considered taking a break from seminary. A wise mentor advised me against walking away. He reminded me that I was facing a renegotiation of life's toughest questions—How do I want to spend my life's work, and whom do I want to spend it with? Thankfully, I realized that the community I had built around me was strong enough to handle hearing my struggles and questions and holding my tears. Staying in seminary and digging deep with my questions was the right path for me. What I learned helped me learn how to sit with people in pain who have experienced the same wonderings and struggles.

Life in seminary continued to provide me with many lessons and chances to try out my new ministry gifts. "You can do anything God calls you to do" continued to be the refrain that popped up during this season in my life. At the insistence of professors, I preached my first sermon and continued preaching throughout my time there. I served as a chaplain intern at a children's hospital and found a love for sitting with people in the joys and pain of life. It was during seminary that I began serving as associate pastor at Peachtree Baptist Church.

What began as a part-time assistant minister role transitioned into my first full-time ministry position after I graduated from seminary. At Peachtree, I served with a supportive staff and lay leadership who encouraged the gifts of young ministers. I was regularly given opportunity to preach, teach Bible studies, and work with children. Our community of faith was a small, diverse group of believers. To many on the outside, it would have seemed like we were struggling. We had a large, historic building. We struggled to meet our budget because of our growing building needs. For those who were part of our community, it was a place where faith questions were welcomed, mission service was integral to our life together, and strangers became family.

They helped me recognize and affirm gifts within myself that I had not yet embraced. When they said they wanted to ordain me, it felt like another affirmation from God that this was the next right step. That October Sunday afternoon felt like a dream I had never allowed myself to believe would come true.

You can do anything God calls you to do. My ordination did not change anything about my job. We laughed that it would grant me access to pastoral visits at the local jail since that was the only place I had ever been denied. What it did is remind me that while God had called me into ministry, I was not going alone. I was surrounded by a crowd of witnesses who had blessed me on this journey, but they weren't abandoning me. They were cheering me on through their prayers, blessings, and presence in my life.

Their presence spurred me on in ministry but also personally. They reminded me that my heart was big enough to love again. When I began dating my now husband, Barry Johns, they cheered me on. There were times when I wished they were not so interested in who I spent my time with, but family is like that, having a hard time not expressing their opinions. They watched and supported us as we fell in love, got engaged, and were married in the same sanctuary where they had ordained me. They were so proud that I found someone who loved me and all of my gifts. He joined with them in being one of my biggest advocates.

They remained our faithful cheerleaders as we discerned a move to California to pursue a grand adventure. Barry was entering a medical fellowship at Stanford University. I was completing another ministry dream—completing the requirements for clinical pastoral education through the Veterans Hospital (VA) in Palo Alto, California. It was not only our chance to create new paths for ourselves professionally; it was also a chance to grow as newlyweds.

When I was applying for chaplaincy programs, I interviewed at three different programs. I was scared to work at the VA. I had never worked with veterans, and a lot of my ministry work had involved working with women. I prayed that God would give me wisdom about which program was the right one for me, but I made sure to declare how uncomfortable I would be working with veterans. God made my decision a lot easier when the only program I was accepted into was the one at the Veterans Hospital. Chaplaincy at this hospital has been one of the highlights of my ministry experience. Sitting with people who have given so much to our country in their toughest times in life were some of the most holy moments. Their love for our country and deep commitment to service made me more thankful for my own places of service as well. You can do anything God calls you to do.

When my residency program ended, I had the opportunity to fill a nine-month position as pastor for an American Baptist Church/ United Church of Christ in San Jose, California. New Community of Faith is an inclusive congregation made up of individuals identifying as gay, straight, and transgender. Some of our church members would drive two hours each Sunday because it was the only church where they felt welcome. For nine months, they taught me how to love unconditionally, create meaningful community, and value our differences. Barry and I announced the news of the anticipation of our first child and his first post-fellowship full-time work contract with this community of faith. They knew our time with them would be limited, but they celebrated these milestones with us.

Barry's work brought us to Macon, Georgia. I was halfway through my pregnancy with our first son, Parker, when we moved. My initial thought was, "Who wants to hire a pregnant minister?" I realize now that in many ways I was my own worst enemy, not believing there would be opportunities. Almost immediately, I received requests to preach for friends when they were out of their pulpits. I was also asked to lead retreats.

Those last few months of my pregnancy in a new town felt isolating and lonely. I was thankful for the work that came along when it did. My plan had been to look for engaging work after Parker was born. I am privileged that I did not have to work immediately, but I did desire to work. Parker's entrance into the world was easy, but that seemed to be the only easy part of motherhood for me. While struggling with breastfeeding, my newborn baby and I both developed an infection. Thankfully, he recovered quickly, but I did not. A few days later, my infection landed me back in the hospital while family cared for my newborn baby. When I returned home, I received IV antibiotics for a month. It was a hard, depressing time for me. I found myself wondering where God was in all of this chaos. Trying to recover, care for a newborn, get used to additional family members in the house helping—it was a difficult time. Thankfully, when Parker was two months old, I was able to come off medicine and our family went home. Over dinner one night, Barry asked if I was still going to meet my goal of looking for a new job. I knew I wasn't ready to find work yet. I needed more time being a mom to my newborn.

At the same time that I was adjusting to my role as a new mom, I was grieving the loss of serving the church through pastoral ministry. We joined a church when we first arrived in Macon, but I cried most Sundays when the loss felt powerful. It felt like I was having to choose between spending time with my child or seeking ministry opportunities. Somewhere the message that you can have both was lost. Thankfully, I continued to receive offers to preach for ministry colleagues, even completing a sabbatical interim for a friend.

Even with ministry opportunities popping up, I struggled with my identity. Since becoming a young adult, I had always had a ministry job and I had been good at ministry positions. However, my ego had me thinking that was the only way I could serve God—as a young, successful female minister. It was difficult to sort out, and sometimes I managed it better than I did at other times.

I still longed for a community similar to the one we had in California, a community of faith that welcomed and loved all people. When a colleague inquired if I would want to help start a new inclusive church in town, it felt like the right thing to do. You can do anything God calls you to do. My prayers felt like they were answered as opportunities kept popping up for us. Saint Clare Baptist Church became the name of our community of faith, one that would welcome all people. We shared life together as folks navigated through divorce, new love for others, and the announcement of another baby for the Johns family. They helped Parker, a young toddler, know how to anticipate and celebrate the joy of being a big brother.

While the community of Saint Clare didn't last together formally for long, they became a part of our lives. They came and snuggled Patrick when he was born. They remained a part of our lives even when the next part of their journey called them from Macon. As for me and my family, we ended up joining First Baptist Church of Christ (FBCX). Several people had reached out to us during our last days at Saint Clare to let us know we would be welcomed as a part of the FBCX community. They embraced us and gave us opportunities to serve almost immediately.

As my boys grew and needed me less, my desire to enter the workforce grew strong again. Late one night as I mindlessly scrolled through Facebook, I ran across an ad for a hospice chaplain at a local hospice company. The ad was placed by an old seminary friend with whom I had not yet reconnected in person since living in Macon. I sent her a message asking if they had room for a PRN chaplain. She immediately wrote back, "Yes! Want to meet for coffee tomorrow?" I panicked. What had I done? I had loved my chaplaincy residency, but hospice? I'm not sure I was the right person. You can do anything God calls you to do.

I'm so glad Tina Clark immediately wrote me back. I think I would have talked myself out of it otherwise. Instead, over coffee, we reminisced and laughed, and she told me about this calling of hospice chaplaincy. We took the next steps towards my employment, and before I knew it I was working with incredible colleagues who were passionate about helping people in their last moments on Earth.

As a hospice chaplain, I was able to sit with patients as they prepared for their final days, hear the sacred stories of their lives, and walk with their loved ones once they had passed away. Two events that we hosted were my favorite activities to be a part of—our children's grief camp for kids grieving some kind of loss and our Annual Memorial Service for families.

For nearly five years I served Hospice Care Options in this position. My duties grew beyond just chaplaincy into teaching and training colleagues. When the Covid-19 pandemic hit, there were fewer opportunities to see patients. I was also helping my own kids as they navigated the virtual learning setting for school. An opportunity was presented to me that I had not considered in over twenty years. I had the opportunity to return to the classroom and work with children who had learning struggles, advocating for them and assisting them in the general education classroom.

You can do anything God calls you to do. While this is not the calling or life in ministry that I would have dreamed of or written for myself, it is better in so many ways. I have more than twenty years of experience in ministry, organizational work, and work with children in a variety of settings to draw on. When I look at my students and colleagues, I see them as the gift that they are to our world—as children of God. I get to be a part of helping raise our next generation of leaders to do good things in the world.

There has been magic and mystery to following God's call upon my life. I remain grateful to family, friends, and colleagues who have cheered, loved, and supported me along the way. And most of all, I am grateful to the author and giver of this call and vocation who helped me believe in my ability, gifts, and growth. Thank you, God.

LeAnn Gunter Johns grew up in Panama City, Florida, and graduated from the University of West Florida. In 2001, she moved to Atlanta to attend McAfee School of Theology. Upon graduation from seminary in 2004, LeAnn transitioned into a full-time associate pastor position with Peachtree Baptist Church. While serving as associate pastor, she also served in a number of volunteer leadership roles, including Baptist Women in Ministry and McAfee School of Theology's Alumni Board. LeAnn completed a chaplain internship program with the Metro Atlanta Women's Prison. In 2007, she married Dr. Barry Johns, and a year later they moved to Mountain View, California, where she completed clinical pastoral education (CPE) through the Veterans Affairs Hospital in Palo Alto. Following CPE completion, she served as interim pastor for New Community of Faith (UCC/ABC affiliated church) in San Jose. She currently lives in Macon, Georgia, with her husband and is a proud mother of Parker and Patrick. She believes in the magic and mystery of God's calling that has led her to various jobs in ministry, from hospice chaplain to, most recently, special education teacher.

The Sixteenth Story

Grateful for Who I Am and What I Do

Pastora Ruth Eunice Rodríguez de Orantes

I was only nineteen years old, just out of high school, when I received my call to serve God and dedicate my life to pastoral ministry. I lived through many experiences throughout these years: victories and defeats, joys and sorrows, difficult times on this long journey. But here I am in my fifty-seventh year of life, grateful to God for who I am and what I do. Being happy is one of God's great gifts to me. Even in the most difficult days, I feel the kind of happiness that remains in my heart no matter what happens.

In 2020 and 2021, Covid-19 claimed the lives of so many people close to me, both church members and their extended families. I lost my "right hand" in the church and then my "left hand." We lost Brother Hugo Orellana, principal of our seminary and a faithful church member. He was a man of God, passionate about preaching, evangelization, and solidarity with the poor.

I lost a piece of my heart when Covid-19 took another faithful church member, Sarita Campos, who was barely thirty-five years old and six months pregnant. While she was in intensive care fighting to live, her baby was born. After spending many weeks in pediatric intensive care and experiencing many crises, Sarita's premature baby survived. When I attended the kindergarten graduation of Sarita's seven-year-old son, Santiago, I learned again that only the strength of

God sustains us in these moments. During Santiago's graduation, his kindergarten presentations offered a tribute to his mother, and I realized that I needed to cry for Sarita because she was like my daughter. Only the strength of God sustains me as a pastor.

In my almost twenty-two years serving as a pastor at Shekina Baptist Church in Santa Ana, El Salvador, I have developed many connections with the extended families of our church members. So I offer care for the people of my church *and* for their family members. Yes, I have been tired during Covid-19, but how deeply I love the people and love to be with them. In spite of our losses, I am a happy person.

Writing my story has caused me to think a lot about my call to ministry. I remember how surprised I was when I first thought I would go to the seminary. I came to the seminary when I was only twenty years old. I was young, and I honestly think I didn't understand what I was doing.

Since I was little, I have wanted to participate in everything the church was doing. I was different from my two brothers and one sister about church attendance. For some reason, I was the person in the family who was most connected with the church since we were little ones. My father took us to church every Sunday. I was so happy to be part of the church.

So, yes, I have thought many times about being so young when I decided to go to the Instituto Teológico Bautista de El Salvador, The Theological Baptist Institute of El Salvador. According to our law, at age twenty I had not yet become an adult. That would happen when I was twenty-one. I wondered if I was doing something wrong because my father at that time said to me, "No, no, no, you cannot go to the seminary."

When I was a little one, very young, I never expected to study at the seminary or be a pastor. My expectation was that I would be an accountant. That was my little girl dream, to be an accountant because I loved numbers. I also planned to work in a bank. My father worked with one of the richest families in El Salvador, a big family who owned many kilometers of land in a coffee plantation. They also owned a bank, and my dream was to work in that bank.

Even in high school, I believed my destination was that big bank. When I graduated from high school, I still had my focus on going to the university to study accounting. I have often thought about how I managed to go from banking and accounting to the seminary. I remember well how I made that decision. It was a beautiful time of my life. At ages eighteen and nineteen, my church was my life. In 1984, one of the young adults from the church set his sights on going to the mission field—the mission field in a nearby town about fifteen kilometers from my First Baptist Church. He said to the church, "You know, we will go to evangelize the people." A group of young people that I was part of in the church were intrigued by this mission opportunity, and we said to him, "Let's do it! We will go with you and support you."

We went to that small town and started to invite people to come to the church we were working with. I remember that we worked with children and their families who had moved from the eastern part of the country to San Salvador due to the harshness of the civil war that they were living through in those days.

Then one day as our small group of young people ate dinner, someone said, "Hey, I feel something in my heart." We asked what he was thinking. "I don't know," he said, "but I feel a fire is in my heart." Others began to say that they, too, felt something. Because of the work we were doing, working through the church and with the people, we all felt something, and we all said, "Hey, I feel the same."

The adults told us that what we were feeling was God calling us. We didn't understand that God was calling us and putting a fire in our hearts. We just felt that we were doing a good thing for God and for the church, but the adults insisted that God was calling us to take another step in life, a step we didn't understand. "What is this step?" we asked. They adults said with conviction, "You have to go to the seminary."

"Okay. Let's do it!"

I told my father first because he was a deacon of the church. My father has always been a strong Christian. When he became a Baptist before his children were born, his conversion was about the kind of life he wanted to give us. A beautiful, happy Christian life! Always he tried to do what was best for us. When I told him I was going to the seminary even when I didn't understand, he immediately spoke up. "What was that?" he said to me. "You cannot do that. You can go work or study, but never go to the seminary."

I went to the seminary!

The truth is that I did everything behind his back. He didn't even know that I went to Santa Ana to take my psychology exam to get my papers. Fifteen days before I left for the seminary, there was a big meeting in the church because the leaders wanted to ask the whole congregation if they would financially support the students attending seminary.

I remember that meeting vividly. The sanctuary of the First Baptist Church was traditional, with benches for the people to sit. My bench was in the same line with my father, but he was sitting on the other side. The secretary of the church began reading the names of the students going to seminary: José Rene Alvarado, Jaime Wilfredo Peña, David Alonzo Mena, Alejandro Emilio Orantes, and Ruth Eunice Rodríguez.

My father was shifting in his seat, looking at me and trying to ask me what was going on without attracting attention. I leaned up and silently said "Shhh" because I didn't want to answer.

I went to the seminary! It was so beautiful for me. Around fifteen years later, a member of the church told me that, in a particular worship service, my father took the microphone and told the people about living that moment when I decided to be a pastor. And he said, "I'm asking God to forgive me, because after these years, I do see my daughter to be a pastor. I made a mistake fifteen years ago."

He said why, and what he said was important to me. He said that he was against my becoming a pastor because he worried about how my life would be. My father was always connected with the pastors. He supported the pastors. He respected the pastor as the leader of the church. He said to the church that day, and later told me, that he had seen how the pastor suffered. He knows that many church members never know when the pastor doesn't have time to eat, when the pastor doesn't have time to sleep, when the pastor is awakened at night because something is wrong with a member of the church.

While other members might say, "That's your job. We pay you for that," my father understood the pastor's struggles. Later, my father said to me, "Daughter, I was telling you not to be a pastor because I know the pastor's suffering. And because you are a woman, I believed that you would suffer even more than the men."

His words were hard for me to hear, but I gave him a big hug. Even though he did not want to see me become a pastor because he knew what could happen to me, he never stopped me. He didn't say anything to hinder my path, even though I was not yet a legal adult. He could have said to me that I had to wait one year or more to decide. He could have said, "Right now you have to stay in my house because you are not an adult! You are not twenty-one years old." Instead, in his own way, he supported me.

Years later, I understood why he said "no" to me, but at the time, I was not obeying him. In spite of my young age, I never felt that I made a mistake. I am so happy with what I am doing, with who I am. Just one year after finishing high school, I believed I was ready to begin my biblical and theological studies. I was ready to expand my mind and see where that knowledge would take me. Where would I go? What kind of ministry could I do? I did not know what I wanted at that point. The only thing I knew was that I wanted to be part of the church, to help the church to do ministry.

I grew up in San Salvador, the capital city, which was sixty kilometers from the seminary in Santa Ana. Studying at the seminary meant that I would be far away from my family. Saying goodbye to my family in 1985 was a big decision. In addition to that hard goodbye, I fully realized that a twenty-year-old female seminary student might be lonely. When I arrived on campus, I saw that I was the only woman in the group that enrolled that year. The next year, 1986, two other women came. Being only one woman in classrooms full of men felt like an obstacle to overcome at the beginning of my ministry. The reality for women called to ministry in the country of El Salvador is that they would be traveling a rocky journey with their pathways to ministry blocked.

Before the eighties, it was impossible to be a woman pastor in El Salvador. Many women went to study at the seminary hoping to serve as a teacher in Christian education. The seminary received the women, never thinking that they would be pastors in the future. I knew in my first year at the seminary that I wanted to be a pastor. I was a little rebel—you know the kind! I was also a bit of a feminist. I did not make a conscious decision to push against the culture, but I had two reasons that, early in my life, I pushed against our customs about the place of women.

One reason is because of my mom's strength and confidence. Even though she was not a feminist, I never saw her asking my father's permission to do something. She always decided what she would do. I used to eavesdrop on my parents' conversations. Once while I was listening, I heard my mom say to my father, "Okay, the next weekend, I will go to visit my family, to visit my mom." She did not ask my father. She decided on her own, so I always saw her as a strong woman. My mom never told me that this was the way to relate to authority figures. I just learned because I saw.

The second reason I clashed with the patriarchal culture is because my father was different. He grew up with his father and one brother. My grandfather taught my father and my uncle to do everything in the house, three men. He taught them to cook, to clean, to make everything. My father lived his life like his father before him. Whenever he asked his children to do a task, he never asked only my sister and me simply because we were the woman of the house. He never said, "You have to do everything for your brothers." He never asked that of us.

I always said, "Thank you, God, for the parents you gave me." The way they lived their lives taught me how to live mine. So for me, to be a pastor was normal, to have the feeling that I wanted to be a pastor was normal. I was not thinking that because I am a woman, I cannot do this since no one in my house has done it. They never taught me that I could not do certain things because I am a woman. Because of my parents, I never believed I could not do something.

I found it hard when I was in other churches that used women only to teach or sing or cook. The people in my home church in San Salvador were a bit more progressive. Although they never had a woman pastor, they were open to new ideas about the roles of women and men.

The majority of the Baptist churches in El Salvador in the seventies and eighties would have never called a woman to be their pastor. Even now, we have many churches that would say, "This is crazy! To have a woman pastor is not normal. It's not biblical."

As a seminary student, I didn't have a problem. Everything I did felt normal and right, and after a while it was normal for my colleagues to have me there. I always loved to study. I was dedicated to it. Ever since I was a little one, I loved to study. My seminary studies were exciting and compelling. I was expanding myself in so many ways. At this point in my life, I thought that if somebody paid me to study, I would study my whole life!

When I came to the seminary in the eighties, it was like a *Kairos*, a time of God, both for me personally and for the country. Many open-minded people had come together. Pastor Ismael Mendoza was returning from his studies in Nicaragua, after the triumph of the Sandinista Revolution, to assume the direction of the Baptist Theological Institute of El Salvador. He was an intelligent man with great theological openness, an excellent teacher.

Around the same time, the Rev. Stan Slade and his family and the Rev. Ruth Mooney were designated by the International Ministries of the American Baptist Churches as missionaries for El Salvador. Both gave a boost to theological education. Other people who were important in the 1980s for a change in understanding the vision and mission of the Baptist churches in El Salvador were the Rev. Carlos I. Sánchez, who served as executive secretary of the denomination. He was theologically prepared with a tremendous ecumenical spirit, a commitment to liturgical renewal and to the integral mission of our churches.

All of them together created a unique, refreshing ecumenical spirit around us. The classes and division in the churches began to change. The Spirit of freedom and liberation was among us. This gathering of open minds taught me not to fight to find my place as a woman. And I think for that reason, I talk about the *Kairos*. My time at the seminary was the God *Kairos* for the Baptists in El Salvador. I knew in my heart that it was also the God *Kairos* for me.

As far as the difficulty of my call, it has been clear to me that I *do* have to win my space. For example, I remember being at the seminary in 1986. The churches in El Salvador were always asking the seminary to send students to them, especially for the weekend. We were in Santa Ana studying from Monday to Friday, full days of study, and on the weekend we traveled to the churches. In my first year, the seminary didn't send us. The only places we went in my first year were classes and classes and more classes. In the second year, a church one hour away on the coast of the Pacific Ocean didn't have a pastor. So they asked the seminary to send them a student. I will always remember what the principal of the seminary said to them.

"Okay, we don't have anyone to send except one student, if you want her. We only have one woman. That's it!"

The church responded, "Oh, my God! Well, okay. Okay, send her."

Their hesitation to receive me was not that hard for me to hear. Their response was okay with me. I think I expected it. I remember the first weekend I went to that church. Two deacons of the church, male deacons, were waiting when I arrived. They stood in the front door of the sanctuary waiting for me as if they were guarding the door. I never had that feeling before or after that day. Their eyes seemed like an X-ray machine. They looked at me from my head to my feet—looking, looking, looking—just to say to me, "Welcome." It was a hard moment for me because I was alone and this was my first experience out of my home church. Still, I always say, "Okay! Let's do this!"

Their decision to invite me was easy because they did not have a choice. Interestingly, a year later when I had to leave that church, the deacons said, "No! You cannot leave. We want you here!"

I said, "No, I have to go. I have to go because this year I end my studies at the institute. I have my graduation and then I go back to my home church to serve on the pastoral team." The whole church was sad when I had to leave, and I was sad for them. But all of it was a good experience for me and has empowered me to say, "I can do this. I can do this!"

Again, I have to say I learned from my family to be positive and confident. Sometimes I took the responsibility of the oldest child in my family. For example, my father is still alive at ninety-nine years old and my mother is eighty-two. Every time something happens with them, my sister and brothers expect me to do something, to be with them, to make decisions and take care of them. This helps me in my ministry. If somebody tells me something has happened, I quickly say, "We have to do this. We can do this. Let's do this." Because of the experience I've had with my family, I'm prepared.

By the way, my parents are always praying for me and my church people, for my life, and for my ministry. They are happy that I am their daughter, that I am a woman, a Christian, a pastor, and a psychologist, and that I am happy.

In my story of call and the journey I traveled, one of my milestone years was 1989. Our community of Baptist churches got an invitation from the United Church of Christ in the United States to receive a couple. They call the program "Missionaries in Reverse"—a person from the south goes to the north to serve as missionary. Our churches decided that my husband and I would be the designated people to go to the United States. We went and spent eleven months with the Illinois conference of the United Church of Christ.

We visited many of their churches in the years that we were there. We also visited the Lions Club, the Kiwanis Club, the schools, and the universities. We talked with hundreds and hundreds of people. It was a good experience for us.

At that time, El Salvador was in a civil war. The war was terrible and seemed to reach its highest peak. The military had killed many people, including six Jesuit priests from the Central American University. In January of 1990, we were supposed to return to El Salvador, but the leader of the churches in El Salvador said, "If you come, the military could kill you. You cannot come to El Salvador."

We had to leave the United States, but we could not go to El Salvador because our lives were at risk. The church leader from El Salvador and the leader from the American Baptist International

Ministries discussed a possible solution: that we would look for a school where we could go to study. So we went directly from the United States to Brazil, and we spent five years there studying at the Methodist University in Sao Paulo.

My studies and experiences in Brazil expanded my biblical and theological knowledge, in addition to my ecumenical spirit. I gave more shape to my feminist ideas and struggles and to my testimonial and theological option for the poor. Eventually, the guerrillas and the army were sitting at a table and signing a peace accord. We were able to return to El Salvador in January of 1995 and went directly to our seminary to teach. I loved the idea of teaching at our seminary. Since there weren't many teachers, we all had to teach courses in different areas. In my case, although my strength was teaching New Testament (The Gospels), I taught classes in liturgy, pastoral administration, Old Testament, and History. Because I loved to study, if they asked me to come up with a new course, my mind started to spin to create a new course outline that I would enjoy teaching.

I love to be with people studying the Bible. For me, it's a big challenge to open the minds of the people in El Salvador through the Bible. The Baptists always say, "The Bible is our only standard of faith and practice!" So any change that is sought in the vision and mission of our churches is achieved by studying the Bible with them. In the specific case of the role of women in churches, it becomes easier to empower women through Bible studies. It has to be reading the Bible with a liberating perspective. This is where liberation theology and feminist movements have contributed greatly to the equality of women in our Salvadoran Baptist churches.

The feminist movement in El Salvador can be credited to a number of factors. These include the conditions resulting from the war, the influence of liberation theology, the international feminist movement, and the growing awareness among Salvadoran women of their own oppression. An interesting article published on the website hosted by CBE International (Christians for Biblical Equality) speaks to this:

> Some Baptist women, such as pastor Ruth Rodriguez and others, have been challenged and changed by liberation theology because, according to Ruth R., "it is a biblical and Christian theology that helps us because it speaks of oppression, which is our reality." Indeed, as women hear their own stories in the stories of the poor, they are beginning to see God as a God who liberates—and themselves in need of liberation.[1]

I feel proud to be part of the group that has had the joy of drinking from liberation theology, being part of the feminist movement and the ecumenical movement. All of this has made me grow as a person, as a woman, and as a Christian. Most of all, I feel so proud to be a Baptist. I have had beautiful experiences in the Baptist church, but because of my experience working with other denominations, my horizons have expanded and I am able to see the beauty of each denomination's faith and practice. I have learned from so many other faith traditions that I can be open with anybody.

During those incredible years in the United States and Brazil, I was in my early twenties. Many times, I have said to people, "That was a big responsibility, and I was so young. Wow, if I were invited to be a missionary in the United States now, maybe I would have to stay here!" But when I was twenty-four, I said, "Yes! Let's do it!"

I thought about teaching for the rest of my ministry, and that would have been an enriching ministry for me. One day, a lady from the Shekina Baptist Church contacted me and said excitedly, "Sister Ruth, I have to talk with you about something." I said, "Can we talk later? I have to lead the worship right now." She quickly responded, "Okay, but I will say to you quickly that the Shekina Baptist Church wants to have you as our pastor." I said, "What?"

At that point, I was not looking to be a pastor working in a local church because I was happy to be teaching at the seminary, but when she told me about the church's invitation, I felt something. I said to myself that I needed to think about this. There were other candidates for the position, and I was surprised when they decided to invite me. I was the only woman in the group of candidates. They didn't know

---

1. Kathleen Hayes, "The Historical, Social, and Religious Context of American Baptist Women in El Salvador," *CBE International,* January 30, 1994, cbeinternational.org/resource/article/priscilla-papers-academic-journal/historical-social-and-religious-context-american.

too much about me, although some of the people in the church were students in the seminary. Still, I was surprised when they said the church decided I would be their pastor.

It's always exciting when something new comes into my life, when I am invited to do something that is new for me. I am afraid, but I always say to myself, "Let's do it. Let me try this new thing!" I knew I would make mistakes, but at that point I was thinking, "Aha! This is why I went to the seminary in the eighties." It was 2000, almost fifteen years later, but I thought, "Oh, oh! This is the reason: to be a pastor." I never expected to be a teacher, but life took me to the United States. I was not able to return, so I was led to Brazil. When I returned to El Salvador, I found myself teaching. My journey to the United States and to Brazil was not my plan. It was a divine plan.

When the church called me, my heart and my mind said, "I am happy."

Shekina is a special church. The members are good people, and I always say to them that to be the pastor of the Shekina Baptist Church is easy because they are an easy people. They are not like other churches that can be difficult. Since the day I started, April 20, 2000, I have found grace serving this congregation. When I came to Shekina, they were a small group. Most of them were women—widows or retired people. They didn't have a temple, a facility. They were renting a house. Now we have a beautiful space, our own space. We have a beautiful community of faith and a connection with other churches around the world like Central Baptist Church in Wayne, Pennsylvania; Wilmore Presbyterian Church, Kentucky; Madison First Baptist Church, Indiana; Immanuel Baptist Church, Rochester, New York; Oscar Romero Inclusive Catholic Church; Iglesia Bautista de Santo Tomás, Heredia, Costa Rica; Protestant Church, Egmond Ann Zee, Holland. And we also have a partnership with the Alliance of Baptists, the Baptist Peace Fellowship of North America (BPFNA-Bautistas por la Paz), and American Baptist Churches, USA.

For me, connections are important. I have enjoyed many connections over the years that have empowered me. To know that somebody is fighting for me, for the church, for our country has been important in my life, because to feel alone is the hardest thing a person can face. But to know that people, even if they are far away, are with you in spirit is a priceless treasure.

For example, during our most difficult times with the Covid-19 pandemic, we knew we needed to help the people. When a country is closed and when the people cannot go outside, it is not easy. We supported twenty-five families from our church and more than three hundred families in the community with the help we received from our friends in the United States, Costa Rica, and Holland. It was a blessing to see the faces of the people when they received help. I said to them that this was not coming from me; this support was coming from our friends, from our brothers and sisters outside the country. Just the feeling that I am not alone at this time when the people need help brightens my heart.

With the help of our brothers and sisters from inside and outside of the church, this year we started a psychological clinic to help the people with their mental health. It has been a great experience to help them, even as we discovered how much pain they have. The people need someone to listen and give them sacred space to share the sufferings of their souls. They need a safe place to cry for as long as they wish. They need somebody who understands and who never will say, "Oh, don't cry. These are small things." I say to them, "Your tears are important to me."

This is the vision I have, that the people can see their church as a sacred place where their pain is important. The most beautiful church is one that offers a place for people in pain to cry and not be afraid that somebody will judge them. I feel that I have been doing the right thing, and I have kept my eyes fixed on the needs of the people over everything else. I know I am not Superwoman. I know the things I have been doing are small, and this a big world. But I'm happy.

When people ask me how I'm feeling, I might say I'm tired or that I feel pain, but something is making me strong—I know I am not alone. I don't have words to express how happy I am and how much I feel gratitude for the prayers of my friends, even when we are separated by many miles. This path has not been free of difficulties; it has had many. But the path has also led to personal satisfaction and achievements.

What would I say to a young woman who felt called to pastoral ministry? I would encourage her to accept the challenge. I would tell her about my experience and would offer myself as her mentor. I would invite her to prepare theologically, and if she could, I would encourage her to study another career so that she would have more tools for life and for her pastoral work. For instance, I studied psychology at the university for six years and received my degree in psychology, specializing in clinical psychology. This has been of great help in my teaching and pastoral ministry.

I constantly pray that God continues to call other women to ministry, and I pray that those women will accept the challenge. I pray that the churches will free themselves from the ties of machismo, patriarchalism, androcentrism, and misogyny and become spaces of freedom where, guided by the Holy Spirit, men and women offer our best gifts and together build the kingdom of God. I pray that the world can see in the church a benchmark of equality and dignity. Together we can help other women to be strong, to experience liberation, and to feel happy to be women.

Today, Baptist women in El Salvador are claiming and using their gifts of teaching, preaching, and pastoring. According to American Baptist missionary Ruth Mooney, "Liberation theology is the predominant theology being taught at the Baptist Theological Institute of El Salvador."[2] Yet Mooney also suggests that only recently have women begun to see liberation theology as having significance for them when she says, "Perhaps together, we must begin challenging others to look at feminism and the empowerment of women as a part of liberation theology."

Even with the expansion of thinking about women ministers, women in El Salvador do not often look toward ordination. It brings me to the question: Why am I not an ordained pastor? Even my church members ask, urging me to be ordained. In a recent meeting

---

2. See Hayes, "The Historical, Social, and Religious Context of American Baptist Women in El Salvador."

in Chile, my colleagues in a group of Latin American female pastors commented on my being a pastor for so many years and yet not being ordained.

It is true that I have resisted being ordained. In the 1980s when I was studying to be a pastor, my thoughts were not focused on ordination but rather on the civil war El Salvadorans were suffering. Many people were simply disappearing, never to be seen again. The United Nations reports that between 1979 and 1992, more than 75,000 people were killed in a civil war that did not end until 2016.

That chaos in my country overshadowed thoughts of ordination for me and for my other seminary classmates, both women and men. Instead, we were learning about our Baptist principles and how to live them out, specifically the principle that teaches that every Christian is a priest. At that time in our history, it was in our hearts to live that principle as pastors. While we studied the movement of Jesus in the Gospels, we also studied Baptist principles, such as the universal priesthood of all believers. I have thought about the distinction between pastors and reverends. I am in a silent revolution, I think. In my thirty-four years of pastoral ministry, I have always preached, baptized, celebrated weddings, dedicated babies, and officiated the sacrament. A title, *reverend*, does not make a distinction between me and other pastors who are ordained, and I don't want a title that places me above my church members. All of us stand on the same foundation of service to God.

With that being said, I strongly support women who want to be ordained. I have always celebrated their ordinations. Ordination is a challenge to them, and they often find that the path to ordination is not welcoming. For women, ordination is an aspiration that is important in affirming them as ministers. More importantly, I recognize the long, difficult path they must follow in order to be encouraged as female ordained Baptist ministers. I may seek ordination myself someday, and when I do, I know that it will be a worship service that will impart a blessing to my ministry and affirm me as a minister of the gospel.

This book shares our stories as women. I can't wait to read all of them, because for me finding another woman pastor is a reason to celebrate! I know that we are all sharing stories in this book that may be painful but also powerful.

In this book of our stories, I am privileged to share my story—the story I tell about my call, my ministry, my life, and the entire journey that has made me who I am. I believe that when we, as women ministers, speak our own stories, we will more fully see God as a God who liberates.

After all is said and done and after all the struggles, it's wonderful to be a woman. It's wonderful to be a woman pastor! To celebrate the unique view of life we have as women, to understand one another, to be midwives birthing new things, to be empowered for ministry, and to do all of these things together in a community of sisters—all of this is amazing. It makes me happy!

Ruth Eunice Rodríguez de Orantes has been a Salvadorean Baptist pastor for more than thirty-three years and is also a clinical psychologist. Ruth has been the pastor for the Shekina Baptist Church in Santa Ana, El Salvador, for twenty-one years. Shekina is a member church of the Baptist Federation of El Salvador (FEBES). Ruth teaches at the Latin-American Baptist Seminary (SEBLA) and is president of its board of directors. She is an active member of the Ecumenical Women for Peace—El Salvador. She has been connected to the Alliance of Baptists for more than fifteen years and is also a member of the Baptist Peace Baptist Fellowship of North America/ Bautistas por la Paz.

She did her primary theological studies at the Baptist Theological Institute of El Salvador (ITBES) from 1985 to 1987. After a year of pastoral work at her mother church, the First Baptist Church of San Salvador, Ruth traveled to the United States in 1989 to start a year of missionary work at the Illinois Conference of United Church of Christ. Faced with the impossibility of returning to her country, given the persecution during the events of the Salvadoran civil war of the eighties, she moved to Sao Paulo, Brazil, where she had the opportunity to continue her theological studies at the Methodist University from 1990 to 1994, supported by the International Ministries of the American Baptist Churches. Ruth is passionate about the study of the Bible, the integral mission of the church, liberation theologies, liturgical renewal, pastoral counseling, mental health, and ecological and feminist struggles, with a deeply ecumenical spirit. She is the proud mother of a twenty-six-year-old son.

The Seventeenth Story

On Being a Soul Friend

Melody Carroll Harrell

When I was invited to write a chapter for this book, I felt like my story did not belong. I have been called to ministry but have not experienced the heartbreaking obstacles in Baptist life that so many friends and colleagues have faced. I have education under my belt but don't have a theological degree. I believe my story is rich and God-filled and I have been a guide to others, but I've never sought ordination or the pulpit. However, the standing invitation the universe offers me is to say yes when I'm asked to show up. And sometimes I find the courage to do it. I am convinced of the truth of the proverb, "God writes straight with crooked lines." And so I offer my crooked lines to this compilation of narratives of God's call among women.

I don't know how to tell the story of my calling without telling the story of my life. My calling has been organic, each experience forming the next, like rings growing inside a tree. It has morphed over time, starting out as one thing and becoming another. My calling has been my teacher, and I have been the student. I have not forged it into being. Yet by some mercy I find myself more aligned now with who I believe I am created to be than I could have ever imagined. I see it as a gift of grace that I feel seen by God and that my work in the world engages matters of the heart.

I have a vivid memory of the first time I sensed God reaching for me. I was seven years old and had just sat through a long church service in Swahili in Jinja, Uganda, with my missionary parents. That Sunday morning at the source of the Nile River was beautiful, a cross-breeze wafting through the open windows of the concrete block church. We were standing to sing the last hymn in Swahili, "What a Friend We Have in Jesus," and I began to cry. I was overwhelmed with a real sense of God's love for me. It was as if I heard, "Melody, I see you. And I deeply love you. We are connected. And this is the beginning of something significant for your life." I was so pierced by that word to my heart, especially in the context of a spoken language I had not yet mastered. It felt personal. Mystical. Special.

Being a child of Africa as a blonde, white girl was both grounding and disorienting. My Southern Baptist parents, first arriving in Tanganyika (now Tanzania) in 1956 and then moving seven years later to Uganda, fit many stereotypes of missionaries in those days. My dad wore khaki shorts and knee socks with the best of his British settler friends and spoke fluent Swahili with a Southern accent. My mom fulfilled her "church and home" role, teaching Sunday school to women and having friendships with all kinds of people, as well as managing a household with helpers, as was the custom in those days. Mama Alice was my nanny, and I spent much of my time on her back, nestled into a colorful cloth she expertly tied around her torso that allowed for attentive but hands-free child care. I felt safe with Mama Alice, and our shared love for one another lasted for many years, well into my adulthood.

Despite decidedly "old school" ways of doing missions, my parents could not be faulted for lack of earnestness or sacrifice. It was a long way from the hills of West Virginia and the sandy soil of Florida to the British protectorate of Uganda, a tropical Eden of a place. They believed wholeheartedly in the truth of the gospel, that everyone could be saved and experience the abundant life found in following Jesus. They felt that they had been specifically brought to this calling. So they spent forty-two years working, living, loving, and undoubtedly making many mistakes, contending with their own personalities and blind spots even as they pointed the way to Christ. My dad was a larger-than-life character, taking up most of the air in the room. And my mom, a reserved, agreeable presence, was always less than confident of her own voice in the world. I never heard her speak to the inner strength it must have taken to live in Africa for forty-two years, especially during many years of political unrest. My dad was not only a man of many words in our family, a master storyteller who easily traded facts for a rapt audience; he also had an uncanny way of being in places when crazy things happened. He lived an overextended life, always engaging in another scheme that he believed would benefit those he served. For my dad, more was always more, which meant more seeds and hoes for the people, more malaria pills, more protein powder for the malnourished babies. More also meant stacks of other stuff people might need filling every inch of our storage spaces—things he was sure he would eventually use, which often he did. He once shared in a letter to supporters that they had been part of the purchasing and shipping of thirty-seven containers of relief supplies to Uganda over the years—everything from liquid malaria medicine to blue jeans to outdated Bible commentaries and more. That was a lot of stuff!

I loved my parents and was proud of them. I sat in church pews on furlough, glowing that the stories my dad told were so captivating. And that I knew them all by heart. I loved living in our sleepy town of Jinja, along with my older brother. I loved attending the local Victoria Nile Primary School, wearing my checked uniform with three yellow buttons down the front, signifying "Moroto," the house I was assigned to for sports days, sometimes getting to add to it a yellow sash when my marks were high enough in the term to make the honor roll. There was no other life than this. The close ties were real with my Ugandan friends in school, with my "aunts and uncles" in our mission family, and with other missionary kids (always known as MKs) who became like siblings. I was at home in Uganda and at home in my innocent heart.

Everything took a turn from 1972–1979 under the rule of Idi Amin, an uneducated and brutal dictator who controlled by methodically killing off the intelligentsia as well as hundreds of thousands of others across the country, with some estimates citing 500,000 people.[1]

---

1. Stan Mooneyham, "Uganda Genocide," *World Vision*, July 1979, worldvision.org/disaster-relief-news-stories/uganda-genocide-nightmare-finally-end.

My parents' decision to stay in the country in solidarity with those to whom they ministered (and in obedience to God) turned my sense of security on its head, and for the first time I began to experience the terrible conflict between believing God could be trusted while at the same time observing terrible human suffering and the crumbling of my sense of safety in the world. It appeared to my childlike eyes that the complexity of this was bigger than God. Or at least that my nightly prayers for an end to it all were going unanswered. As the horror of the news of people we knew being killed became more and more of a reality, anxiety settled into my gut as a nauseating and constant companion. My sense of what was too much to endure was not sought, as the bravado displayed by my dad, perhaps for his own survival, carried the narrative. I remember him returning home one day with bullet holes in the side of the car. "Oh, they weren't shooting at me!" he said, nervously chuckling as he told yet another story of being stopped at an armed roadblock and witnessing some horrific scenario play out where someone else was beaten or worse. The only response available to me as such a young child was to listen and internalize my fear.

With the deterioration of infrastructure, it was decided that I would begin attending boarding school, a day's drive away in Kenya. I was nine years old and in the fourth grade. Part of it was heaven in a Harry Potter kind of way. Not that the facility was castle-like, but the British-run Anglican school was an enigma, and I loved pretending I, too, was British, taking on a British accent to fit the scenario. Our blazered uniforms with the school's coat of arms sewn on the left side of the lapel made me feel important, and our Saturday "Tuck Box" hour was a sweet tooth's dream come true, an opportunity to delve into the candy and treats our parents had sent for the term. I loved chapel on Sundays, the day we wore said blazer and participated in a service using Anglican liturgy.

I formed my identity around my Christian faith as well as being concerned for others who were away from home and in need of support. I listened, provided a shoulder to cry on, and performed some sort of role of encouragement. I played guitar and often graced those in my dormitory with worship songs, which I interspersed with

"Killing Me Softly" and a little Neil Diamond when the worship songs felt like they might be falling on bored ears.

Some years later, I transitioned for high school to another boarding school, Rift Valley Academy (RVA), a mission school in Kenya with an American curriculum. I was well versed by now in the independence that comes with living away from home, but I was still a child in so many ways. I gave myself to leadership opportunities as they arose and nurtured the conservative contents in the container of my spiritual life. Quiet times and memorizing Scripture verses from a Navigator program were the things that made me feel I was on track with God. I didn't question social structures and have been sobered in recent years by stories from my schoolmates from other countries about what it was like to be a student at RVA as a person of color. Not long ago, after I sent an affirming message of support on Facebook to a former classmate (a Kenyan) upon learning about the death of his partner, he responded by thanking me and citing the kindness he felt from me in high school. I felt gratitude in the depths of my being that this was what someone remembered about how I had treated them—not my naive way of looking at the world that assumed so much and didn't have the maturity or life experience to recognize that not everyone was living easy.

Towards the end of high school, I experienced my first dark night of the soul, a dark night that turned into several years of losing ground and wandering in the wilderness. As a minor caught up in the advances of a married, male missionary teacher, a two-year relationship ensued that consumed me and stole from me any normalcy that might be expected of a high school experience. Overnight, I compartmentalized my faith and fell victim to a feeling of despair deeper than I had ever known before. My inner compass was shattered, and I lost touch with the truth. Truth about myself. About the destructive circumstance I was in. About the pain it would cause others. And about the way forward. I experienced all the things a victim of sexual abuse is dealt. It was a confusing time in my life and lasted for several years. It's a wonder to me that I kept living, performing required obligations as a student, and giving the appearance that all was well while the ground beneath me was quicksand and threatened to swallow me whole.

By the grace of the calendar, I graduated and moved to the States for college, which provided the severing of the relationship that I needed. Over the course of some time, I faced the destructive patterns I had succumbed to and found my way back to myself and to a sense of my own place in the world as a young woman who could make choices for her own good.

I studied elementary and early childhood education and, through my first job in the inner city, began to feel a sense of call. I imagined returning to Kenya at some point, to do what, I wasn't sure. But working with these children from difficult circumstances gave me purpose and meaning. I was mentored by a gifted African American female principal who held a high bar for the students at our school as far as who they could be. I began to feel again that I had something to give, I experienced the gift described in the beautiful words of Mother Teresa, "Not all of us can do great things. But we can do small things with great love." To be sure, working with these children was overwhelming in lots of ways, fourteen-year-olds in the fourth grade who had been held back repeatedly because they couldn't yet read. Belligerent kids who wielded foul mouths as distractions against their own uncertainties and lack. And insecurity within the community itself. It was always noteworthy to me that the only place I experienced a mugging one morning when coming to work was not overseas but on this block in Birmingham, Alabama, where my elementary school was housed.

I could not have been more surprised when the man who became my husband reached out one day out of the blue. I had known Sam Harrell all my life. He was back in the States after working for a while in Kenya for a Muslim furniture maker and was pursuing the completion of his master of divinity (MDiv) degree. Sam had also grown up in Kenya with Southern Baptist missionary parents. He knew the details of my background as it was his background too, and he shared a love and deep connection with Kenya. He knew he would return to work there, but for now he felt it was important to finish his degree.

From our first phone calls, we connected quickly and easily as if we had never been apart. On the one hand, it seemed unbelievable to both of us that, after other relationships each of us had experienced, we would find one another again and fall in love so quickly. On the other hand, it made perfect sense. I was open with him about what had happened to me in high school and my subsequent disorientation. He received it with acceptance and mercy, even while being sobered by the complexities of it all. I remember thinking, "So this is what grace is—the mercy of being given a beautiful relationship on the heels of a journey that has made me feel I might never experience such a thing." It felt like a miracle to me, and I knew that God specifically wanted me to have this good gift.

We were talking about marriage days later. Our parents expressed both their concern and joy, cautioning us that we might be rushing things while at the same time remembering warmly a supposed photo somewhere (which we've never seen) in which we are holding hands as three-year-olds. To this day, we say we had an arranged marriage! Our joy (and the only way it could be) was holding our ceremony in Kenya, surrounded by friends and family. My white dress for the ceremony, Sam's kanzu, and my Ugandan basuuti for the reception were all homages to our rootedness in East Africa. Our guest list included forty Ugandan friends whom my dad brought to Kenya for the ceremony, well over two hundred Kenyans, and a smattering of missionaries. The live goat presented during gift giving, as well as drums and traditional dancing, brought a rural ease to an otherwise formal affair.

While Sam's MDiv was in process, we investigated the possibility of field service overseas with the International Mission Board, the only game in town at the time. We will never forget the awkward and difficult interview process that for the first time presented a barrier to our calling. It seemed that our own vision of how we would return to East Africa did not fit into the prescribed format of the agency or the interviewer. Our sharp knee knocks under that interview table confirmed for each of us that, indeed, this would not be the way forward for us.

While this "No" was a closing door, we kept moving forward, moving back to Kenya for a time and engaging various opportunities available to us. After about five years, we returned to enroll at Baptist Theological Seminary at Richmond, where Sam finally completed his MDiv degree. At that point, we turned to the newly formed Cooperative Baptist Fellowship (CBF) and began to sense that this might be a way into the future for us. But it would be three years before alignment about possibilities in Kenya and funding for a new position would come together to allow us to become field personnel. While we waited, we started a nonprofit, Africa Exchange, drawn forward despite the risks by what we knew was a summons back to Kenya. We couldn't ignore it.

Our three sons were born from 1991–1995, and another facet of God's call on my life came into clear focus. Motherhood was something I deeply wanted, and it was so much more than a role to me. I gave myself to it wholeheartedly. I wanted to be home with them for as long as I could and be a trusted presence in their lives, fostering rhythm, routine, and security. Living in Kenya again, Sam and I both eased into the natural and familiar space of raising our boys in the place we knew so well. They ran around outside barefoot, dirty, and free, conversing in Swahili words with James and Janet, who were an integral part of our world around our home. The equatorial climate meant we spent as much time on the verandah as in our living room, the lines between inside and outside wonderfully obscured.

As the first iteration of our ministry took shape, we worked with street children, at the time numbering some 60,000 in Nairobi. They moved in groups, sniffing glue to mask cold and hunger, occasionally finding some familial contact in one of the sprawling urban slums. They ranged in age from six to sixty, with a smattering of baby siblings in the mix, secured to only slightly older backs. Our Anglican church had started an organization called Kids to Kids that we partnered with, eventually taking on most of the onus for its development. It was grueling work with little evidence of hopeful outcomes besides knowing that for this day at least, those in our program were attended to with food, basic education, and lots of love.

During these years, I joined a women's spiritual formation group called "Women at 10" (we coined a bunch of other cheeky taglines in keeping with where we found ourselves, like "Women at Lunch" or "Women on Retreat"). These women came from everywhere: Kenya, South Africa, the United States, England, Sri Lanka, Ireland, India, Australia. Some were professionals and others had followed spouses to work and live in Kenya. We studied books together written by Christian authors like Yancey, Foster, Thompson, and others and talked through them in terms of our own faith, sharing our day-to-day lives and praying with one another. We learned contemplative practices and moved silently from the large group to solitude in the garden to practice them. We began a tradition of making a creative craft together during our retreat times, and to this day, I still have decoupage trays, dessert stands (which we would use for Communion), prayer beads, iron and glass garden ornaments, and beaded crosses, which are all precious possessions holding significant memories. And we learned that the gift was not so much in which book we were studying but in the months and years of being in community together.

A few years into the group, I began to notice others speaking to something they saw in me. "I have never told anyone this," one of them would say when we found ourselves alone and sharing with one another. "I can't believe I am telling you this," another would say as she bore her heart and soul about something she was dealing with in her life. It felt like I was developing a third eye, a perception of noticing and gathering attention around deep things in other people. I found myself becoming the spacious place for those things to come to the surface. I realize now that this was part of the groundwork for my calling to a ministry of companioning. I became a key leader in the group and was looked to for navigating a space where every woman's journey was honored and respected while, at the same time, the values of the group were upheld. It became more than a women's group. It became central for our spiritual journeys and significant in cultivating in me what it meant to be a soul friend.

By now, Sam and I were well down the road as CBF field personnel, and our ministry began to shift. We realized we needed to focus less of our efforts on the triage work with street children and more on what issues could be addressed before children found themselves caught up in the urban sprawl. We needed to look to rural settings outside of Nairobi, where the children were coming from, and see if we could work with communities to create systems whereby families did not need to send their children to the big city to look for further opportunities. We started visioning what that might look like, and Sam, along with input from local leaders, began to develop the concept of integrated child development centers (ICDCs).

A shared priority of both Africa Exchange and of CBF at the time was working with marginalized people. So we looked to the poorest districts in Kenya as the places where we would build these ICDCs. The concept was a simple two-classroom building in the heart of the community, offering basic education for children ages four to six. Each center could accommodate eighty children. They would be fed a highly nutritious porridge snack and a healthy lunch each day. We would attend to basic health needs including deworming and malaria prevention and ensure that each center had a clean water source. The teachers were enabled to gain certification, and the ICDC was governed by a committee made up of parents, teachers, community leaders, a pastor, and a local chief.

Over the next ten years, this is what consumed us. Those who took the most ownership became the most successful. But we worked alongside all of them, in times of faltering as well as times of strength. Sam was often out of town, building and then visiting the centers to grow local leadership capacity. We hosted church and student groups from the US, in some cases building the facilities and in others implementing programming. It was good work, and we remain grateful to have played this role in the lives of so many Kenyan children for so many years. The ICDCs continue to this day throughout Kenya under local leadership and continue to holistically impact a thousand children and their communities each year.

In about 2013, we began to realize something new was calling to us. Our three sons had moved back to the States for their university studies, and we recognized that our aging parents were living their last years, with new complications arising for each of them in their eighties. We knew they needed help and felt we could be a support to them, but we could hardly imagine leaving the country and work we had given our lives to. The grief began to take hold, even as we watched ourselves exploring options for a transition. It felt like transition was happening *to* us, and the idea of moving towards such unknowns felt like more than we could manage. But the ball was rolling and already becoming bigger than we could stop. How strange to move forward when one is not sure it is the right thing! How unnerving to know that no space in life is all good or all bad and that the creature we are staring down is multifaceted. We faced the incredible grief of leaving Kenya coupled with new opportunities and the gift of being closer to our aging parents.

Sam was offered the job of associate coordinator of global missions with CBF and, in 2015 we moved to Atlanta, Georgia, the one city on the map in which I would never have chosen to live. As we tried to cope with the transition, we reached out to others who had gone before, believing if they hadn't died in the transition, perhaps we wouldn't either. We read a lot and looked for trusted guides to make sense of a path we felt guided to but so challenged by. One of the most impactful learnings was from William Bridges.[2] He talked about the experience of transition as being "the process of letting go of the way things used to be and then taking hold of the way they subsequently become. In between the letting go and the taking hold again there is a chaotic but potentially creative 'neutral zone' when things aren't the old way but aren't a new way yet either."

What? How could the death we were experiencing lead to creativity? And could the new possibilities we were reaching for alleviate our distress in leaving the life we had known for so long?

I began to explore what could be ahead for me. What could this new space yield in terms of opportunity that would further equip me to live into my calling? It wasn't long before I came across a certification program in spiritual direction through the Haden Institute in North Carolina. The more I read the details of the two-year program, the more excited I got. This was me! The approach of the program rooted in the Christian faith through an Episcopal lens incorporated

---

2. W. Bridges, *The Way of Transition: Embracing Life's Most Difficult Moments* (Lebanon, IN: Da Capo Lifelong Books, 2001).

Jungian psychology, poetry, the enneagram, Celtic spirituality, and dreamwork among other topics, all my cups of tea poured out of the same teapot! I enrolled and began the training in January. Not only was there so much new and engaging material, but I was also reminded that being a soul friend has been understood and practiced in other traditions for centuries. I felt late to the game of this rich and life-giving tradition, but I knew it would mean life blood for other ministers I might work with in Baptist life and beyond.

My ears have always listened for "the thing behind the thing" and the "space" for whatever has led to a deeper journey with God, both for myself and for those I companion. It seems timely that I find myself here now in this place in time, when distracted living is our modus operandi. I believe our longing for connection and for taking time to remember ourselves is an invitation we often hear whispered from within. Sometimes we listen and respond. But often, we are just too busy doing the next thing to stop and be still. It feels indulgent and even unproductive, until we recognize that a practice that allows us to get in touch with our spacious hearts is what gives us any hope of living whole in the world. More and more ministers across CBF life, men and women, are reaching out for spiritual direction—pastors, youth ministers, state coordinators, children's ministers, and chaplains. It's like there is a rising tide that, while we know we are responsible for our own lives in Christ, we're also recognizing life is too hard to go it alone. This age-old tradition of *Anam Cara*[3] offers a trusted place for remembering the story of our lives in God. The monthly sessions add up one by one to create a beautiful narrative of one person's journey in the world and how they see God interacting with them. We look with gratitude at strengths and gifts and with humility and courage at weaknesses and liabilities. We remember them, name them, and hold them all in the light of God's mercy and love. We practice together *Lectio Divina*, the *Examen*, and contemplative prayer. We celebrate with thanksgiving the gift of gentle accountability that comes with meeting together and urges us to live awake, rather than moving numb through our days.

---

3. J. O'Donohue, *Anam Cara: A Book of Celtic Wisdom* (New York: Harper Perennial, 1998).

My work extends beyond CBF life to intersect with my experience of living and serving overseas. I meet with men and women who are involved in field service with other organizations in places around the world. The distance has not been a barrier to the work of spiritual direction, nor has the strike of a global pandemic. If anything, it has offered a touchstone for assimilating spiritual journeys in these challenging days.

There have been many influences in my work, but one of the most notable is the work of Matthew Fox, specifically his *Four Paths of Spirituality*[4] (gleaned from the writings of Thomas Merton). I share this here as a glimpse into some of the things my directees and I talk about together. The first path, "Fall in Love at Least Three Times a Day," invites us to the path of wonder and awe. It asks us to notice the things and people around us and to pay attention to what causes a rise in our own hearts each day. The second path, "Dare the Dark," is the path of letting go and letting be. It asks us to undergo grief and sorrow about the wrongs in the world but also regard our own shadow. It allows for confession, truth telling, and repentance as we own up to our tendencies and ways of being. The third path, "Don't Be Afraid to Give Birth," invites us to celebrate and to co-create along with the Holy Spirit in the world. It admits God's life pulses through us and creates good in all kinds of ways if we will allow it. The fourth path, "Be You Compassionate as your Father in Heaven is Compassionate," is the path of compassion and justice. It is the path of being involved in making things right in the world as they should be for all people.

As I conclude this writing, fall has turned the leaves on the trees that stand sentinel around our property into hues of golden yellow and red. The air is turning cool and crisp, and the evenings are reflecting autumnal rose on the lake. I recognize, as I often do, that I have traded equatorial living for a seasonal rhythm of days. The little blonde girl with an African heart has become a woman living her second half of life, deeply informed by what was, but living where she is now with all its gifts. I thank God for my calling and for the slow

---

4. M. Fox, *Creation Spirituality: Liberating Gifts for the Peoples of the Earth* (New York: HarperOne, 1991).

and sometimes unseen blessings that come into focus, only when we look back and remember that it is in God that we live and move and have our being. Thanks be to God.

Melody Carroll Harrell was born in Uganda, East Africa, to missionary parents. She lived in East Africa until graduating from high school, when she returned to the United States for her college education at Samford University. From 1998, she served for seventeen years with her husband, Sam, in Kenya as field personnel with the Cooperative Baptist Fellowship. Her work during those years was multifaceted. She worked with marginalized children and communities, focusing primarily on developing integrated child development centers in the nine poorest counties of the country. She taught regularly with an urban early education center located in the slum of Kibera in Nairobi. She also worked with urban women from all walks of life in personal and communal spiritual formation. This led her (upon her transition back to the US) to certify as a spiritual director with the Haden Institute in North Carolina. Her personal study of the enneagram for many years led her to training with the Enneagram Institute and is one of the tools she uses in her practice.

Working as a spiritual director has pulled together many parts of Melody's journey. She works with people across CBF life (pastors, associate pastors, youth ministers, state coordinators, chaplains, and laypeople) as well as individuals ministering overseas with other organizations. She believes deeply in the value of being an *anam cara*, a soul friend, as we follow Jesus on the way. Melody believes in the gift of gracious living, and as such she creates peaceful spaces in her home, loves cooking delicious meals, and sets a welcoming table (either inside or out). Her creativity feels like a north star around which she orients, finding expression through gardening, photography, writing, watercolor, and soul collage. She has three handsome and artistically talented sons, one beautiful daughter-in-law, and one adorable granddaughter who is one and a half years old.

The Eighteenth Story

If the Shoes Fit

Rev. Kelsey Stillwell

The First

My words poured out of me with enthusiasm as I simultaneously recounted and verbally processed my experience. Over dinner in a restaurant with two friends, I talked about the weekend I spent at the Festival of Young Preachers Conference in Louisville, Kentucky, where I preached my first sermon. I had never imagined myself preaching, much less enjoying it.

My roommate crowded next to me in the booth and leaned in, and I received her genuine curiosity as support, the assurance I didn't know I would need as the conversation unfolded. Across from us, the bench shook as Bryan kept shifting his weight, restless and visibly uncomfortable. I was slow to register that his discomfort grew the more I spoke. As he got antsy in his seat and turned a brighter than usual shade of red, I paused to ask, "Are you okay?" It did not register that his discomfort was because of me.

What we felt in that moment is a tension I have experienced countless times since then. It's a tension women know well and can usually see coming. But this time, the first time, was when my relationship with this nameless tension began.

Bryan searched for the words to say, weighing his convictions in his mind. He was faced, maybe for the first time, with something that challenged a belief he held strongly. Just how tightly he was holding on to that belief was tested the more I spoke. His inner distress bounced so violently within his head that his body moved along with it. Eventually, he hesitantly chirped out broken sentences that, strung together, said something like, "I don't know how to respond to what you are saying. I don't believe women should be allowed to preach."

This was the first time these words were ever said directly to me. I know they had been said in my presence before, but those instances weren't memorable. I always wrote the comment off as idiotic, surprised that someone was dumb enough to say it out loud. (Ah, the confidence of a teenage girl. Where has she gone?) But in that restaurant, a dear friend with full conviction said it to my face. His words hung in silence for a moment before they fell with the weight of all who say the same, and I heard them, all of them, for myself for the first time. It felt like I had run into a glass door, a barrier I didn't see in front of me, but I do not remember how I responded. We shook it off and moved on.

Years later, when we were students at McAfee School of Theology in Atlanta, Georgia, I shared this memory with Bryan. He was mortified to remember that he ever said this to me, much less that he was the first person to do so. And then we laughed about it, a lot. Bryan and I had remained friends in college as the few students studying Interior Design. He was active in his home church, and I worked as a youth ministry intern at mine. This was something we had in common, so we learned how to carefully talk about church with each other, knowing our theology differed greatly. After graduating with a BFA from Eastern Kentucky University, we had both stayed in Richmond, worked in design, and became close friends. Curious about seminary, we took a class at the Baptist Seminary of Kentucky and explored seminaries to attend. Together, we moved to Atlanta to attend McAfee. We supported each other and understood each other as artists trying to negotiate our identities as both designer and minister. My experience in seminary was made all the more special because we journeyed together, sharing the things that challenged us, growing, and becoming more ourselves. I enjoyed sharing my story of the first time someone told me women couldn't preach, mostly because of the reaction that followed when I revealed it was Bryan who said it. We were such close friends that this was unbelievable and comical for anyone who knew us. Of all the people to say those words to me, it was Bryan, one of my best friends, with whom I grew into my calling.

This story has taken on greater significance since then. I tell it now from a place of deep gratitude. That conversation in the restaurant came full circle and ended in a way that I know I am lucky to have experienced. Not all moments like these are so beautifully resolved. That first time of facing opposition as a woman exploring ministry is a memory I think of fondly. It reminds me of a beautiful friendship and how it protected me from the trauma that could have come from facing it more harshly later, from someone else. "Women cannot be called to ministry" is a message that has been spoken to me directly and demonstrated through actions countless times, but I was first introduced to this thinking by a friend when I was a college student. I know this is not the case for most women. The traumatic experiences of my sisters being told this for the first time breaks my heart and causes me to hold my own story carefully, honestly, and with gratitude.

I cannot begin to tell my call story without first naming where I started in the larger story of women in ministry. I began my journey farther down a paved road, a road that women before me have traveled for a long time, paving and preparing a smoother way for those coming behind them. This road still extends far ahead of us, still farther to go, and must now be made wider for all to travel together, not narrow for just a few.

It was not long into seminary that I learned how much women had been through before even starting their first class. I needed to look at my own experience more intentionally to see where I had escaped the belief that there are limits to whom God can call. In the same way, I also had to uncover the many ways patriarchal systems had influenced and limited what I imagined was possible. With this in mind, I revisit the stories that shaped me and brought me here.

Home

My call to ministry was gradual, muddled with my experience as a pastor's kid, and met with my stubborn and skeptical self. I grew up the daughter of a minister and a teacher. I am the pastor that I am today because of what I learned from my parents' professions and passions. My dad is a Baptist minister and worked in various associate pastor roles for thirty years. I saw him as "pastor of all the things except preaching every week." He had a passion for missions and education. His is the voice in my head that reminds me to approach missions intentionally and with an open mind to learn. My mom is a gifted teacher who taught in an elementary school and with hearing impaired students for a total of thirty-four years. Hers is the voice in my head that reminds me of the importance of a teachable moment and to guide with patience. She is also where I get my love of dance and movement. Most of my childhood was spent in a classroom and the church.

When I was in fifth grade, my dad was called to a new church, and so we moved from Western to Central Kentucky. Apart from my dramatic response as a child who felt the world was ending, I didn't realize the significance of this move until years later. My older sister and I would eventually come to understand that this move happened after the Southern Baptist Convention (SBC) takeover and as the Cooperative Baptist Fellowship (CBF) was getting started. It was clear that the church in Western Kentucky was staying with the SBC and opposed women in ministry. It was because of this, among other things, that my dad looked for other churches to find a place that welcomed women's leadership. This decision means the world to me, and I cannot imagine how differently my life could have been had my parents not made that decision when they did.

Lexington Avenue Baptist Church in Danville, Kentucky, is the church I called home. I grew up knowing every hallway, every hidden closet, and which Sunday school classes had the best candy. I entertained myself during Dad's meetings, attended every mission trip, and was a committed member of a small youth group. The church raised me, supported my leadership, mentored me, showed me the power of relational ministry, taught me intentional missional theology, gave me the opportunity to learn from other cultures, and was comfortable letting me speak, and eventually preach, in worship. I started working in the church when the youth minister moved, and I, along with three other college students, served as youth ministry interns. A job that was only supposed to last a few months turned out to be a part-time job that I kept for three years, taking the lead. The pastor, and one of my most impactful mentors, Tommy Valentine, was brave enough to trust us and gently nudged me along as I resisted a calling that became more evident as it unfolded. Working with the youth, having the chance to preach and lead in that church, is where it began.

Saints

Dianne Stillwell (my mom) wrote this about her mother Pat Cummins (my grandmother):

> My mom was loved by so many, especially the young adult ladies at church. She taught a Sunday school class of young women and loved them dearly. I can remember her waking early on Sunday mornings and spending time reviewing her lesson at the kitchen table while enjoying her coffee. She prayed and cared for them regularly. She knew their fears, concerns, and needs and checked on them often.
>
> It was not uncommon for the phone to ring, and it would be "one of her girls" on the other end, sharing something urgent with my mom. She would listen, help reassure, encourage, and often head out the door to go be with them wherever they might be to offer support and comfort . . . often right in the middle of our family dinners. She loved them well. She wasn't just there for them on Sunday mornings during class, but she showed up for them while doing life. They adored her and valued her greatly. That was evident to me. She modeled to so many that loving and caring for others took more than just words. It involved investment. She was never actually an ordained deacon but was approached and asked to consider it. She was always appreciative but turned the opportunity down, anticipating that serving as a woman deacon might be a hindrance for some and not desiring to muddy the waters. She was content to serve behind the scenes without drawing attention to herself. But there is no doubt that she served in that capacity well without the title.

I did not know my grandmother for long. She died when I was young, but I know of her love for people and for me because it shows up in every old family photo and in the stories we share of her. This strong and compassionate woman, who made a difficult decision in her time to turn down being a deacon, is a part of me. She is the wisdom and persistence in my heart when I am angered at how far we still have to go. She is the confidence in my spirit when I need to remember that my calling is true and not a mistake. My grandmother, along with all the saints of strong women who have gone before, stays with me.

Identity

At CBF of Kentucky gatherings, I was often identified as "Keith's daughter." This evolved to "Brittany's sister" when my older sister started seminary at Baptist Seminary of Kentucky and became more involved in CBF life. Don't get me wrong; these identities were never a bad thing. They did, however, play into my already skeptical personality, suggesting that I needed to be absolutely sure I was cut out for ministry and that I wasn't sensing a call simply because it was what my family did. So to test this, I intentionally chose a seminary out of state, where I did not have any connections. I chose McAfee and moved to Atlanta. I did this for me. I'm glad I did.

"Artist" and "designer" were what I had known myself to be, not "minister." I thought that to pursue ministry meant starting over and giving up what I had been studying. I was wrong. I never stopped being an artist. Even though it was not what I had imagined for myself, it transformed into something better. Inspired by other women, I discovered how leaning into my identity as an artist made me a better minister. This was true of other identities I have claimed for myself along the way. Art, movement, design, and creating sacred space are at the heart of my call to ministry. God's calling is for all of me, including the parts that make me an artist.

I do not have a romantic story of when I first felt called by God to ministry. At some point during college while working on a small team of youth interns, the shift began. It started as a job I knew how to do because I grew up in the church. It evolved into a job that

I was good at because I loved it, was energized by it, and wanted to keep learning more. This was evident to people around me who voiced what God had been saying, that I should be open to the call to ministry. I was still hesitant and skeptical. What had previously sounded like a whisper, which I feared was my own voice, became a clearer calling when I removed myself from the context I had always known. There, I was still drawn to ministry, captivated by the God who pulled me to and was present in spaces outside my comfort. I listened more carefully there and could trust that this calling was from God, not from me.

The call to ministry was intimate and personal as I saw how God could use all of me. I could use my passions and gifts in ministry; I could expand my identity as an artist to something bigger. Art and movement became my spiritual practices, my way of connecting with the Divine. In this connection, I felt that I was called by name by a God who knew me completely. I have since built on this, but it was here that I first felt seen by God. The answer to God's calling was a scared but assured "Yes."

Seen

In this collection of women's voices, I am a young one, still processing some of the trauma and still learning how to confront the more nuanced challenges that women in ministry face now. I have experienced the power of hearing stories from other women that sound familiar to my own. It can offer some relief to be reminded that these moments are real and unfair and that we are not alone. For this reason, I share my memories. They are small moments that hold joy and despair in tension, validation that should not be so rare.

A group of high school girls, after much anticipation, rushed to me with an indescribable excitement to meet me. At a church that had a long history of hiring summer youth interns, I was the first female intern they had ever had. I love those students and my time with them. The power of seeing women in ministry and representation of all kinds of people is real and holy.

I can recall the first time a layperson introduced me, outside of church, as a pastor to someone else. I was the youth minister at a

Baptist church after graduating from seminary. A church member was the vice principal of the local high school and was giving me a tour of the school. When we passed a teacher in the hallway, he introduced me by saying, "This is Reverend Kelsey Stillwell, a pastor at my church." Simple recognition and respect have power. It was startling, unfamiliar, and wonderful. What followed was the frustration of realizing that this had never happened before. It still doesn't happen often. Context is important and informs which titles carry weight, but honest respect and validation make the difference. You know it when you feel it. I wish we felt it more often.

An old sanctuary had a temperamental sound system, and I was given notes on how to adjust my voice most every week. It became difficult to tell the difference between critique that was about delivery and critique of the sound of my voice. The latter is discouraging and unfair. For months I accepted the fact that I needed to try harder to adjust my voice and that half of the congregation would never be able to hear me until the sound system was replaced.

"Stop sending women to preach in pulpits without doing a sound check! Giving women the chance to be heard means adjusting mics to their voices." Someone said this in a group discussion hosted for women to share what they wish church leaders would understand. This was a frustration I understood; I needed to hear I wasn't the only one. Eventually one of our sound techs approached me to set a mic specifically for me. What a relief to finally be heard. It was long overdue.

Defending my call to ministry as a woman was something I anticipated. I did not, however, expect to feel the added controversy of being a single female minister. Not only was I not married when I started my first full-time ministry position out of seminary, but I was also not actively pursuing a partner and did not care to. As a response to my search for volunteers, I was told countless times how my predecessor had a husband who helped with the youth. I was asked about my personal life with questions that were loaded with judgment. For years I felt that I weirded out church members because I was not married, but I couldn't put my finger on it apart from snide comments. It also seemed too ridiculous to be true. In my exit interview from that first church, I was told multiple times that the youth parents wanted the next minister to be married, which was not at all relevant to the meeting but a way for them to drive home this point one last time. This is a church that I still love dearly. It is full of incredible people and fond memories I hold close to my heart. They loved me well in many ways. Even still, when it came to my singleness, I did not live up to the expectations within that context and gave them a new reason to question my abilities as a minister. When I started at my next church, I was no longer made to feel that being single made me less valuable. I welcomed questions about my personal life because they came from a genuine desire to get to know me. I didn't know how much it had affected me until I found myself in a place without it. What a relief.

It became an inside joke of ours. "Nice shoes!" he would say as he left worship. First of all, I love shoes. I have fun trying different styles, and to me they are a small space for self-expression since robes cover everything else (similar to how men wear fun ties or socks). For a long time, comments on my shoes were not compliments; it was the most some people could say to me after worship rather than comment on my preaching or worship leadership. They were uncomfortable and didn't know how to talk to me like they did the pastor, but they felt they had to say something. Commenting on my shoes was the best they could come up with. At some point the topic arose in a conversation with this man, who thought it absurd to find out that this is what I heard week after week. Then he started saying it too, but exaggerated and with a smirk, making a joke of the people who said it, not of me. I absolutely loved it. He saw me as a pastor with cool shoes. Now, in a different context, comments on my shoes (or anything else) do not come from people uncomfortable with my worship leadership. I know and trust that my awesome shoes are not all that they see of me.

Authenticity

Starting with seminary, I have grown as a minister from wherever I was, within the limits of the spaces that held me. Each place comes with its own expectations, standards, or ideas of "good" that I try to mimic. In each church I have served, I have learned new aspects of ministry. I also see how I measured myself differently in each location, using rules of the congregation's culture that I picked up. I am always me, but a part of me is a mimic of what is seen as "good," and that is most often the voice and leadership of men. Finding your own voice is hard to do when what we hear most are the voices of men. It is even more difficult when the ears of congregations are only tuned to hear men's voices.

In 2020 when Covid-19 changed how we did life and church, I lived alone during quarantine. Those months allowed space for introspection without church walls and offered a lot of time with myself. The search for authenticity became a complex riddle that I didn't have the tools to solve. Painful as it was, I felt that it was even more imperative that I tried. Some of the best advice I heard during that time was from Angel Pitman: "Do the work of finding your authentic self." It is definitely work—hard work.

There were no standards for Zoom church or virtual worship. I got a break from comparing myself to the standard and had time to "do the work" to find who my authentic self is. It was (and still is) a painful and holy process. What I know right now is that it requires confidence, trusting myself, and vulnerability. It made the return to church in person more difficult than before, back to old molds that no longer fit. I hope to pass along the advice that was shared with me. It has made all the difference.

I choose to take on the challenges that come with authenticity. I choose to use my gifts unapologetically in the face of patriarchal systems that remain in the church even if they differ from how things have always been done. I choose to risk failing every now and then for the sake of creating something that fits me. I do this for myself because I must—because God called me, not a poor mimic of someone else.

Middle

My call to ministry is still unfolding before me, so I am not sure how to end a story that I am still in the middle of. I do know that in sharing my story, I want to be honest with myself about the privileges that play a role in making my journey easier. I cannot look back without seeing the many people and stories that shaped and affirmed me. I am grateful for them. I must also recognize how God has been present, calling me by name.

So this is where I leave it, anxious about how I might one day look back on these words and see how far I still needed to grow, hopeful for what is ahead because of where we've come from, compelled to join those already working to widen the road, willing to live authentically, and still called by a God whose mission is bigger than us.

Kelsey Stillwell serves as the associate pastor of youth and missions at the First Baptist Church of Christ in Macon, Georgia. Kelsey grew up in Central Kentucky. She studied and worked in interior design before discerning her call to ministry. An appreciation of beautiful and thoughtfully designed spaces remains a part of her identity and connection to spirituality. She attended the McAfee School of Theology at Mercer University in Atlanta, focusing on global Christianity. Her call to ministry is centered on a curiosity of the world and God's work in it, as well as intentional relationships with young people who have much to teach us. She finds a connection with the Divine through art, dance, and nature. She will likely mention pickleball, her dog Eliza, and cat Higgins when given the chance. She finds home in her parents' kitchen, in long phone calls with her sister, in her Macon community, in Bali, in pet snuggles, in dancing music, in good burgers, in Marvel movies, and in adventures with her partner, Bren.

The Nineteenth Story

This Labyrinthine Calling

Rev. Julie Pennington-Russell

As a child I loved to crawl in my father's lap after supper. Sitting in our porch swing with his arms around me on those evenings, my face pressed into the fabric of his shirt, I would close my eyes and inhale. To this day, the faint memory of beer mingled with Old Spice and tobacco still makes me smile. On such evenings, as Dad and I rocked back and forth in the swing, it wasn't unusual to hear from inside the house my mother singing the words to some old gospel hymn: "Every day with Jesus is sweeter than the day before. Every day with Jesus . . . I love him more and more."

I grew up in a home marked by a kind of spiritual duality that had a profound and lasting effect on me. My mother, Barbara, who professed her faith at the age of twenty-one after an encounter with two Southern Baptist door-to-door evangelists in Bermuda, is to this day a fundamentalist Christian who loves nothing more than studying the Bible. At the other end of the spiritual spectrum was my father, Ron. Baptized as a boy at the 35th Avenue Baptist Church in Birmingham, Dad ushered organized religion to the margins of his life when he enlisted in the US Air Force at the age of twenty.

As a military family, we lived not so much on borrowed time as in borrowed towns—one lily pad to the next. Throughout my childhood I was drawn to the rhythms of faith to which my mother moved. I also loved the earthy, funny, off-color ways of my father. My mother taught me by example that following Christ means plunging all the way in, not dabbling one's toes at the edge of the water. At the same time, my father, who had a fondness for just about every vice on the Baptist "Thou Shalt Not" list, was also the kindest, humblest, most generous person I knew. This was a signal to me from childhood that the lines we sometimes draw and the labels we assign—good/bad, saint/sinner, saved/unsaved—never tell the whole story about any person.

Mom imparted to me her love of Jesus. Dad taught me not to muck up my faith by confusing it with religion. Best of all, my nuclear family gave me the gift of feeling equally at home with people of deep faith and people of little or no faith.

The other adult who deeply influenced my young life was my maternal grandmother, Velma Aileen Mabry, whom I adored. Aileen lost her first husband in a coal mine explosion and her second husband to alcoholism. Had you asked my grandmother about her relationship with God, I think she'd have responded, "It's complicated." Aileen loved watching Billy Graham crusades on TV and often sang along in her gravelly smoker's voice as I played "How Great Thou Art" and "The Old Rugged Cross" on the piano. Raised in the Methodist church, Aileen had an appreciation for the things of God. She also appreciated bourbon, Winston cigarettes, and nickel slot machines and often peppered her conversations with colorful expletives that made me laugh. I grew up calling her "Grandma Who Goes to Work." As an insurance agent with City Federal Insurance Company, Aileen was the first woman in our extended family to work outside the home.

During summer vacations at Aileen's small Birmingham apartment, I would rise early each morning so we could share "grown-up time." Drinking coffee together at her tiny Formica table, I felt so worldly wise. As I watched my grandmother get ready for work, I was fascinated by every choreographed detail of her morning ritual: the cold cream, the lipstick and rouge, the Chanel Number Five. When Grandma Who Goes to Work emerged from the bedroom in her smart office suit with those impeccable red nails and chestnut beehive, I was convinced that "office girl" was the most exciting thing anyone could ever aspire to be.

I professed my faith at the age of nine. In 1969, our family was living in the tranquil days of pre-Disney World Orlando where Dad was stationed at McCoy Air Force Base. At the time, Walt Disney was quietly purchasing some 27,000 acres of orange groves and pristine farmland in Central Florida, preparing to build the mother of all theme parks. This was big news.

Down at our little Southern Baptist church, however, the rapture was getting a lot more attention than the Magic Kingdom. Obsession with the end times was building. While my father was largely bemused by apocalyptic predictions, my mother couldn't get enough. At the dinner table she talked of the antichrist, trumpet judgments, and whether Mrs. Jones next door, who smoked Virginia Slims and drank Schlitz beer straight from the can, would survive the great tribulation after the rest of us were caught up in the air. I'm pretty sure my initial decision to give my life to Christ was based on my love for God and a child's dread of the Four Horsemen.

I've heard faith described as "giving all of yourself you can to all of the Christ you know," and that is what I did when I knelt beside my bed on that summer evening. Following the guidance of my Sunday school teacher, I confessed to God all the sins I could think of and asked Jesus to "come into my heart." Then I got off my knees and went into the living room to share with my family the happy news of my salvation. Dad was on a tour of duty in Vietnam, but my mother and grandmothers were there, watching a television show. They turned the volume down when I asked them to. Suddenly, with three pairs of eyes focused on me, I felt self-conscious and only managed to sputter, "Well, I guess I'm saved."

"Praise the Lord!" said Mom. "Hot damn!" said Grandma Who Goes to Work. They celebrated my news for a few moments, then cranked the TV back up. That was it. My conversion is forever linked in my mind to the theme song from *Mission Impossible*.

A piece of my early story has to do with God's providence at work, even before I was alive. In 1956, four years before I was born, it became apparent to my father that he was not going to be able to go to college because he needed to work to help support his widowed mother and younger sister. Dad's decision to enlist in the Air Force rearranged the trajectory of my life because it removed my family from Alabama, essentially forever. My parents always spoke fondly to me of growing up in Alabama. However, Birmingham in the 1960s was a broken city.

So, while my cousins were growing up in a place of fire hoses and church bombings and the ubiquitous "White Only" and "Colored" signs, my brother and I were living out in central California, in military housing with our neighbors—the Washingtons who were African American, the Schwartzes who were Jewish, and the Awohis who were Pacific Islander. Their children were our best friends. The racial and cultural diversity I experienced shaped my young life in important ways.

What's more, at that time in California the women's liberation movement was in full swing. In those days Helen Reddy was singing, "I am woman, hear me roar." My sixth grade teacher, Mrs. Petker, wore hotpants and go-go boots and quoted Gloria Steinem. As I listened to older generations of women find and use their voices, inside my young heart a seed was planted. I concluded that I could be anything God wanted me to be.

The years we spent in the San Joaquin Valley of California when I was in junior high and high school were some of the most formative of my life. Memories of those days would draw me back to the West Coast several years later when I decided to enter seminary. When I think about it now, it feels as though God the Beloved somehow took my father's shattered dream of college and fashioned from those broken pieces a path for my life that still feels beautiful beneath my feet.

The discernment process that let me to seminary was flimsy at best. My father had retired from the Air Force, and we were living once again in Orlando. I was about to graduate from the University of Central Florida, and the only thing in life I *was* sure about was that I did not want to be a speech pathologist—something I had just spent three years learning how to become.

I also was a devoted member of the largest Southern Baptist church in Orlando: worship twice on Sundays, prayer meeting on Wednesdays, "Evangelism Explosion" on Monday nights. As it happened, among the college students at this church there was a peculiar assumption that following Jesus in earnest automatically included going to seminary. It was the "spiritual" thing to do. No call? No problem. Go to seminary and see if you get one. The array of possibilities for God's call was much narrower for the young women in that college group than for the young men.

But in 1982, six months after my college graduation, with no idea where it would lead and without any clear sense of being "called" to a particular ministry, I boarded a Delta jet in Orlando, bound for San Francisco. Tucked inside my carry-on bag was a leather Bible, a homemade journal covered in bright-yellow gingham, and an acceptance letter from Golden Gate Baptist Theological Seminary. I'll repeat: my vocational discernment process was uninspiring. But in hindsight, that experience taught me that God can take half-baked motives, convoluted theology, and a general lack of maturity and craft from these a surprising recipe for a call.

When I think of those days, I want to remember myself as an independent young woman who swash-buckled her way into a new life on the West Coast. In truth, by the end of my first week in seminary I was pummeled by waves of doubt and anxiety and cried myself into a three-day migraine. I didn't have words for it then, but I believe my angst was tied to assumptions I carried about God.

A Catholic priest and friend, Phil, once observed to me how important it is, especially when we are in the throes of discernment, to ask, "Who is the God I pray to? Am I praying to the God *out there*? The God *up there*? The God I need to satisfy or placate? Or do I pray to the God *in here*, who dwells in me in love?" At the time I entered seminary, I hadn't yet met that latter God.

I arrived at Golden Gate as thoroughly Southern Baptist as I could be. As a young woman steeped in fundamentalism, I was certain I wasn't called to lead a church. Every morning during that first semester I got up an hour early and headed to the little prayer room in my dormitory where I fell on my knees and prayed for all the confused, misguided women in my classes who thought God was calling them to be pastors. The theological systems I'd been swimming in since childhood had left me with an acute case of spiritual pride coupled with deep feelings of shame and unworthiness.

But during my years at Golden Gate, God slowly peeled back the roof of my life and ushered in fresh light. Layers of fear-based, fundamentalist dogma began to give way to new understandings and intuitions about God and myself that were broader and freer, more generous and hopeful than I'd ever experienced before.

While at seminary I also met a California-born, Hawaii-raised free spirit named Tim Russell. When we met, to put it in musical terms, Tim was jazz improvisation, flush with breezy spontaneity. I, on the other hand, was a crisp Mozart minuet, determined to follow every note on the page. For nearly four decades now, we have been learning from each other both the joy of winging it and the importance of making plans. Tim is the best life partner I could ask for.

A series of pivotal moments occurred for me while in California. First, on a chilly, foggy Sunday morning in spring 1983, I visited a small, two-story wooden church on a main thoroughfare in San Francisco, two blocks from Golden Gate Park. From the moment I walked through the front door of Nineteenth Avenue Baptist Church, I knew there was something special about this community. The spirit of life and joy radiating from the congregation was palpable. And from what I could tell, everyone was invited to serve according to their giftedness and passion. There wasn't a single ministry role at NABC that was off-limits to women.

When I began worshiping at Nineteenth Avenue, the church needed a music minister. I possessed some modest musical skills and applied for the job. When the congregation asked me to serve, I felt a holy nudge and said yes. Later that year when the pastor, Bill Smith, was preparing for vacation, he said to me casually, "Of course I'll need you to preach while I'm away." Bill's confidence that I could lead and proclaim in his absence contributed more to my life and calling than he'll ever know. I owe him an enormous debt of gratitude.

When I graduated from seminary two years later, that church asked, "Will you become our associate pastor?" More discernment:

God, what are your intentions for me? Are you leading me through this door? Again, I perceived a Divine "Yes," as I would seven years later when that same community asked me to become their pastor. Over a period of fourteen years at Nineteenth Avenue Baptist Church, I served in three different roles.

Since those first years in California, our family has moved three more times, following my call to Calvary Baptist Church in Waco, Texas; First Baptist Church of Decatur, Georgia; and now First Baptist Church of Washington, DC. At each of these junctures I've needed to pause—most recently, for a period of six months—and listen for hints of guidance and grace. My experience of call is that it rarely comes with trumpets and bright lights but almost always dawns on me by inches and hunches and best guesses. Following the Spirit has felt less like cruising down a wide, well-lighted freeway and more like walking a labyrinth in the middle of the night, holding a birthday candle.

Early in 2015, after thirty-two years of committee meetings, programs, bylaws revisions, stewardship campaigns, staff brawls, frustrating justice work, a bruising journey with my third congregation on our way to LGBTQ+ inclusion, and the recurrent feeling that my family was suffering from church conflict, I hit a wall, emotionally and spiritually.

When we think of calling, I think we most often imagine a call *to* something. But sometimes the Divine calls us away. In my experience, this call is harder to discern because the human mind has endless avenues for second-guessing itself. Fortunately, the Creator has placed within each of us a resource deeper than the analytical mind: our "knowing" heart. Especially when we become still and silent for a time, in the deep places of ourselves something will begin to stir. We may have no words yet for this stirring. No matter. Eventually, the way forward will come and lay a hand on our shoulder.

My "hand" came in the form of dreams. In one memorable dream, I was at work, but not in my study at church. I was in an underground room, a claustrophobic space with one naked light bulb overhead. In my dream I was fiddling with wires, switches, tubes—basically the things I'm no good at—while trapped in the most uninspiring environment imaginable. When I told my spiritual director about the dream she said, "Yes, this space you're in feels claustrophobic spiritually, emotionally, and psychologically." Then she gave me a compassionate smile and said, "Julie, you can only operate so long from grim determination." I knew she was right, but how does a pastor walk away from her church?

In 2006, the Canadian advertising agency Ogilvy Mather created an award-winning commercial in which two executives are riding a tall escalator in a spacious, lovely, multi-story atrium. When the moving stairway unexpectedly stops, the two executives begin to show signs of panic. Neither has a phone, so they begin hollering for help—*from the middle of an escalator*. Eventually a mechanic comes to their aid, riding a separate escalator from the floor below, but his escalator lurches to a stop as well. The commercial ends with all three, the two executives and the mechanic, huddled on their separate, stalled escalator steps, awaiting rescue. The fifteen-second commercial went viral, doubtless because it connected with this paralyzing illusion people carry inside of being stuck, when all we need to do is take a step, then another.

My discernment process in 2015 included my dear husband, listening friends, a week-long retreat at a mountain cabin, and long conversations with trusted mentors and my discerning spiritual director, Tavye. It was in Tavye's office the Monday after Easter that I said the words aloud for the first time: "I have to go." It was time to walk off the escalator. Once I arrived at that conclusion, the process unfolded quickly. I shared my decision with the church's compassionate deacon chair the next day and notified my church several weeks later, making every effort to bless and encourage the people on my way out.

I spent nearly half a year pondering my call. I allowed myself the freedom to put church ministry aside for a while. I wasn't sure I had the heart to return. I took some trips, led some retreats, hiked Stone Mountain, joined a writing group, worshiped (though not every Sunday) with a diversity of congregations, and essentially let myself dwell in a liminal space for a while, resisting the temptation to obsess about the path forward. As Gregg Levoy put it, thinking too much about a calling is like leaving a hot iron too long in one place while trying to smooth the wrinkles out of your shirt. I put the iron down and let the wrinkles stay wrinkly.

Finally it was time to reengage the questions, though it's not like there is a definitive checklist. I was back in the labyrinth at night with the birthday candle. I did conduct a kind of SWOT analysis of myself—strengths, weaknesses, opportunities, threats—but mostly I paid attention to my intuition and my body, both of which are usually way ahead of the rational, analytical mind. While I grappled with issues of purpose and passion, an unexpected face swam to the surface of my memory—the face of Clemmie, an elderly woman I had known years before, when I was a young pastor.

Clemmie had slipped beneath our church's radar as she became too old and frail to attend worship. "Out of sight, out of mind" is never good enough in the body of Christ, but it happens more often than we want to admit. Our office received word that Clemmie had taken a fall. I felt the knot tighten in my stomach as I drove to the hospital, knowing I had dropped the pastoral-care ball in a big way. There was a noticeable frost in the air when I introduced myself to Clemmie. Understandably, she was hurt that her pastor hadn't been to see her and that her church seemed to have forgotten her address. But she did receive my fumbling apology. Her face relaxed a little, and I ventured to pull up a chair.

I asked Clemmie to tell me about herself and her family. For the better part of an hour, she recounted story after story, going all the way back to World War II. Eventually she grew tired from talking and I thanked her for sharing pieces of her life with me. I held her hand and offered a prayer, then said goodbye. When I returned a few days later, Clemmie's family was visiting. They were as chilly toward me as Clemmie had been earlier and I felt my face grow hot with embarrassment. This time, though, Clemmie broke into a wide smile as she called out my name. Then, grabbing my hand, she announced to her family, "This is my *pastor*."

Years later, over the course of that extended period of discernment in 2015, a quiet awareness tucked itself inside the folds of my heart: *I love congregational ministry.* I cherish the honor of being invited into people's innermost, vulnerable spaces. What's more, I have experienced firsthand the strength and joy that flow through people's lives when their church is a mostly healthy community, and I enjoy helping broken congregational systems become more whole, less burdensome. And I do treasure the preaching life, especially among people who are skeptical of the Divine. Whether I am doing these things well, or clumsily, or miserably, for nearly forty years now they have answered a desire in me deeper than words can express. I wound up engaging in conversations with three urban churches in three unique cities. Over time, Tim and I felt drawn to the First Baptist Church of the City of Washington, DC, a historic church in the Dupont Circle neighborhood of Washington, seven blocks from the White House.

Mindful of the spiritual and mental exhaustion I had experienced earlier, I was eager to make a different kind of start with this new congregation. I wanted to lead and live from a more heartful place, a grounded-in-God place. Soon after arriving in the District I was introduced to another wise and wonderful spiritual director, Charlotte, and I enrolled in the Shalem Institute's Going Deeper: Clergy Spiritual Life and Leadership Program. Though I hadn't thought of myself as contemplative, as it turned out, it was the contemplative path I was craving.

God's labyrinthine call upon my life has brought me now to what I would describe as the sweetest season so far. The seventeenth-century Jesuit priest Jean Pierre de Caussade said that when a person is fully present with God, the soul is light as a feather, liquid as water, simple as a child, and easily moved as a ball by every inspiration of grace—to which my grateful soul would offer a hearty *amen*. These days find me endeavoring to tap into what the twentieth-century contemplative Gerald May called "the power of the slowing"—easing back the throttle and letting myself notice when the velocity at which I'm moving and thinking exceeds my ability to be fully present. In this rocket-speed age, I am taking intentional care with my horse-and-buggy soul while inviting my beloved church family to that beautiful venture as well.

As for the shape my calling may take in the future, I am entrusting the labyrinth to God. As the contemplative teacher Rose Mary Dougherty observed, "Here is the grace of it all, the hope for our spiritual lives. We may never clearly discern all the intricacies of our prayer; we may never be able to depend on our desire. But God's prayer in us is constant, as is God's love. And in God's loving prayer our hearts can rest."[1]

Julie Pennington-Russell became senior minister of the First Baptist Church of the City of Washington, DC, in 2016. Ordained in 1986, she also has served churches in Decatur, Georgia; Waco, Texas; and San Francisco, California, and was the first woman to serve as senior pastor of a Baptist church in the state of Texas. A pilgrim on the contemplative path, Julie co-directs the Shalem Institute's Going Deeper: Clergy Spiritual Life and Leadership Program. She is a graduate of the University of Central Florida and Golden Gate Baptist Theological Seminary. Her messages have been featured on the television broadcast *30 Good Minutes*, on Day-1 Radio, and at the Festival of Homiletics. Julie is married to Tim Pennington-Russell. They have two adult children, Taylor and Lucy, and a pony-sized Great Dane named Charlie.

---

1. Rose Mary Dougherty, *Group Spiritual Direction: Community for Discernment* (Makati City, Metro Manila: St. Pauls, 1997), 30.

The Continuing Story

Then, Now, and Dreams to Come

Rev. Kathy Manis Findley

Within these pages, you have walked nineteen journeys alongside nineteen women, dreamers all. At one moment in their lives, or maybe through many moments in their lives, they fixed their eyes on a dream that seemed tenuous, if not impossible. Still, they sensed an ethereal presence of a dream that was a call to vocation, a call to serve as Baptist ministers. Each of them traveled a labyrinthine path that led them, as Julie Pennington-Russell described, on a journey not unlike "walking a labyrinth in the middle of the night, holding a birthday candle." Some of them started their journeys of call more than sixty years ago, while some have more recently found their way to ministry as Baptist women.

Their journeys, taken together, span decades. In those decades, they realized that they traveled against a backdrop of history that held the power to change their trajectory or even stop them right where they stood—abruptly, harshly. With dreams in their souls, they walked on with courage and persistence. They also walked smack dab through the turmoil of Southern Baptist denominational change that began in the late 1970s and resulted in ripples of division and exclusion that continue to this day. How important is societal context? One may think that the societal context of denominational angst had nothing to do with these women directly, yet it had *everything* to do with them.

The denomination they had known as "home" was changing, even crumbling. The names they had always counted on began to feel distant and unfamiliar. The Southern Baptist Convention—their overarching name for "home"—would eventually fade from their consciousness.

Dreams shattered? Not at all! They would wander into other "homes"—the Alliance of Baptists, the Cooperative Baptist Fellowship, the Baptist Peace Fellowship of North America: Bautistas por la Paz, the Association of Welcoming and Affirming Baptists, Equity for Women in the Church, and many other organizations—"homes" that would open their hearts, accept them, and invite them in.

They now heard names of places that suddenly felt disturbingly unfamiliar. The names that once had been safe places were now transitioning out of their minds. The Southern Baptist Theological Seminary, Southwestern, New Orleans, Golden Gate, Midwestern, Southeastern—names of the schools they had loved began to feel distant to them. These names of the theological homes they had long known would be replaced by other names.

Dreaming still, they gravitated toward these new names in other places. Baptist Theological Seminary at Richmond, George W. Truett Theological Seminary, Campbell University Divinity School, Baptist Seminary of Kentucky, Central Baptist Theological Seminary, Wake Forest Divinity School, Duke Divinity School, McAfee School of Theology, and Brite Divinity School are only a few of the names the women began to hear, and in the halls of these seminaries the women found "home" again, maybe for the first time.

The journeys these women continue to travel have been marked with change, loss, displacement, mourning, and then rejoicing when they found new places to call home. The Baptist landscape changed as they traveled, and the backdrop of Baptist history/herstory continues to change, ever evolving into pockets of inclusion and nurture for women whose path led them to ministry.

Nineteen women followed twisting and winding pathways, grieving the loss of what had been and then finding "home" again. They learned to recognize the names and the places that promised inclusion and acceptance. They embraced frightening but refreshing change.

Oh yes, a shifting and unsettled Baptist landscape was the backdrop of their journeys. Yet their journeys continue—the past completed, the present full of the movement of Spirit wind, the future made of the dreams they dreamed while looking up into a dark void that suddenly, miraculously, lit up with stars. Thanks be to God.

Every great dream begins with a dreamer. Always remember, you have within you the strength, the patience, and the passion to reach for the stars to change the world. —Unknown

Afterword

On the Meaning of Baptist-ness

Rev. Suzii Paynter March

Ministry. Sometimes a calling and sometimes falling. The whisper of God's voice was an echo and calling to Kathy Manis Findley from a young age. Her Greek Orthodox heritage and roots provided the cadence and encounters with the spirit. For Nancy Sehested, the voices of women leaders and women preachers patterned her calling, even though they were never acknowledged as preachers in their own right. For Anika Whitfield, even the voices and examples of ancestors carried the whisper of calling.

The wording of God's whispers in these stories is varied and sometimes conditional. Like Carolyn Hale Cubbedge voicing to herself, "I would be a preacher when I grow up, if I were a boy." If . . . , if . . . , if . . . . So many women experience the conditional path of "if" and its twin sister "if only" on the way to ordination and committed ministry. The strength and resilience required to overcome the conditional path strewn with obstacles builds a certain sinewy musculature for ministry. Woman after woman in these stories finds herself expressing ministry through various positions, denominations, churches, organizations, and institutions. In watching ministry flourish after many *if* and *if only* moments, the parable of the soils comes to mind.

Can a call to ministry transcend the call's origin and context? Resoundingly, yes! We are called forward toward ministry, but whatever nursery births these notes of curiosity and inquisitiveness, each woman here as the carrier of the calling embellishes the calling with vision, ambition, and energy. After a while, a minister can indeed see and feel beyond the context that was the birthplace of calling and the context of inherent restraint.

For Rhonda Blevins, Julie Whidden Long, and Lynn Brinkley, the experience of finding ministry began with the love affair of immersion in a youth group, a college ministry family, and the fellowship of a church's embrace. Falling into ministry meant feeling the love abounding in friendship, support, and collegiality of terrific people, at least until the emerging gifts of leadership pressed into the expected roles of the day.

Each of these stories is punctuated by at least one experience of burnout, rejection, or confrontation: ministry with hurdles. Resiliency in ministry is contextual across every story. The dream and the lived calling are always shaped by geographical context, mentoring, support, relationships, and the ebb and flow of opportunities. But the identification of "opportunities" is tricky for these women in ministry. Heeding Rhonda Blevins's sage advice to be careful, we are cautioned not to be so hungry for opportunity that we "paint the red flags green"! The desire for an opportunity can lead us to deceive ourselves.

In these stories, there are beautiful, memorable, and precious moments of "YES." These affirmations and callings by congregations do not come easily or often. Carolyn Hale Cubbedge had the joy of learning that the "deacons had unanimously recommended me." Unanimous is a blessing and is wind in the weary sails of many in ministry. Christine Wiley is a legendary long-term minister with an unusual story of thirty-seven years in ministry with the same congregation. But although the location has been the same, the ministry has changed over time as she "followed the winds of the spirit."

Often in women's studies, much is made of the shaping of women's identities by the roles we occupy—daughter, mother, aunt, grandmother, wife, sister, employer, employee. I am struck in these stories of women exhibiting authentic gifts of leadership as highly proficient administrative or executive leaders in faith. The capacity of women to traverse many roles becomes a highly developed skill, and this expression is often recognized, even by notoriously lagging denominational bodies, as giftedness for administrative leadership.

Carolyn Yeldell Staley took administrative gifts of ministry to the highest levels—even to United States presidential levels—as God wove the relationships of childhood friendships into opportunities for extraordinary service. The success of women as administrative leaders throughout a career in multiple organizations can garner great accolades given for their superlative work. Soaring accomplishments! Only there is yet the often regrettable caveat in Baptist life: "as long as it is not in the role of pastor."

Baptist-ness is a theme in each story. Whether it is one woman saying, "I am no longer this kind of Baptist but another," or another woman saying, "I used to be Baptist," or the fierce *Baptist-ness* of independence and soul freedom, each woman offers a great lesson about their identity and affiliation. Our religious expressions and our ministerial identities are birthed and then later shaped by communities, churches, mentors, sisters, brothers, families, and many who are held in the cloud of witnesses around us.

I heard God's call to ministry myself long before my imagination could even vaguely see me as an executive for state, national, and international religious bodies. I never imagined myself as CEO of the Cooperative Baptist Fellowship or as executive director of the Texas Baptist Christian Life Commission. That is not to say that I didn't see myself a CEO or executive; I did. I just imagined myself in secular positions, not faith and denominational ones.

However, my love, commitment, and call to care for God's people were intensifying even as these secular gifts of administration were strengthened in a professional education career. The streams of love for God's folk and my administrative career merged when I was invited to interview as a candidate to be the lobbyist for the Baptist Convention of Texas. Within a few weeks, I was advocating at the state legislature for the people benefiting from the missions and ministries of Texas Baptist churches.

I believed God could use whatever meager gifts I gave over to the mysterious power of the Holy Spirit. It was as if I was giving the most mundane and dutiful tasks of administration to God, asking, "Can you make something of this?" But what transformed my skills to ministry on behalf of God's purpose was turning my love for God's people into the action of advocacy—being the advocate for women in prison who needed more time with their children, legislating for the simple dignity of having clothing and proper shoes, adding hospitality houses for traveling families of the incarcerated, and adding chaplains to state prisons. The un-sacramental tasks of law making were developing into ministry by working for years to bring a "life without parole" sentence to a place with the highest death sentence rate in the free world. Drafting, amending, persuading for legislation is essentially dull work until the work is ignited by love. I was working to add more full and compassionate services to children in foster care. I was lobbying for immigrants seeking asylum. I was getting college tuition for Dreamers and providing services to navigate the labyrinth of immigration law. I was fighting to tighten the accountability for predatory lenders who were seemingly able to make a loophole of abuse at every turn.

So in my own ministry journey I offered the pedantic gifts of administration, and God ignited them to sear my heart and catapult me as a magnified voice on behalf of suffering. It was a meager handful I gave to God; there was a harvest a hundredfold.

Who knew that the thick skin and seasoned executive skills I learned wrangling with Texas legislators would be later put to some holy purposes to raise millions for international ministry and encourage Christian social innovation? Who knew that the same thick-skinned executive leadership would later enable me to weather the storms of personal betrayal and denominational controversy?

For each of the women in this book, ministry roles have changed and evolved—pastor, chaplain, missionary, associate pastor, denominational leader, clergy staff, laity staff, part time, full time, volunteer, on call. The work products, too, are diverse—sermons, stories, curriculum, liturgy, art, poetry, spoken word, lyrics, libretto, screenplays, paintings, devotions, essays, testimony, witness, advocacy, autobiography, and biography. My own ministry adds legislation, amendment, and policy.

I am reminded of Hildegard of Bingen, the anchorite child who, when exposed to God outdoors, felt a greening of the spirit as she took on new expressions of ministry in art, pharmaceuticals, song, policy, and preaching. This is what she wrote: "We cannot live in a world that is not our own, in a world that is interpreted for us by others. An interpreted world is not a home. . . . Part of the terror is to take back our own listening, to use our own voice, to see our own light."[1]

How did these nineteen women see their own light and dare to use their voices? What catalyst expands ministry? What fertilizer makes ministry bloom? And what fruit abounds and will abound in the yet-to-come days? In their journeys, these women build their ministries as a strong foundation, an investment of hope that what they have built will support other women, especially young women and girls who will come behind them.

How can you help build a bridge to strengthen other people's ministry when your own bridge or foundation is so rickety and fragile itself? Perhaps the way is the miraculous catalyst of generosity, a power seen throughout these stories. One striking similarity and thread throughout these remarkable stories is the willingness of women in ministry to give away, to generously share with a true faith in fertility and abundance. While their circumstance does not provide largess (no stately barns of wealth or amassed power to draw from), these women are giving seed, tending growth, and reaping harvest. Each is giving to others, not from a stock of extra and discretionary storage but from the actual overflow from the precious but small stream of grace generating from within her own ministry.

We might name it real-time sharing with no assurance that there will be enough for me, but giving anyway. There is genuine sharing. There is genuine hope that the vessel will be refilled and that their

---

1. Quoted by Allison L. Boden, "In the Hand of God," address presented at the Princeton Theological Seminary Chapel, December 21, 2019.

gifts will be returned to them: "pressed down, shaken together, overflowing into their laps. Measure for measure."[2]

Suzii Paynter March is a graduate of Baylor University, with a lifetime of experience in organizational leadership and public advocacy. In September 2019, Suzii became executive director of Prosper Waco. Suzii has held advocacy and leadership roles with the Southwest Educational Development Laboratory, the Christian Life Commission, the Cooperative Baptist Fellowship, and Pastors for Texas Children. Through these endeavors and her affiliations with many other associations and groups, she has worked on issues ranging from education to poverty to prison reform. Suzii's recent work with Pastors for Texas Children has been recognized for advancing education funding in the 2019 legislative session. For ten years, she has helped vulnerable people recover from and prevent predatory lending.

She has been honored as a distinguished alumnus of Baylor University and holds an honorary doctorate from Dallas Baptist University. Her personal honors include recognition for her work in ethics and cross-cultural and women's leadership. In addition to her Baylor bachelor's and doctorate degrees, Suzii holds a master's degree in education from Stephen F. Austin University. She is married to longtime resident of Waco, Ben March.

---

2. Author's paraphrase of Luke 6:38.